THE INHERITORS

The Inheritors

A Study of America's Great Fortunes
and What Happened to Them

JOHN TEBBEL

G. P. PUTNAM'S SONS

NEW YORK

A Note on Sources

Anyone who writes social history of the kind contained in this book must acknowledge certain primary sources, past and present. Gustavus Myers' *History of the Great American Fortunes* remains such a source for this and many other volumes, as does the formidable collection of data compiled by Ferdinand Lundberg for his landmark book in this field, *America's Sixty Families*.

Among the modern chroniclers, I am much indebted to Stewart H. Holbrook, who has written so ably of the nineteenth-century accumulators in *The Age of the Moguls*, and to Cleveland Amory, who has definitively chronicled the lives and times of the inheritors with such wit and charm in *Who Killed Society?*, *The Last Resorts* and *The Proper Bostonians*.

For the rest, I have consulted the usual secondary sources, the files of newspapers and magazines, and a few manuscript sources which I have been permitted to examine in confidence. A portion of the book is based on personal experience and observation, including conversations with the people involved.

Contents

[*Three*]
CONSERVATORS AND EXPANDERS

[*Four*]
LORDS AND LADIES BOUNTIFUL

Illustrations will be found following pages 136 and 232

$ *One* $

THE ACCUMULATORS

$ 1 $

A Preface to Wealth

"For the love of money," Paul reminded Timothy, "is the root of all evil," an admonition which must have fallen ruefully on the ears of the good Bishop of Ephesus, laboring toward martyrdom among a flock scarcely distinguished for its wealth. Looking about him in the cruel uncertainties of the first century A.D., Timothy may have observed that the lot of no man was easy, but conceivably he might have had a passing doubt that those who erred from the faith by pursuing wealth had really "pierced themselves through with many sorrows," as Paul asserted with ascetic zeal.

Scholars may debate the authenticity of Paul's letter, but the moral truth of his pronouncement, a cliché in our time, is still generally accepted by generation after generation. We accept it, yet we doubt it, and therein lies one of the major paradoxes of human affairs. "Money won't buy happiness," we tell ourselves sagely, meanwhile sacrificing everything, or nearly everything, to attain it. If money does not buy happiness, one might reasonably ask, why do people pursue it beyond whatever is necessary for the simple necessities of life? Some people don't. The rest of us say these people have no ambition; they do not share the common interest of getting ahead in life. In brief, they are queer.

To a Christian aesthete like Paul, the evil of money was plain enough, whether a man was rich or impoverished. If he loved money more, he could not fail to love God less. The corrupting influence of money was seen plainly, then and now, as a revelation of human weakness. Money has always betrayed man's better instincts in a thousand ways. The ultimate betrayal, to those of the Christian faith, was a matter of only thirty pieces of silver.

Yet there has existed for centuries the undeniable fact that the rich appear to be having a good time, and the poor are beset by anxieties and must be content with meager comforts. The rich are not truly happy, we tell ourselves, and create the stereotypes of the poor little rich girl who cannot find happiness for all her money, and the hagridden financier who suffers gout and ulcers in the hectic scramble to get and keep his wealth. Whenever one of the rich appears in a courtroom, the wolves slavering at his throat, or kills himself in the library of his magnificent mansion, we nod and say, "You see? All that money, and he was miserable."

The doubt remains, and gnaws. Was J. P. Morgan miserable, sitting on the spacious deck of the *Corsair*, smoking an opulent cigar? We peer into the television set on a Saturday afternoon in June and watch the beneficiaries of Eastern wealth promenading in the paddock at Belmont before the horses momentarily eclipse them. Are all these ladies in their chic dresses in reality dying for the simple pleasures of the kitchen and the nursery? The housewife ventures to doubt it. Are the sleek gentlemen in their $300 silk suits, owners of horseflesh worth more on the hoof than most of the television watchers, betting more than the average man's annual salary on the day's racing—are these fortunate ones

secretly longing to be at home with a bottle of beer amid the luxury of three and a half rooms with kitchenette? None but the fatuous could believe it.

We like to think that in America the distance between the haves and the have-nots is negligible. After all, we have the highest standard of living in the world. To the destitute masses of Asia and Africa and South America, the poorest of our citizens may seem like a rich Uncle Sam. It is often forgotten, however, by these trumpeters of the American Century, that our rich men are comparatively richer, on the whole. There is little more quantitative difference between rich and poor here than elsewhere. What sets off America is the size and affluence of its middle class, whose members support the comfortable illusion that they are or may soon become well off themselves. The reality is that they are the victims of a constant struggle to maintain or increase their status in layers of social strata which are constantly shifting under economic pressures. "We earn $20,000 a year and we're broke," the blurb in a national magazine proclaimed the other day. It was a morbid reminder of the essential insecurity of middle-class life.

For the gulf that separates the rich from all the others is not only a matter of income. Wealth is also a state of mind. Words take on different meanings in the world of the financially secure. "Struggle" does not equate with "survival." For these people the everyday struggle of humanity for the essentials of life, no matter at what level it is lived, has ceased to exist. To struggle at the economic peak is to play the game for its own sake. In so doing, one may have the soberest feelings of responsibility, but in the end there is the knowledge that, no matter what the outcome, the way of life is not threatened. Even for the totally incompetent, it is no easy matter to dissipate twenty-five, or fifty, or a hundred million dollars, although some have tried it with considerable success.

The feeling was summed up, on a lower and far more sordid plane, by the well-heeled television personality who was fond of saying to any guest who pressed him too hard in the public view: "I'm going home in my Cadillac tonight after the show. How are you going home?" The public, of course, was spared this little homily.

It is difficult for outsiders to comprehend what it is like to live in the private world of wealth. Motion pictures and television and the idle chatter of newspapers have done virtually nothing to illuminate the subject, except possibly to underline its unreal aspects. It is harder for us to understand the possession of wealth than its acquisition, because only a few serious novelists have succeeded in portraying the lives of the rich with insight and accuracy, while the lives and times of the accumulators have been chronicled at length by literally hundreds of writers, in terms that any reasonably literate person can understand.

The difference between acquisition and possession is the essence of this book. In the pages that follow, some but by no means all of the great nineteenth-century American accumulators of wealth will be examined with the idea of perhaps understanding better what manner of men they were, what drove them on, what the amassing of money meant to them.

Then will come the more complicated matter of the people who inherited this vast agglomeration of wealth. They seem to divide roughly into three classes. There were those, first of all, who simply spent it. Born to wealth, they could conceive of nothing else to do with money except to maintain and expand the luxury in which they found themselves. Some spent their money lavishly out of sheer boredom; without any inner resources of their own, they had to depend on exterior stimulation for what interest they could extract from life. Clothes, horses, mansions, jewels, art they seldom looked at, beautifully bound books they never read, travel from one rich man's hotel to another with no more than a passing view of the countries they journeyed through—these were the stimuli wealth could buy, which made life endurable.

Other spenders pursued different chimera. The struggle of the Vanderbilt women to be leaders of society, the pursuit of similar eminence by the Astor wives, were symptomatic of how far human pride and vanity could go, once wedded to unlimited wealth. There were a few among the men who spent to compensate for the satisfactions they had to deny themselves because of their failure to make human contacts in the essentially unreal world of the very rich. Finally, among the spenders were those who took pleasure in possession of particular objects. With several of these the object was horseflesh; with others it was art, and with a good many it was women. Again, one might say, these were compensations for the emptiness of lives from which all striving had been removed.

The second large category of inheritors would be those who spent a major part of their time in conserving and expanding the wealth left to them. Many of these were men who inherited, besides money, a preoccupation with it, and a sense of duty to it, almost as though money were a beloved child to be tended and carefully reared. Others, no doubt, were ridden by a sense of guilt which was translated into an enveloping sense of responsibility, as in the case of John D. Rockefeller, Jr., who devoted his life and fortune to rectifying the wrongs his father had done to society. Still others were those who found as much satisfaction in using wealth to make more wealth as their forebears had in acquiring it.

The third broad category of inheritors are those with an inherited or acquired sense of social responsibility, whose sense of obligation to humanity, like that of Carnegie and Rosenwald, led them to spend their wealth for the benefit of mankind, according to their own conception of how mankind might best be helped. It is interesting to note that the old-fashioned idea of *noblesse oblige* was not the motivation of these men so much as a genuine and constructive knowledge of what wealth could do to make the world better.

Mention of names like Rockefeller, Carnegie and Rosenwald underscores the impossibility of making rigid classifications. Rockefeller, for example, was a conservator and expander, certainly, but his main activity was in the direction of spending money for the public good; therefore he is classified among the "Lords and Ladies Bountiful." Carnegie acquired his fortune in the nineteenth century and spent most of it himself in the twentieth, so that in a sense he was at once an accumulator and an inheritor. The foundations he established were the practical inheritors, but the American people themselves were the real beneficiaries, as will be pointed out. Rosenwald was, again, both an accumulator and an inheritor, in the same fashion as Carnegie, and he overspread the two centuries in a similar manner. Henry Ford was a nineteenth-century figure in spirit and in the manner of his accumulating, yet chronologically his fortune was made in the early years of the twentieth. Thus, in logic if not in fact, one can "revisit" him in the company of the robber barons, and yet observe elsewhere the uses he made of his own wealth, before his sons took charge of it.

There is more such overlapping in the pages that follow, but it appears unavoidable. Within the same family there often exist completely different philosophies of what to do with inherited money. It would be frivolous to pretend that one individual can stand for an entire family. The impact of inherited wealth on the personalities within a family is also varied, making playboys out of some Vanderbilts, for instance, and conscientious businessmen out of others, depending on those imponderables of human character that only a psychoanalyst can unravel. One analyst who did just that was Dr. Gregory Zilboorg, whose analysis changed Marshall Field III from a confused and unhappy spender to a happy, if not entirely resolved, participant in public affairs.

One may quibble, too, about words. "Wasters" carries an implication of irresponsibility, of careless dissipation, and while there are individuals in nearly all the families discussed in that section of the book who would qualify as both irresponsible and careless, others in the families were spenders for the more complicated reasons already described. Similarly, some "conservators and expanders" were not strangers to ostentation, or opulent spending, but the trend of their lives was to conserve their wealth and expand it. Thus the three categories of inheritors are necessarily broad and rough, with frequent overlapping.

Taken together, the lives of these people make clear once again the dramatic change in American life which has occurred in this century. Taxes, wars and depressions have ended forever the bold and unhampered individualism which marked the nineteenth-century accumulators. The death of *laissez faire* as a national economic policy was also their death. Their successors have been circumscribed by trusts and foundations and income fluctuating with the value of stocks and bonds. Some have made more money; a much higher percentage have not. For the most part, the great fortunes have fragmented, passing into many hands and becoming less liquid as time went on.

We have, it is true, a new breed of accumulators today. Probably they are as ruthless a lot at heart as the robber barons themselves, but government is now a powerful counterbalance to wealth, and the practices of the nineteenth century have been restricted by a veritable forest of regulations, enforced by a series of court decisions, which effectively curb the merciless exploitation of the public and each other so characteristic of financiers in the days of the senior Rockefeller and the first Mellon.

It is often said that regulations, combined with taxes, have made it impossible for anyone to accumulate great wealth today, but Paul Getty, for one, has contrived to amass a fortune that equals if it does not surpass any of the legendary treasuries of the past, nor are the Texas monoliths far behind. By comparison, the inheritors have become somewhat small potatoes in many instances. One can understand the absolute sincerity of Bernard Baruch's wry observation: "I would be a rich man today if I had stayed out of public life." To Mr. Baruch, a fortune of approximately twenty-five million dollars is nothing to brag about in comparison with the wealth accumulated by his contemporaries, to say nothing of the Texas monarchs and the wizards of international finance who are with us today.

These newer twentieth-century accumulators have been omitted from the considerations that follow. Not that they are to be disdained, but they are another story. The continuous narrative offered here concerns the rise of nineteenth-century wealth and its uses and abuses in this century by the men and women into whose hands it fell. Somewhere in the examination may emerge an answer to the paradox St. Paul has bequeathed us.

$ 2 $

The Robber Barons Revisited

A school of revisionist historians has arisen in the past few years to challenge the assumption that there was ever any such thing as a robber baron. They were, it appears, empire builders in the grand tradition who made America what it is today, and if they used methods which are frowned upon in our time, such chicanery must be viewed in the context of a period when rough methods were essential to the shaping of American industry and finance.

There can be no real quarrel with this thesis. In the long view of history, the late nineteenth-century industrial figures seem no better nor worse than those who came before or after them. Surely their sins were no more venal than those of the speculators and merchants in the early part of the century, whose activities were merely on a much smaller scale. Rascality, sharp dealing, ruthlessness and vaunting ambition did not die with the end of the last century. In our time these normal attributes of business have been converted by the ritual of transformation known as public relations into respectable corporate images, until it has become somehow un-American to say or imply that business is anything but the last best hope of free men.

The long struggle between capital and labor, beginning
with the advent of the Industrial Revolution, has done a
disservice to history by giving a black-and-white aspect to
the public consciousness of business and businessmen. If our
sympathies lie on the right, we take whole the revisionist
view of the robber barons and sanction everything that has
happened since in the blessed name of free enterprise. If we
turn left of center, the barons become even worse than they
have been painted, and what has happened since is seen as a
continuing struggle for the rights of workers against predatory capitalism.

We need to take a calmer view, perhaps, not in the interests of persuading General Motors and Walter Reuther to lie
down together as lambs, but for the sake of simple accuracy.
There is no better eminence from which to take such a view
than the era of the robber barons, removed as it is from the
partisan passions of the present and documented so amply
that it can be studied in depth and in perspective.

What, then, is the view from Morgan's head?

First of all, it seems inevitable that great fortunes should
have been accumulated in the nineteenth century; the expansion of business and industry could no more have been
controlled or avoided than could the total defeat of the Indians who lived on the country we took from them. Second,
the nature of man and society dictated that these fortunes
should be made by ruthless, often dishonest means, in a
period of unrestrained competition. But it did not dictate
that *every* fortune should be made by these means, or that
every robber baron should be a Fisk, a Gould or a Ryan.
Some, indeed, were neither robbers nor barons.

Similarly, it was not ordained by historical process that the
fortunes, made by whatever means, should be used primarily
for ostentation, or to make rich men richer. If it is true that

the *laissez-faire* moguls precipitated decades of bitter struggle between the haves and have-nots, which did not end until government became as large and formidable as both, it is also true that their money is responsible for the better part of American culture today.

For years it was fashionable to attribute this tremendous outpouring of wealth into the fabric of society to nothing more than the guilty conscience of the rich. It may have been so in a few cases, but the motivation seems immaterial and the result absolutely vital to our national life. That result lies all about us, on the campuses of our universities, in art galleries, libraries, concert halls, parks, civic activities of every kind, hospitals, research laboratories, and nearly every other field of human activity. Take away the wealth of the robber barons from these areas, and there would be precious little left to contemplate.

Let us not, therefore, consider the great accumulators as entirely greedy and conscienceless pirates, nor yet as anointed saints of the free enterprise system, but as men representative of their times who had the good fortune to be born in the era when industrial America was forged. They were a breed of individualists now largely vanished, most of them somewhat larger than life, possessed of certain common vices and virtues.

Perhaps the largest single fact in their lives, as it was for so many Americans, was the Civil War. A negligible number of them fought in it. Some were too young, but for other accumulators it was the golden chance to begin accumulating. Tacitly they followed the counsel of Andrew Mellon's father: "It is only greenhorns who enlist." Those who did not begin by supplying the armies started by filling the bottomless pit of civilian needs after the war.

An omniscient eye looking down upon America in mid-nineteenth century could have seen the future accumulators on the march. They had several characteristics in common. Mostly they came from the farms and small towns; they had little use for formal education, and most of them quit school as soon as they were old enough to work. They were one and all possessed by a driving ambition which had to do not so much with making money for its own sake as with playing the great American national game of business, and playing it to win. Only this peculiar kind of ambition can explain their single-minded devotion and their inability to stop until long after there was any reason to accumulate more wealth. One sees this trait today, as characteristic now as it was then, in industrial leaders who play the all-absorbing game for the fun of it because it is their passion in life; they are no less dedicated than the virtuoso pianist or the baseball player.

The game was new and shiny then, a game for individual stars, not for committees and teams, and they came to it eagerly, out of poverty, struggling competitively for a new life beyond mere subsistence.

Here was Peter Arrell Brown Widener, through with high school after two years, working as a butcher's boy in his brother's meat shop and examining the Republican Party with the profound fascination of a cat among the beef kidneys. Farther north in the Puritan precincts of Eastham, Massachusetts, twenty-year-old Gustavus Franklin Swift was opening his first butcher shop, after four years of adolescent slaughtering, while his future Chicago rival, Philip Danforth Armour, a New York State boy himself, was far away from meat and home, laboring with thirty other Oneida men in the gold mines of California.

Leland Stanford, another York State lad who was to find gold of a different kind in California, was practicing law in Port Washington, Wisconsin, and preparing to marry an Albany girl. Thomas Fortune Ryan was a lean, hungry Virginia farm boy, about to be thrown on the world orphaned and penniless, but little more than two decades away from a seat on the New York Stock Exchange.

In the village of Parma, Ohio, John D. and William Rockefeller were waiting for their father, a patent medicine spellbinder, to move at last into Cleveland, where oil and incredible fortune awaited them. Down the river in Pittsburgh, Henry Phipps, always a cautious man, was a thirteen-year-old clerk in a jewelry store, who read poetry at night and was seemingly a long day's journey from a fortune in steel.

John Pierpont Morgan was studying mathematics at the University of Göttingen, certain of a job in his father's banking house, while in upstate New York a boy surveyor named Jay Gould was making maps of the countryside and assiduously saving $5000 before he was twenty-one so that he might ultimately become a thorn in Mr. Morgan's financial flesh. Farther south, in the anthracite fields of Pennsylvania, housewives were opening their doors to a bearded young peddler of stove polish, Meyer Guggenheim, who was about to found one of the astonishing dynasties of the century. And in nearby Delaware the Du Pont dynasty to end all dynasties was already in full cry.

Thus they came on, all sorts and conditions, and slowly a pattern began to form as they drifted into the major new industries of expanding America and began to dominate them. Oil, railroads, steel, meat packing, banking, automobiles at last—these were the major fields on which they fought each other and the government.

The most successful of them were three quiet men whose immense fortunes were made almost by stealth, cold men whose only interest was business, slight men physically whose presences were not impressive. Other accumulators were often flamboyant, or they were sportsmen, or they loved good living, and almost without exception they were big men of commanding presence. But not the three giants, the three billionaires of our time: Andrew W. Mellon, John D. Rockefeller and Henry Ford. Ford, perhaps, requires a word of explanation. As explained earlier, he overlapped the two centuries in spirit and in fact, although his fortune was made in this century. In the public mind, he would not have fitted into the image of Mellon and Rockefeller, but in reality he was as cold and quiet as they; physically slight and unimpressive; interested almost exclusively in business, although his other interests were far better publicized; he became a billionaire not only because he made a product so many people wanted, but because he was a ruthless and talented behind-the-scenes manipulator of men and managements.

Of the three, however, Mellon remains the apotheosis of great power concentrated in a man whose whole personality was so withdrawn that he was an anonymous figure even to his contemporaries. He came by it honestly. His father, Judge Thomas Mellon, a Pennsylvania farm boy who came of frugal Ulster stock, was described as a "cold, impenetrable person, hardly human, a granite-like figure," who called his marriage a "transaction," and wrote of it: "There was no love making. Had I been rejected, I would have left neither sad nor depressed nor greatly disappointed, only annoyed at the loss of time."

Judge Mellon made the bulk of his fortune out of the Civil War and, when it was over, began the bank that was to be the foundation of Andrew's wealth. The judge had been cold but forceful. His son, one of eight other children, was shy and wispy. In Stewart Holbrook's memorable phrase he looked "like someone just leaving the room," yet he became a titan of finance. How did he do it, and so unobtrusively that at sixty-six, involved as official or director in companies capitalized at two billion dollars, he was still unknown? He paid attention to business and nothing else. Instead of building railroads or steel mills or oil refineries, he provided the money for the builders, always acquiring a part of what he sponsored, until the growth of these basic industries built his own fortune, all of them contributing to it.

In the lives of the accumulators, as in other men, there is always a point on which destiny pivots. But what seems a matter of chance or luck in others becomes prescience in the man of business genius, a kind of sixth sense. How else can one explain Mellon's action in listening to a young inventor named Charles Hall, who had already been turned down by responsible capitalists in Boston and Cleveland when he went to them with his idea for making aluminum? Mellon not only helped him start the Pittsburgh Reduction Company, retaining part of it, but instigated that noted infringement-of-patent suit which ended in a decision by a federal judge in Cleveland, William Howard Taft. The decision was favorable to Hall and worth, so it was estimated, a hundred million dollars to the Mellons. For the road was then clear to the creation of an aluminum trust; eventually the Pittsburgh Reduction Company's name was changed to the Aluminum Company of America.

Mellon became the great supplier of capital to industry, one industry leading into another like a nest of boxes. Bauxite was the basis of aluminum, and when Mellon controlled the supply, he was in the wire and radiator businesses, to name only two. Aluminum was also a prime ingredient of automobiles. He organized the Union Steel Company, whose steel went into his Standard Steel Car Company, and the bridges built by his McClintic-Marshall Construction Company. Then, having built this little empire, he sold its base, the

Union Steel Company, to the burgeoning colossus of United States Steel for a good deal more than it was worth.

Thus the Mellon organization grew, stretching out arms of substantial interest and sometimes control into dozens of organizations. Ranks of underlings stood between these companies and the man at the center, but there was nothing particularly sinister about it. The muckrakers who later pictured Andrew Mellon as an octopus secluded in a Pittsburgh cavern, extending in every direction to strangle American business to his own advantage, failed to understand that Mellon had no power complex and no particular interest in money for its own sake. He knew nothing at all about the enjoyment of money and took no pleasure in spending it. His joy was organization, building pyramids of business blocks like a child at play.

As he had befriended Charles Hall, so did he extend his help to another inventor, Dr. Heinrich Koppers, whose coke-making process Mellon acquired for an insignificant $300,000 —plant, patents and all. In four years, thanks to the First World War, this enterprise was worth $15,500,000, and when the war was over, Mellon built another of his fantastic pyramids upon it, a holding company composed of fifty-seven different corporations. This was the Koppers Company of Delaware. A similar empire, of twenty-four subsidiaries, was Pittsburgh Coal. Never was there mention of Mellon's name in these or other businesses. He was involved with at least six holding companies, and innumerable single corporations, yet his was the silent hand in their operation. His name never appeared.

What a lonely man he must have been, self-isolated from other human beings, unable or unwilling to be a part of the human race. His Irish wife, she that was Nora McMullen of Dublin, could not stand the gloom of Pittsburgh or her husband and went home in 1909. Mellon's only concern, it appears, was to keep the matter private. He went so far as to use his political power for the passage of a new state divorce law permitting courts to appoint masters who could hear evidence in private. That was how the Mellon evidence was heard in 1912. When it was over, he went right on living in his somber Pittsburgh mansion, sometimes turning an "ice-water smile" upon his son Paul.

Lucius Beebe, who knew him, told Stewart Holbrook, who reported it in his *Age of the Moguls,* that he was having breakfast with Mellon one morning, and the master was enjoying his favorite thin hot cakes and sausages when a servant brought in a telephone with the advice that the French Minister of Finance was waiting to speak with him. Mellon was irritated. "Not with the hot cakes," he protested, and then to Beebe: "These foreigners have no sense of propriety."

Mellon was sometimes pictured as a greedy miser whose passion was accumulation, but this was the man who burned the notes of small debtors at Christmastime and gave away his money in large bundles with the greatest secrecy. He shuddered at the idea of good will or personal popularity. A chain smoker, he could have bought the finest Havanas in carload lots, but he smoked a small cigar called Between the Acts, ten for fifteen cents. He had one extravagance, though, a custom-built car, every part of which came from some product he dominated. It cost forty thousand dollars, and of course most of its construction was aluminum.

No one would ever have heard of Andrew Mellon, outside of the business world, if he had not been proposed to President Harding as Secretary of the Treasury. "Who's he?" inquired Harding, a calm man himself. He had never heard of the richest mogul in America. But Mellon was Harding's kind of Secretary, and even more so Coolidge's and Hoover's, both of whom he served well, earning himself a place in history as the last Secretary to succeed in reducing the national debt. Understandably, Mellon favored reducing income taxes and surtaxes. As have so many other less fortunate Americans, Mellon had his own tax return for 1931 investigated in 1935, but he did not live to see himself exonerated two years later.

Perhaps the Internal Revenue Bureau simply wore itself out investigating. Mellon no doubt had the most complicated personal tax situation of any living citizen. His dividends in 1929 from his banking interests alone had amounted to nearly four million dollars, and his profits from bonds and shares were more than ninety million. No political appointee ever had more conflicts of interest to avoid; when Harding appointed him, he had to resign from the boards of fifty-one corporations.

Having finally emerged in the public eye, Mellon was sometimes ridiculed for political reasons, but he was seldom reviled as the prototype of the evil rich man except by a few militant writers. John Davison Rockefeller was not so lucky. It was hard for the public to hate Mellon, about whom they knew so little and whose pictures made him look like the tired little bookkeeper afraid of losing his job, whom everyone knew at the office. Rockefeller, however, who lived to see nearly a century of life in America, endured what to most people would have been an intolerable burden—the general hatred and fear of his fellow men. If it troubled Rockefeller, no one knew. He was totally anesthetic to public opinion and, like Mellon, he was isolated from everyone. In later years he fed his thin body on graham crackers and milk, but his mind constantly subsisted on the always nourishing matter of business.

Rockefeller, the second of the three American billionaires,

resembled the others in that he had no taste for the things money could buy. He had Mellon's enjoyment of manipulation, of building, of sitting at the center of an intricate and complex web. These men were essentially creators of wealth.

John D.'s father, William, had hoped to create wealth too, but he chose what seemed an easier road, calling himself Doctor and selling dubious patent medicines from hotel rooms and wagons in the grand style of the American pitchman. He was a breezy man; Mellon's father would have hated him on sight. His two sons, John and William, knew him as a traveling man who was often away from home, leaving them little to eat and wear in the New York State village of Richford where the family lived when the boys were growing up.

Yet it was the old pitchman who gave his hardheaded son John a start in the business world, and he made a sharp deal of it, too, by asking ten per cent interest on the thousand dollars he was lending to help the eighteen-year-old start a commission firm. Father William made a handsome gesture, however. If John made his interest payments regularly, he could have the principal as a gift when he was twenty-one. John D. had no trouble paying the interest. Out of his $3.50 a week salary, he had already been giving $1.80 a month in religious philanthropy. The fact that he wore the same shabby clothes summer and winter did not concern him.

By this time the family was living in Cleveland, where John started his new firm. His father had made a good investment and could have made a far better deal if he had possessed his son's business sense, because the newly founded commission house did a gross business of nearly a half million dollars in its first year. It was a modest start toward a billion. None of his associates thought at first that the thin and pious young man was the kind of fellow who could amass such wealth.

He accomplished it somewhat as Mellon had, by pyramiding, but the manner was different because he concentrated on one industry, oil, and he knew how to work with other men. Cold and single-minded he may have been, but he did not possess Mellon's pathological shyness. He surrounded himself with able associates who were, oddly enough, very like his father in temperament and quite unlike himself.

Henry Morrison Flagler was one of these, a medicine man of finance, uninhibited and looking sharply for the main chance. The chance was Rockefeller. To John D., Flagler was a means of getting the uncle of his new partner's wife, Stephen V. Harkness, an Ohio whiskey king, to put money into a new refinery. At the same time Rockefeller brought in his brother William. They could scarcely have been more dissimilar. William had inherited his father's jovial disposition and something else his brother wanted—an extraordinary talent for selling.

John D. went on acquiring partners who were equally useful, and with whom he had little in common. John Dustin Archbold, the competitor he bought out, was also a Baptist, but he was a poker-playing persuader and an aggressive businessman who loved battle. Henry H. Rogers, a Fair Haven, Massachusetts, boy whose Brooklyn refinery John D. acquired, was a profane young man Rockefeller never liked, but he was tough and able and without visible scruples.

The story of how these men, with Rockefeller the master mind directing them, built the Standard Oil Company is a familiar one. John D.'s notorious economy and his incredible efficiency were factors in his success, but it was achieved chiefly by the ruthless crushing of competitors, which made him a villain. He honestly could not understand why he was hanged and burned in effigy at Titusville, nor why a congressional investigating committee termed his attempt to elim-

inate competition in Pennsylvania "one of the most gigantic and dangerous conspiracies ever conceived." John D. was shocked by such language. Nor could he see anything wrong in building Standard Oil into the first American trust. Monopoly was simply the most efficient way to do business; it was the opposite of waste, which he hated. It was also, and he saw this quite clearly, the way all American business was tending in the latter years of the nineteenth century.

By the time he had created his trust, business was full of them, and they were being busted by Teddy Roosevelt and exposed by the muckraking magazines, which were now reaching a newly created mass audience. Standard Oil was the most obvious target. Other trusts were bad, but Standard was the public's favorite whipping boy, particularly when it was discovered that the United States Senate was virtually its subsidiary. Naturally, the man who headed it became the archvillain of the era, and remained so until he died, in another era when capitalism was also unpopular.

Probably no other rich man has been so bitterly attacked, and while John D. failed to understand it, he took the same kind of attitude toward public abuse that he had taken toward business, in which he succeeded, so he remarked, because "we never deceived ourselves." True, he told his Sunday school class that it was wrong "to assume that men of immense wealth are always unhappy," but it is unlikely that Rockefeller ever experienced any worse unhappiness than he did on the day in 1911 when the Supreme Court dissolved Standard Oil and cast its refineries, pipe lines, oil fields, ship lines and other related industries to the corporate wolves.

The dissolution hardly disturbed the Rockefeller fortune. John D. had amassed more than two hundred million dollars for himself in thirty years, before he retired in 1896. His brother William had laid by only a little less, somewhere between a hundred and fifty and two hundred million dollars. By the time the Supreme Court got around to tampering with the source of this wealth, John D.'s fortune had reached a billion without his having to turn a hand. He had made his money from kerosene; then the automobile was invented and he made it five times over in gasoline.

If he had cared anything about money, John D. might have blessed the name of Henry Ford as he sat in retirement among the Pocantico Hills near Tarrytown, New York. But he was an ascetic, as he had always been, and utterly incapable of enjoying his wealth. There was the tray with his milk and graham crackers, which he munched while he read Ella Wheeler Wilcox. Rockefeller was not literary; he had never taken the time to read. He neither smoked nor drank. Golf was his only recreation, and even there his dime tips only brought more ridicule upon him. But presumably he never asked himself, What was it all for? Virtue and business had been their own reward.

Henry Ford was curiously like him. As the last billionaire, his fortune was a product of the twentieth century, but he himself was a true son of the nineteenth. There was nothing of the modern man about Henry; he was the perpetual farm boy with a mechanical turn of mind, disdainful of book learning but curious about a great many things. Like Mellon and Rockefeller, he was an organizer, but he lacked Mellon's financial genius and Rockefeller's superb grasp of corporate management. Ford was not an originator, a creator; his talent lay in organizing methods already extant and improving on them until they approached perfection. He was a gaunt, angular man like Rockefeller, more of an individualist and totally self-centered, an attribute he shared with the other accumulators.

After the Ford Motor Company was launched in 1903 with

twelve partners, it grew in competition with the other auto manufacturers at a respectable rate. Fortunately for Ford, five of the partners were impatient with the rate of progress and permitted Ford to buy them out. The majority control thus acquired gave him freedom to carry out the dream that made him famous and earned his fortune. He wanted to make a thousand cars a day, to sell for about the same price as a horse and buggy, machines that could be repaired easily and cheaply—in brief, transportation for the masses. It was a revolutionary idea for a time that considered the automobile a symbol of the well to do, "of the arrogance of wealth, with all its independence and carelessness," as the president of Princeton, Woodrow Wilson, put it.

Everyone knows how the Model T revolutionized American life, except possibly the people who share Ford's distaste for history and in any case cannot visualize life without a machine which is at once necessity, social symbol and love substitute. Ford revolutionized industrial life too, with the five-dollar day, which his business manager, James Couzens, invented to circumvent a labor insurrection within the plant and the threat of union organization without.

As time went on, and the Ford Motor Company waxed great and powerful, its founder retreated more and more into a dream world which had little relation to the business community in which his enterprise operated. Always more or less out of touch with reality, he could not understand what was happening in the America of the twenties, or what his competitors were up to. His Model A, introduced in 1928, was good for only five years, where the Model T had lasted twenty, because other auto makers were rapidly educating the public to buy a new car every year, and were far outstripping Ford in styling.

Nor could the country mechanic comprehend the revolution in national life of the thirties. He fought against collective bargaining and the rise of big unions with every weapon, fair and foul, at his command. The strategy was terror. Before it was over, and the UAW got the best contract of any in the industry, some of the blackest pages in the history of industrial management had been written by the company.

But it is idle to write objectively about Henry Ford. The public will have none of it. People much prefer the legend, which was propagated by one of the most astute and successful public relations efforts ever seen in industry. Ford has emerged from it as a kind of rustic American saint, against whom it is heresy to speak evil. He is, indeed, a phenomenon among the accumulators, since he is the only one of them— and a billionaire at that—who escaped popular attack as a capitalist, bloated or not.

That, of course, is because the propagators had an ideal subject. Ford was a man of the people, particularly the rural people. He was the stereotyped figure of the shrewd farmer come to town, making his way successfully against the city slickers. His distrust of banks and bankers was well known. He preached the gospel of hard work, low prices and simplicity. The richer he became the more he denounced the money-changers, and to the horror of his fellow capitalists, he even came out strongly against the profit motive.

When the Chicago *Tribune's* lawyers had Ford on the stand in the famous libel case of 1919, exposing his ignorance and his virtual illiteracy, they discovered that it was really rural America that was on trial. The solemn observation of *The New York Times* that Ford had been "submitted to a severe examination of his intellectual qualities," and that he had "not received a passing degree" only amused the company's advertising and public relations experts. They were not concerned with what the *Times* thought; they were interested in Main Street's opinion. The trial had confirmed the admiration of Main Street for this typical citizen of the American prairie country, who had come of age in 1884, married a country girl of his own kind, and whose philosophy came unashamedly out of the cracker barrel. He was one of Main Street's own citizens.

Nevertheless, an effort was made to strengthen further the Ford public image when the trial was over. A staff of writers in Detroit began to turn out books and smaller compositions under Ford's name, and eventually the man who had defined "ballyhoo" on the stand as "a blackguard or something of that nature" became an author, with cards under his name in library files, reviewed in the newspapers, and quoted widely by press and public.

Ford stands alone among the accumulators. When he died in 1947, no one could really estimate his wealth, except that it was in the neighborhood of a billion, yet to the end he lived like the simple man he truly was, in spite of the physical luxury of his surroundings. The kerosene lamp by which he died, a storm having snuffed out the normal power, illumined the thin, lined face of a man who had been consistently himself all his life. That he was an anachronism never occurred to him; it was the rest of the world that was out of step.

The gulf that separates Ford, Rockefeller and Mellon from the other accumulators is not merely one of comparative wealth. It is a matter of spirit, and the lives of the railroad builders well exemplify it. There is a vigor about them, a healthy rascality that makes them seem far more alive than the billionaires. Pirates they were, with few scruples to detain them, and there is no doubt it is primarily these men who deserve the epithet "robber barons," but as personalities they stand by themselves, rugged and unrepentant.

Somehow the Vanderbilt family, at least its nineteenth-century progenitors, has come to stand for the whole breed, dominated by the overpowering figure of the first Cornelius Vanderbilt, who stormed out of Port Richmond, Staten Island, in the early years of the nineteenth century to found a transportation empire. What a loudmouthed, profane, tobacco-chewing, hardheaded old rogue he was, and yet possessed of a splendid courage and a vision almost too broad for his times.

The Commodore, as he came to be known, was out of school at eleven and in business for himself at sixteen, ferrying passengers and freight between Staten Island and New York in a sailing vessel. War helped him, as it did so many accumulators. In 1812 he bustled around New York Harbor supplying the forts in and near it under government contract. After it was over he sold his boats and went to work for Thomas Gibbons, who plied a ferry between New Brunswick and New York when he wasn't trying to save himself from being overwhelmed by the steam navigation monopoly which the New York legislature had thoughtfully granted to Robert Fulton.

The Commodore knew what to do about monopoly: create a better one. He made Gibbons' boat show a profit within a single year, and within a decade he was able to go into the steamboat business himself, up the Hudson to Albany, up and down Long Island Sound, and along the coast to Providence and Boston. In five years he had made a half million dollars; in another ten he was a millionaire. It was time to move into New York society then, and he began to build a fine town house for himself on Washington Place, but his wife tearfully, stubbornly refused to move into the city.

Sophia, his cousin, who had been his neighbor when he married her at nineteen, was an otherwise faithful wife. She had, after all, given him thirteen children. But Vanderbilt would not tolerate defiance of his wishes; he could not, in fact, understand it, and simply had Sophia committed as insane for a few months until she was ready, meek and subdued again, to be mistress of the New York house.

He was, however, a kindly family man, or so it seemed in 1853 when he took his first vacation. Into his steam yacht *North Star* he packed his entire family, including sons-in-law and grandchildren, along with a few invited guests and an official chronicler of the expedition, and proceeded to tour Europe in the manner of an Eastern potentate.

Vanderbilt was nearly seventy when he turned from steamboats to railroads, but in a few years he contrived to make his name memorable. He got control of the New York Central, fought Drew, Gould and Fisk for the Erie, and in little more than five years created one of the great American transportation systems, which paid its dividends as usual during the panic of 1873 while Vanderbilt was calmly letting contracts for the building of Grand Central Terminal.

After what might be described as a full life, the Commodore died in 1877, having lingered for eight months as a result of his admirable constitution. He left behind him his second wife of seven years, a Southern young lady from Mobile with the unlikely name of Frank Armstrong Crawford, and a fortune estimated at more than $100,000,000. Nearly all of it, $90,000,000, went to his son William Henry, while William's four sons got $7,500,000. Four million was to be divided among his eight daughters. His wife had to be content with $500,000 in cash, the home her predecessor had been so reluctant to live in, and two thousand shares of New York Central stock, worth considerably more than their weight in gold. The Commodore had cut off the women in his life with a comparative pittance. That was because he neither trusted nor liked females.

Late in his life Vanderbilt discovered philanthropy and gave a million dollars to Vanderbilt University, in effect founding it. His only other charity appears to have been $50,000 given to the Church of the Strangers, in New York, whose pastor was his friend.

His son William, then fifty-six, assumed control of the family fortune. William had survived what might have been ruinous to the psyches of some children: growing up in the knowledge of his powerful father's contempt because he appeared to be weak physically and hardly forceful mentally. He had further offended his father by marrying at nineteen, as the Commodore himself had done. The elder Vanderbilt, however, thought it foolish for anyone who was as weak and had as few prospects as William to get married at all. His foreboding seemed justified when William's health began to fail soon after the marriage. Disgustedly, considering his son a failure, the Commodore set him up on a seventy-acre farm at New Dorp, on Staten Island, and left him on it, to die or vegetate. There William began the long climb back to favor.

He began by putting the farm on a paying basis, increasing it to three hundred and fifty acres and populating it with four sons and four daughters. Then he persuaded his father to get him appointed as receiver for the Staten Island Railroad, a decrepit line with thirteen miles of trackage which was about to go under in the depression of 1857. William nursed this tottering rural line back to health, and thus, while his father was still in the steamboat business, he became a railroad executive.

This was the kind of accomplishment the Commodore could understand. He rescued his son from rural exile, gave him a house on Fifth Avenue, and made him vice-president of the New York & Harlem Railroad. It was too late, however, to mend the relations between father and son. By this time William was understandably a bitter and cynical man, and although he accepted the new role his father had assigned him, he knew himself to be still in the shadow—knew it because his father refused to make him a full executive until the old man's health began to fail. William then had only nine years of his own life remaining, but he spent them in demonstrating that he knew how to manage and expand railroad properties.

He showed himself a man of more generous nature than his father. When the Commodore's will was contested by his second son, Cornelius Jeremiah, an epileptic ne'er-do-well, who had been left with only $200,000, and two of the eight daughters, who felt themselves cheated, William did not rest on the court victory awarded him by a surrogate but by means of a secret compromise guaranteed Jeremiah the income from a million dollars and gave each of his eight sisters an additional half million in bonds.

To the men who worked for him he was no less generous, in an era when such generosity was virtually unknown. His trainmen and laborers, who were loyal to him in the railroad strike of 1877 even after their wages were cut, were rewarded with the distribution of $100,000.

Although he must have hated his father, William was like him in several respects. He was a horse lover, as all the Vanderbilts seem to be, and besides owning some race horses, liked to drive his fast trotters about the roads of upper Manhattan. He also took the Commodore's constructive attitude about the expansion of the railroads. But he was fond of painting and sculpture, something his father had no time for, and installed a fine collection in the splendid Fifth Avenue home he built. In 1884 he went out of his way to rectify one of his father's business deals, in which the Commodore had lent $150,000 to General Ulysses S. Grant and taken in security several real estate parcels, the general's swords and medals, his art collection and several precious objects given to him by foreign governments. Grant had never been able to repay the loan. William gave the entire security back to his widow.

In business, William operated in a quieter way than his father, but in the eight years during which he held the reins himself, he managed nearly to double the family fortune, and he made careful plans for its distribution after his death, which came suddenly in 1885. Each of his eight children got ten million dollars, half outright and half in trust; most of them had already been given mansions. Cornelius, his eldest son, was given two million more, with another million to a grandson Cornelius. A million was divided among missions, churches, hospitals, the YMCA, the Metropolitan Museum and Vanderbilt University, to which he had given $450,000 in his lifetime, along with $50,000 to St. Bartholomew's Church and $500,000 to the College of Physicians and Surgeons.

The remainder of the estate he divided between his two eldest sons, Cornelius and William Kissam, except for the payment of a $200,000 annuity to his widow, Maria, who was also given the house and his art collection, both of which would go to another son, George, upon her death.

There were small touches in the will that were typical of William. He provided enough money to rebuild the Moravian Church at New Dorp; his father and mother had been parishioners there, and in it he and his brothers and sisters had been christened.

Thus passed the second generation of Vanderbilts. The

Commodore and his son had accumulated the wealth, some $200,000,000 of it. It remained for three of William's sons to build further on it and carry the fortune into the twentieth century.

On balance, and as railroad tycoons, the Vanderbilts were admirable people, if one discounts old Cornelius' rough methods in founding the fortune. But the Commodore at his worst could not have competed with the chicanery that distinguished many of the other railroad builders. One of them, Jay Gould, became a symbol of predatory accumulating.

As did so many of the barons, Gould rose from poverty. Born on a scrabbly hill farm in Roxbury, New York, he started life as a blacksmith, then as a clerk in a country store. But from the start he exhibited his one great and useful talent: he knew instinctively how to make money. By the time he was twenty-one, he had five thousand dollars of it, earned through surveying, and he was off on a career hard to match for sheer, unabashed rascality.

His first venture was a tannery in northern Pennsylvania. The New York leather merchant who helped him gain control of it regretted the day he allied himself with Gould, whose speculations probably drove his partner to suicide.

With his tannery money as a backlog, Gould turned his attention to railroads, beginning in a small way by speculating with the minor lines. Then, in 1867, occurred the fateful amalgamation of fortunes when Gould and James Fisk joined Daniel Drew in the complicated career of the Erie Railroad, and there followed an epic battle with old Cornelius Vanderbilt for control of the line, during which injunctions were defied and the New York State legislature bribed. When the smoke cleared, Vanderbilt was defeated, Drew had retired, and Gould and Fisk were in the saddle. This precious pair proceeded to compound their villainy by systematically loot-ing the company, in concert with the infamous Tammany leader William Tweed and others.

Having made millions by watering down the stock of the Erie, Gould and his friends branched out into the credit, produce and export markets of the nation, and tried to corner the gold market. Even for a wild and lawless era in business, it was too much. The newspapers informed the public, and the public rose in anger. Fisk escaped the consequences by tumbling down the marble staircase of the Broadway Central Hotel, two bullets in his body from the jealous hand of Edward S. Stokes, his rival for the favors of Josie Mansfield. Tweed was tracked down and broken by *The New York Times*. Gould suffered the least. He lost control of the Erie, but he consoled himself with the knowledge that his other assets totaled twenty-five million dollars.

Gould next turned his speculative talents toward the young railroads of the new West, and there he bought into the lines that crisscrossed the Southwest—the Union Pacific and the Kansas Pacific, the Denver Pacific and the Central Pacific, and the Missouri Pacific. He owned half of the Southwest's total trackage by 1890. In New York, he acquired the New York *World*, not yet a great newspaper, most of the elevated railways, and all of Western Union.

Gould, indeed, had everything but friends. It was not alone that he was an unscrupulous man whom other men had learned not to trust. He was a calculating human being whom it was impossible to like. Not that Gould appeared to care. His only diversions outside of making money were books and gardening, but he had little time for either, and death by tuberculosis overtook him at fifty-six before he learned to enjoy his money, if in fact he could ever have done so. By that time it was 1892 and the era of the moguls was nearly over. The era had done well by Jay, christened Jason, Gould. It had given him a fortune estimated at well over $200,000,000.

In his Western foray, Gould had encountered but wisely avoided taking on the railroad magnate of the Coast, Collis Potter Huntington. This native of Connecticut, another poor boy who had begun to support himself at fourteen, was a Californian by adoption. Huntington arrived with the gold rush in 1849, but a day of scrabbling in the mountains convinced him that there was more gold to be found in supplying the miners. Thus he built the firm of Huntington & Hopkins, and laid the cornerstone of his fortune.

Huntington soon became a powerful figure in California. A big man physically—over six feet, weighing more than two hundred pounds—he had the sheer exuberant drive to dominate such strong partners as Leland Stanford, Mark Hopkins and Charles Crocker, and with them to get the Central Pacific built across the Sierra Nevada Mountains, hooking up with the Union Pacific in 1869 to make a transcontinental rail route. Huntington risked everything he owned in the project, but he wound up controlling it. With this line as a starting point, he gathered in other California lines and out of them formed the Southern Pacific in 1884.

He had the feeling of the true creator, but he was also in railroading for power and profit. In Washington, lobbying for his company's interests, he was known as a profane and cynical man, not above bribery, although there was never any direct evidence of it. In the business world he was known from Nob Hill to Fifth Avenue (he had homes in both these places) as a man who collected transportation systems as other men did books. He owned all or parts of such diverse and scattered properties as the Chesapeake & Ohio Railroad, the Pacific Mail Steamship Company, the Mexican International Railway Company, the United States & Brazil Steamship Company, the Old Dominion Steamship Company, the Market Street Railway of San Francisco, and several small railroads in Kentucky, Ohio and Indiana.

He left the Southern Pacific as his monument, blessed and cursed by his fellow Californians, depending on whether his indomitable course had affected their lives for good or ill. When people accused him of being unscrupulous, he could always point to the fact that he broke with Leland Stanford because he suspected the senator of using Southern Pacific influence for his own advantage, although Huntington himself never hesitated to use it.

There was never a public accounting of the profits accruing from the construction of the Central Pacific and Southern Pacific, but the relative strength of the men involved in it can be judged by the size of their estates. When the plundering was done at last, Stanford's estate was appraised at more than nineteen million dollars, Charles Crocker's at about twenty-four million, Hopkins' at somewhat less than either, and Huntington's at between fifty and eighty million.

The immoral, and often illegal, means by which these Western freebooters accumulated their wealth were various. As governor of California, for example, Stanford influenced legislation which meant the diverting of nearly a million dollars in public money to the Central Pacific, of which he was also president. He was equally adept at manipulating the law and the courts, when his railroad interests were involved, and he acted as front man for the others on public occasions.

The chief instrument of corruption used by the Big Four, however, was the Contract & Finance Company, which they organized themselves. With this paper dummy they contracted to build the Central Pacific, and it was not long before they had acquired by that device several millions of personal profit from investors' money. Later, they thoughtfully destroyed all the records of this useful corporation, just before the government was about to examine them.

In combining all the small Western lines in sight with the Central Pacific to form the monopoly known as the Southern Pacific, the Big Four did not balk at any form of chicanery. They bought members of the California legislature as easily as Standard Oil later purchased United States senators, and the Big Four anticipated the oil gang in Washington, too, where they sometimes dispensed a half million dollars' worth of bribes in a single session. Sacramento only cost them half as much.

When their monopoly was complete, the Big Four held California in a position of virtual blackmail. Their tariffs were the highest in America, but any industry in which they held an interest could be certain of a rebate. Nothing could move on rails within the state except on the terms of these four ruthless men. If anyone or anything blocked them, or a piece of legislation was required to accomplish some new outrage, the well-greased California legislature could be counted upon to do what was needed. County and city governments were even more subservient. If settlers along the right-of-way revolted when the Southern Pacific wanted their lands, as they did in 1880, they were shot, and if railroad men were killed in the shooting, along with the farmers, it was the farmers who went to prison.

No wonder Frank Norris called his thinly disguised book about the Big Four and its workings *The Octopus*.

By the peculiar logic of wealth, Huntington and his associates escaped the kind of public anger that Gould inspired. Fraud and theft were the stock in trade of the railroad barons, but somehow Gould had emerged as a wrecker, while the Huntington crowd, which had accomplished as much damage in its own way, was accepted by society, and even honored, although they made it quite plain they considered that railroads or their owners owed no obligation to the public. Stanford was elected to the United States Senate by the very people he had plundered, and he generously rewarded them with Leland Stanford University. Huntington was not a giver. His justification was the splendid railway system he had created, which had meant so much to the economic life of the country.

There, once more, lay the paradox. These men were unquestionably builders of the nation. The methods they used to do it were, without doubt, immoral by any reasonable standard, yet consistent with the morality of nineteenth-century accumulation, and only different in degree and kind from what came before and after.

Sometimes an accumulator ran the gamut from attack to eulogy in his lifetime. Such a man was James Jerome Hill, who came from the poverty of an Ontario village, minus one eye which had been shot out by an arrow, and landed in St. Paul in 1856, just too late to join a brigade of trappers and traders setting out on their annual push to the West Coast. Hill perforce had to stay in St. Paul for another year, and from that little trading station of 5000 people he embarked on the adventure that made him an immense fortune. However, he had become attached to St. Paul and thereafter considered it his home.

Hill got his wealth by creating the Great Northern Railway, fighting off Edward Harriman to do it. The methods he used were no different from Huntington's or Gould's. When he made his start as a railroader by buying the nearly defunct St. Paul & Pacific Railroad, with some associates, he got it at a bargain by taking the bondholders' committee of the bankrupt line over the worst parts of the roadbed in the worst rolling stock he could find. When he began rebuilding

the road, renamed the Great Northern, and pushed it west-
ward to the Pacific, he punished towns along the route which
refused to co-operate with him on his terms by by-passing
them entirely. When he had to fight Harriman for rights of
way along the Columbia River, he did it with tough, armed
gangs of men as well as legal skirmishing. Later, this battle
was fought on a larger scale in Central Oregon, with shovels,
crowbars, pick handles and dynamite as the weapons, and
numerous casualties as the result. In brief, Hill was a talented
man who fought hard and aggressively in the field or on the
Stock Exchange, where, with the help of Morgan money, he
manipulated railroad stocks in the traditional manner.

Still, he was one of the lesser villains of railroading. The
holding company he created in 1901 to control his properties
was attacked as contrary to the anti-trust law, and in 1904
the Supreme Court ordered its dissolution. Hill insisted he
hadn't known the Sherman Act applied to railroads, and it
may be he was telling the truth. In combining the Northern
Pacific, Great Northern and Burlington roads under one
financial roof, so that money could be shifted from one to
the other without public knowledge, he was only doing what
was common practice in building the financial empires of
those days, before the Supreme Court began upsetting these
combinations in restraint of trade. To Hill, restraining the
trade of his competitors was only the obvious result of good
business.

Later in his life Hill was widely admired, at least in some
sections of the press. His devotion to stockholders was
praised, and it was undeniable that he loved books. The Hill
Reference Library in St. Paul was his gift to the city. He also
collected modern French art, fine rugs and jewels. Like
Hearst, he was a knowledgeable collector who knew what
he was buying.

In Minnesota, Hill was a favorite son who could have had virtually anything he wanted from the state, and even liberals who had a built-in suspicion of capitalists warmed up to Hill when it turned out that he was a Democrat who worked hard for Cleveland and became a trusted adviser and friend when his man was installed in the White House.

Thus Hill came out of the railroad-building era somewhat better off than his friends. Perhaps it was because he was out of the immediate reach of the New York papers, which were suspicious, with reason, of anyone who had made a fortune in transportation. New York had not only suffered the machinations of the Gould crowd, but it also had to contend with the likes of Thomas Fortune Ryan, yet another penniless farm boy who had come into the city lean and hungry, eager to start as a messenger, or "pad shover," in a Wall Street broker's office, at the tender age of twenty-one. Two years later he had a seat on the Exchange.

He spent ten years learning the ins and outs of the Street and getting to know the right people, until at thirty-three this tall, slender six-footer, well dressed and devoid of scruples, was ready for his grand opportunity. It came as a result of the battle to obtain street railway franchises, and into that unholy fray Ryan plunged with enthusiasm and enormous talent. By 1886, only two years after he began, he had created America's first holding company, the Metropolitan Traction Company, which he called "the great tin box," and by 1900 he had nearly every line in the city secured within the capacious pocket of the Metropolitan Street Railway Company.

The device of the holding company, which Ryan had the ingenuity to invent, was something new added to the scandalous business of traction monopoly. Until then, the standard method of operation, already practiced with success in Philadelphia and Chicago, had been to buy an existing line, then extend it into new areas after carefully (and secretly) buying up land along the proposed right of way for virtually nothing, then selling the land to the traction company for a high figure. The original buyer, of course, would also have a large interest in the company. By this means, enough capital and trackage would be created to force other companies into ruinous competition, or else force them to sell, until eventually a monopoly would be created.

Ryan's device meant that a single, monopolistic company could hold within its corporate jaws a collection of other companies in which the holding company's officers would have varying interests. These interests could then be manipulated wherever money was needed, by milking one to reinforce another, or by shifting stock. That was why Ryan called his Metropolitan Traction Company "the great tin box," because the money of the companies comprising it rolled around in a single container which he controlled. The holding company itself, one may add, is a legitimate device when it does not constitute a monopoly, and is otherwise restricted.

Challenged by August Belmont, who had created the Interborough Rapid Transit Company, Ryan eventually swallowed up that line too. But then in 1906 he suddenly deserted the traction field and left it to its own devices. Everyone was quickly aware on what kind of ground Ryan's traction companies had been built. They were bankrupt in no time.

Early in his career Ryan had fought William C. Whitney for control of the Broadway surface lines. In the nineties he and Whitney joined forces and organized the American Tobacco Company. In two decades it had such a strangle hold on the entire industry that the Supreme Court dissolved it as a monopoly, compelling the company to divest itself of many of the rival companies it had acquired.

Like the racketeers of our own era, Ryan was often indicted but never convicted. Robert M. La Follette denounced him on the Senate floor as having used "methods which should have committed many of the participants to the penitentiary." Nothing came of it but indignation. Ryan and Whitney were both charged with violating the state banking laws by using their State Trust Company to cover up the sins of the traction company and grease the rails of its financial operation. Two state investigations failed to produce any concrete result. The New York *World* gave wide public notice to the last investigation, which clearly implicated the Ryan crowd, but aside from the usual public indignation, again nothing happened. Later Ryan embarked on questionable adventures with insurance companies, notably the Equitable Life, and this time there was a federal investigation, in 1905, which once again resulted in nothing more than headlines. Indeed, King Leopold of Belgium now invited Ryan to develop the Congo.

At the Democratic convention of 1912, Ryan encountered that redoubtable caster-out of money-changers, William Jennings Bryan, whose famous speech to the convention denounced Ryan and August Belmont for coming to Baltimore with "their paid attorneys," seeking "secret counsel with the managers of this party," and charging them with trying to control the nominations, which of course was exactly what they intended. By sheer oratorical power, Bryan forced the convention to pass a resolution putting itself on record as "opposed to the nomination of any candidate for president who is the representative of or under obligation to" any of the Ryan crowd, including Belmont and J. P. Morgan.

At sixty, Ryan began to retire. There were really no more worlds to conquer. In his Fifth Avenue mansion, where a private garden occupied a third of a block, he lived amid his statuary, his priceless Limoges enamels, his tapestries, bronzes and other works of art. There he contemplated the world with the satisfaction that only $200,000,000 and the knowledge that he had worsted his enemies could bring to a man.

The pattern of the railroad builders becomes distressingly similar after a time. Here is Edward Henry Harriman, still another penniless New Yorker, who started his career at fourteen as an office boy in Wall Street and by the time he was twenty-one had a seat on the Exchange. Harriman made his entree into railroading by marrying Mary Averell, the daughter of an Ogdensburg banker who was president of the Ogdensburg & Lake Champlain Railroad, but in two years he was able to strike out on his own.

By a kind of merciless logic he moved from one railway to another, first controlling the Illinois Central, then dominating the Union Pacific, next buying out Huntington's holdings in the Southern Pacific, and so onward. He began this career with money made in the stock market, but continued it with his profitable operation of the lines he bought. There was no question that he was a superb organizer and administrator of his properties; he was genuinely admired by other railroad empire builders. But soon came the inevitable investigation, by the Interstate Commerce Commission in 1906–7, which raised its eyebrows in horror over his "indefensible financing," but could find no basis for prosecution, although it was known that he had juggled the capitalization and surplus of at least one company in order to make a better deal for a purchasing syndicate. On the stand, Harriman made it clear that only the government could stop him from doing whatever he pleased, in whatever way he chose.

Harriman was caught up with Ryan and others in the 1905 investigation of the Equitable Life Assurance Company, yet the investigators could not indict him. But this publicity, following the ICC examination of his activities and a much-publicized break with President Roosevelt, made him one of the public whipping boys for the evils of all his fellow capitalists, who just then were at the peak of their unpopularity. Harriman's excursions into monopoly, his manipulation of corporations, bribery of willing politicians and questionable speculations were no worse than those of his comrades of the board rooms, but he became the focal point for everyone's sins. He answered the storm of abuse with a characteristic silence. Harriman was a cold man, like many of the others, and he remained secure behind the barricade of his millions. The mob could say whatever it liked.

Strangely, Harriman's philanthropy took a truly public-spirited direction. In the San Francisco earthquake and fire, it was Harriman who led the relief parade. In the Imperial Valley, it was Harriman who organized a major effort to stop the disastrous floods. In New York, it was Harriman who organized the Tompkins Square Boys' Club, on the East Side, perhaps the first of its kind. In Orange County, New York, where he lived, it was Harriman who snatched the wild forest from the predatory clutches of the timber interests. He did not believe in free enterprise when it was his own resources that were elected for exploitation. And he was like the Vanderbilts: he loved horses, which convinced many people that the man had a great deal of good in him, as perhaps he did.

One could go on with the lives and times of the Chicago merchants, the multiple careers of the great dynasties of Du Pont and Guggenheim, the lordly façades of the Morgans, and the profitable lifetimes of a dozen lesser accumulators. They will not be neglected in the pages that follow. But the point need be labored no longer.

The accumulators of the great nineteenth-century fortunes, it is plain, were men of exceptional vigor and purpose, operating within an existing framework of morality which is basically the morality of business, at a time when certain social controls had not yet shaped and altered that morality to another mold.

Whether conservative financiers or flamboyant scoundrels, it is evident that their essential similarities outweigh their differences. The wealth they accumulated was made wealth—that is, created out of nothing by their own talents. The cost was enormous—in the ruined lives and fortunes of millions whom their onrushing chariots touched, and in the lives of the women they married and the children they begot. This human wreckage included stockholders caught up in the battles of the titans, who found their holdings, often representing a lifetime's savings, utterly worthless as the result of a company's deliberate ruin. It included property owners swindled by traction and rail operators, and businessmen who entrusted their money and livelihood to unscrupulous men who discarded them when they were no longer useful. It included, too, thousands of small cogs in the machines, like the clerk Hill once fired because he didn't like his name, and the men killed in the railroad wars, and thousands who lost their jobs in the elimination of rival companies.

This was the kind of human destruction the accumulators left behind them, never giving it a thought, because they were men of such acute insensitivity it never even occurred to them that their wives and children were human beings, not ornaments or decorations to enhance their mansions. They were constantly surprised to find that their sons, the inheritors, were people with ideas and personalities of their own.

It is impossible to estimate fortunes accurately. Secrecy surrounds the figures themselves, and only the lawyers and tax experts who tend and water each financial garden know how the money is divided.

On the basis of gross estimates, however, and making due allowance for various unmeasurable factors, it is safe to say that the nineteenth-century accumulators passed on somewhere between ten and twelve billion dollars to their wives, sons and daughters, foundations and other inheritors. These fortunes have been so fragmented in our time that no one could trace where all the money went. We do know how a good part of it was spent, however, and considerably more about the spenders. For it is the manner in which these billions were expended, and the personalities of those who inherited the money, which hold the interest of less solvent mortals, just as we are fascinated by the accumulators as men, and by the manner of their accumulating.

In the pages that follow, it should be borne in mind, as previously noted, that the somewhat arbitrary distinctions among families entail some overlapping. Obviously not every member of a family fits in a particular classification. Only the general direction of each fortune's disposition can be indicated. Here, then, is where all that money went, who got it, and what they did with it.

$ *Two* $

THE WASTERS

Getting and Spending: The Astors

Six generations of the Astor family in America have proved beyond doubt that, once a fortune is made, even the most assiduous hacking away at it will do no more than break the substance into substantial chunks. Anyone who has attacked fifty pounds of ice with a pick will understand the metaphor.

The Astor family history is instructive in other ways. It demonstrates that real estate is a commodity as basic as oil, steel, or railroads, and that $25 will get you $300,000,000 if you deal in the property of a growing country. Such was the acquisition of the Astor fortune by a family which, as Cleveland Amory observed, "has made and kept more money, and for a longer length of time, than any other in American history."

At its base stands the figure so familiar in the history of American wealth: the nearly penniless boy, starting somewhere below the bottom of the ladder, climbing to riches in an incredibly short time by virtue of the most intense concentration on making money, at the cost of everything else. Small wonder this has become a dominant theme in American life.

The Astor founder was the prototype of his kind. John Jacob Astor came from the tiny village of Waldorf, in the German Duchy of Baden, where he was born in 1763 to a good-natured butcher who preferred the beer-house to chopping pork or, for that matter, to the pleasures of domestic society. Young John set out at seventeen to make his own fortune, armed with a set of resolutions foreshadowing the Alger litany: to be honest, to be industrious, and never to gamble. For a man about to make a fortune in real estate, the last was scarcely a durable resolve.

Taking ship for America in 1783, his tangible assets were twenty-five dollars in cash; seven flutes secured from his older brother George, who sold musical instruments in London; and a piece of paper entitling him to steerage passage, complete with salt beef and biscuit. Amory tells the story of John's arrival off the coast of America, in the January ice of Chesapeake Bay which threatened to sink the vessel. When the captain ordered everyone on deck, ready to abandon ship if necessary, he observed that John Jacob Astor was dressed as for the last night out, rather than for disaster.

"What are you all dressed up for?" the captain bellowed.

Astor answered, in the German-comic dialect he was never able to lose: "If ve are saved, I haf my Sunday suit on. If ve are drowned, it von't make no difference vot kind of clothes I haf on."

He was saved, best suit and all, because the captain wisely decided to stay outside the ice barrier until he could get into the harbor. That became a matter of two months, and some of the more impatient passengers made their way ashore over the ice, but Astor demonstrated the financial acumen which was to make his fortune by staying with the ship, where his ticket guaranteed him food until the voyage was completed. Meanwhile, he passed the time of day with those who had elected to stay with him, and discovered they were in the fur business, members of the Hudson's Bay Company. This, he concluded, was the business for him to follow in America. He could almost smell the money.

Arriving in New York in March 1784, he found the city bustling and growing in the aftermath of the Revolution, as it had been before war interrupted and made it a stronghold of Tory corruption. Things were booming. His brother Heinrich was doing extremely well with a butcher shop in the Bowery and John could have joined him, but he had furs on his mind, as well as his landlady's daughter, Sarah Todd, a reserved but nevertheless proud and ambitious girl, who consented to marry him within a few months after he put up at her mother's boardinghouse.

Sarah brought John Jacob several valuable attributes, not the least of which was three hundred dollars in cash. She had, in the bargain, a good head for business and a certain social position, since she was distantly related to an old New York family, the Brevoorts, who had lost virtually everything but their pride. Any social status at all was one step up the ladder for John Jacob.

With Sarah's help and encouragement he plunged into the fur trade and worked at it with that fierce concentration which marked the great accumulators. In a scant fifteen years he had a fortune of $250,000, and at thirty-seven was considered to be the foremost fur merchant in America. Everywhere he turned he displayed the authentic genius of the moneyman. When he opened up a foreign trade through the East India Company, the first ship he sent out to Canton earned him $50,000.

John Jacob could no doubt have made himself a rich man in the fur business, but he was by nature a greedy and acquisitive soul who was always willing to listen to a little deal.

One of these prospective deals came his way in 1809 when a lawyer of his acquaintance told him that some seven hundred families were living illegally on farms they had bought from New York State, covering 51,012 acres in Putnam County. The land, the lawyer said, had been the life-lease property of the Tory, Roger Morris, and as such it could not be taken from him legally. In reality it belonged to Morris' heirs, who were scattered about England.

Once he was sure of his ground, Astor moved with dispatch and a fine disregard for the families who were living on a third of Putnam County in good faith. He bought out the heirs for about $100,000, and then informed the poor farmers that they were trespassing on his property. There was, of course, a struggle in the courts. Astor did not get everything he claimed, but he did get a compromise settlement of $500,000. He also achieved a public unpopularity which clung to the family for years but, again displaying the true accumulator's temperament, he cared not at all what people thought of him.

Having had a taste of real estate profits, Astor wanted more. He was the apotheosis of the conscienceless landlord, buying heavily mortgaged farms on Manhattan for virtually nothing and foreclosing right and left in periods of financial distress. These tactics made him the richest man in America and impelled him to do something about his own real estate. He had lived, during his first seventeen years of infamous progress, in extremely unappetizing quarters, but in 1801 he moved to a handsome house farther uptown, at 223 Broadway, where the Astor House would one day rise. Still later, he moved north to a splendid place on Lafayette Street, but wherever he went he remained an uncouth figure, never accepted by society. That he was a miser, an indifferent dresser, a grasping landlord, were facts known to everyone, but those who saw him plain were appalled, if they happened to be men of breeding and refinement. Albert Gallatin observed, with horror, John Jacob eating both ice cream and peas with his knife. Gallatin's son saw him, at a quiet family dinner in the Gallatin home, wipe his fingers on the sleeves of the fresh white jacket belonging to the host's sister, who sat next to him.

Nevertheless, he was the richest of them all by far, and getting richer with every new development in America's history. The Louisiana Purchase and the explorations of Lewis and Clark meant only that it was easier for Astor to consolidate his interests in the American Fur Company, the nation's first monopoly. On the West Coast he organized the Pacific Fur Company in 1810, and later established the first permanent settlement in the Northwest, Astoria, a town whose story he hired Washington Irving to write, in the same manner that large corporations buy authors to write company histories today.

The War of 1812, with its complex and tragic issues, meant to Astor only that he lost his fur posts in the embattled Northwest Territory, but on the other hand, he was able to lend money to the government, at substantial interest, for the conduct of the war. Near the close of the war, in 1814, when the cost of fighting the British had reduced the new nation to near bankruptcy, Astor and two Philadelphia friends consented to bail it out by purchasing a large block of bonds. They were bought at prices ranging from eighty to eighty-two cents on the dollar; the bank notes their purchasers gave the government were worth no more than half their face value.

After the war Astor went back into the fur business for a time, but he found the real estate business increasingly more profitable. In a later day it would have been said of him that he "thought big." This contemporary phrase certainly describes the high and handsome way he operated in New York City.

In time, however, he seemed to weary of accumulating wealth—of being, as the New York *Herald* described him, "a self-invented money-making machine." He sold his fur interests in 1834 and devoted the rest of his life to managing the affairs of the House of Astor, in a sense the first American "royal" family, and in trying to assure the impossible—that his fortune would be carried on into future generations unimpaired.

He must have appeared to his contemporaries, in these latter days, as an aging monarch of enormous wealth and power, but lonely and ill and therefore vulnerable. His loneliness was understandable; probably no man in New York City was more cordially hated and feared. He tried to mitigate his isolation by placing one of his few friends, the noted librarian Joseph Green Cogswell, on a retainer simply to speak German with him, to be his more or less constant companion and, as Philip Hone put it in his diary, "to be Astor's train bearer and prime minister." Cogswell used his position to fulfill an unselfish ambition of his own. He persuaded Astor to make one of the few generous gestures of his life by bequeathing $400,000 in his will to establish the Astor Library.

As Astor saw death approaching he was in some ways a pitiable figure. Unloved, so ill with a stomach disease that he could take but a little milk from a wet nurse's breast, he had only one son to inherit his fortune of twenty million dollars, the largest in America. Of his eight children, three had died young, three were daughters, and one son was feeble-minded as the result of a childhood fall. There remained William Backhouse Astor, the old man's partner, advantageously married to Margaret Armstrong, who was descended from the Livingstons and a member of one of New York State's first families. Old Jacob was pleased with her social standing but he did not want her to be in a position to get any of his money. The marriage settlement he devised was a piece of bribery, by which Miss Armstrong (or her family) for a price gave up her dower rights in case her husband died.

William was both like and unlike his father. He loved money too, but he did not have his father's bold originality. As "the landlord of New York," the title by which he came to be known, he merely built on the foundations John Jacob had laid so well, although he had enjoyed the advantages of a good education at Heidelberg and Göttingen. For him there was really no necessity to make money. His father had left him $18,000,000, and another $500,000 legacy came from his uncle, Henry Astor. There was, naturally, a steady flow of income from the numerous Astor properties, which were rapidly deteriorating into miserable slums as the city's population increased, and as William consistently refused to do anything whatever about rehabilitating his properties. William was against building new buildings or refurbishing old ones, or even improving the city's streets. When he finally changed his mind in 1861 and began to renovate some of the worst of his rat palaces, it was too late. If William did anything creative in his life, it was to create the slums of nineteenth-century New York.

John Jacob had been a rather short man (five feet, nine inches), with heavy features and an urbane but humorless manner, who never mastered the English language. He liked to think of himself as a patriot, even a humanitarian, but no one could doubt that his only passion was money. William was taller and heavier, but less urbane. The piggish eyes in his heavy features stared out at the world without the slight-

est understanding of other human beings. He was a methodical man, and if he was able to rise to a social position above
his father's, it was because he had patiently doubled the old
man's fortune, and it was difficult for anyone to ignore forty
million dollars.

There was one odd difference between father and son. For
reasons still unclear, William exhibited a greater benevolence
than John Jacob was capable of displaying. During his lifetime he gave the Astor Library another $550,000, and pre-
sented St. Luke's Hospital with $50,000. He also corrected
one of his father's heavy-handed jokes by raising to $1500
the $200 annuity left to John Jacob's long-time secretary, the
poet Fitz-Greene Halleck, who had once made the mistake
of telling the old man that he would be content to live on
$200 a year for the rest of his life if he could be certain of
the money. John Jacob had made him certain in his will.

When he came to die, however, William proved to be no
more charitable than his father, leaving exactly the same
amount, $500,000, to good causes. To dispose of what re-
mained, estimated variously between $40,000,000 and $80,-
000,000, he found himself only one son better off than John
Jacob. Margaret had given him three daughters and three
sons. One daughter, Laura, had married Franklin H. Delano
and so had begun a relationship with the Roosevelt family.
Another, Alida, was also married and she and her sister were
each given $1,000,000. Their sister Emily, who had died
after her marriage into the Chanler family, had left behind
a daughter, Margaret Astor Ward Chanler, who got $700,000.
William's youngest son was cut off in a codicil with only
$30,000. As one of the "queer" Astors he had been in line to
receive a somewhat larger sop, $350,000, but he had proved
his eccentricity, in his father's eyes, by marrying a Dutchess

County girl whom William uncharitably described as a "peasant."

There were two sons remaining, and William divided his fortune equally between them. But he favored the older, John Jacob Astor III, by giving him most of the family's real estate holdings, a symbolic gesture toward the founder of the house, one supposes, although it may be doubted that William was capable of symbolism. The other son, another William Backhouse, emerged with considerably less than his brother, but it was enough to finance more than comfortably his wife's struggle for social position.

It was this struggle, indeed, which now occupied the Astor family. As the nineteenth century waned, the accumulating began to taper off and the fortunes of the moguls increased by the less exciting means of normal investment. With the creation of wealth no longer a preoccupation, the Astors, as did some others, turned to using their money as a means of maintaining a dominant position in society.

There began the greatest social war in history, never approached in its bad taste and calculated to give society a Bad Name, although it was watched with fascination by millions of less fortunate Americans. The tale of the struggle to determine who would be *the* Mrs. Astor has been told often enough, but its possibilities as a demonstration lesson in the uses of inherited wealth are hardly exhausted.

It began, in reality, with the difference between the two brothers. John Jacob III was an aristocrat, in bearing, appearance and manners, and was so regarded by the rest of the family. He had been educated at Columbia, Göttingen and Harvard Law School, from which he had emerged as the most polished of the Astors up to that time. Then he had married a poor but socially prominent South Carolina girl, Charlotte Gibbes; she was *the* Mrs. Astor by seniority, but like the true member of a first Southern family that she was, Charlotte did not feel it necessary to lay public claim to the title.

Her husband led as blameless a life as she did. He continued his father's career in real estate, with the typically shrewd Astor eye for bargains, and invested some of his profits in new industries, such as Western Union, or in the always reliable banks. A tall, ruddy-faced man, much like his father, he was solidly in the Astor tradition, devoted to business—he refused Rutherford Hayes's offer to make him minister to Great Britain—and a tight man with a dollar. He was known to pore over a telegram, trying to rewrite it to save a word. His wife, however, lured him away from the natural simplicities his predecessors had insisted on maintaining at home. It was Charlotte who introduced him to entertaining, paintings, furniture and books. Carried away with the knowledge of what his money could buy, he even hired a superb chef and set himself up as a connoisseur of fine wines and good cigars.

This liberality marked a breaking away from Astor tradition, and John Jacob III displayed it too in his benevolences, which totaled about $700,000 privately, along with the usual gifts to the Astor Library and St. Luke's and the Metropolitan Museum. Some of his money went to Trinity Church, where he served as vestryman. There was a good deal of it left over after charity, however, ready for his son, William Waldorf Astor, to carry on.

William Waldorf had un-Astor-like ideas about carrying on, as it turned out. After his graduation from Columbia Law School he began the usual course in learning how to administer the estate, but to his father's astonishment and considerable chagrin, one may assume, he announced that he was bored with the occupation which was supposed to make all Astors happy. Instead, he declared, he preferred to go into politics. He began modestly with the state legislature and did well. He was elected in 1877 as a Republican assemblyman, then two years later achieved the Senate. Intoxicated with success, he ran twice for Congress and failed. After that he gave up politics, accepting as a consolation prize President Arthur's appointment of him as minister to Italy in 1882.

Old John Jacob would have been mortified by what occurred next. William Waldorf concluded that his true vocation was writing. In 1885, using his three years in Italy as background, he wrote *Valentino: An Historical Romance of the Sixteenth Century in Italy.* He followed this with *Sforza, A Story of Milan,* and *Pharaoh's Daughter and Other Stories.*

These creations were respectably reviewed in the respectable press, but the author's literary life had already been disgracefully interrupted by the series of social events which was to change his life, and that of the Astor family as well. He had married in 1878 a Philadelphia lady named Mary Dahlgren Paul, of impeccable family and no social climber. When she came back from Italy with her husband, however, William Waldorf made it quite plain that he considered his wife *the* Mrs. Astor.

The obstacle to this claim was the formidable figure of William Waldorf's aunt, the wife of his father's brother, William Backhouse, Jr. Whereas John Jacob III was the aristocrat, Junior was considered by the family as decadent, which may be translated as weak, and as weak men are inclined to do, he married a strong woman. She was Caroline Webster Schermerhorn. Her family was older than the Astors, but of course not nearly as rich. What Caroline lacked in beauty, a not inconsiderable deficit, she more than made up in sheer majesty. Cleveland Amory has called her "the most famous lady in the history of Society," a distinction she would no doubt agree with wholeheartedly.

Caroline announced, in effect, that any other claimants to the Astor throne were in error, and that she herself was in truth *the* Mrs. Astor. To prove it, she not only persuaded her husband to drop "Backhouse," a name she loathed, but then on her own initiative she dropped "William" as well. That left only Astor, as she intended.

On the playing fields of Newport and New York, Caroline and Mary fought a desperate game. In Newport, among the magnificent summer cottages, total confusion reigned. Mary had a house called Beaulieu (after all, the William Waldorfs were the international Astors at the time), and Caroline had one named Beechwood. Unless these place name were on envelopes, the bewildered postman had no way of making deliveries, since both ladies insisted that their mail be addressed simply to "Mrs. Astor." Presumably no one dared address a letter by the title Caroline was given among her followers, "the Mystic Rose."

As the struggle went on Caroline acquired a powerful general, the redoubtable Ward McAllister, who compiled the list that came to be known as the Four Hundred, and lo! Caroline's name led all the rest of the socially elite around whom McAllister had drawn a charmed circle. With this kind of generalship, it was inevitable that Caroline should win, particularly against a dignified Philadelphia lady whose heart was probably not in the game.

At any rate, Caroline emerged at sixty as the *only* Mrs. Astor, so recognized by the nation, in which she was an institution. Her parties, her idle comments, the state of her jewelry were all reported meticulously in the newspapers. She reigned supreme, in trailing clouds of glory.

If Mary could accept defeat with elegant grace, William Waldorf was in no mood to do so. After his father died in 1890, compelling him to take over as manager of a $100,000,-

ooo fortune, he concluded that he would leave the United States forever—leave it to the Irish politicians who had kept him out of Congress and to the socially ambitious aunts who were ruining society. "America is not a fit place for a gentleman to live," he declared.

Before he departed, William Waldorf was in a state of mind to do something mean to his aunt, and he hit upon a truly diabolical revenge. Caroline's mansion stood at the southwest corner of Fifth Avenue and Thirty-fourth Street; a block south, on the northwest corner of Fifth and Thirty-third, rose the stately home of John Jacob III, which William Waldorf had inherited from his father. Spitefully, he ordered it torn down and built the thirteen-story Waldorf Hotel on the spot. It opened in 1894, and within a year the commercial traffic flowed so heavily around the beleaguered Caroline's doorstep that she was compelled to move uptown.

But if social ambition had divided the family, greed brought them together again. Caroline's son, John Jacob IV, trying to decide the fate of the abandoned mansion and observing the success of the Waldorf, in 1897 built the seventeen-story Astor House on the site of his mother's former triumphs, and arranged for passages to be built between the two hostelries. In a filial gesture toward Caroline, or perhaps simply with an access of Astor caution, he wrote a stipulation into the agreement that he could board up the passages any time he pleased. He never pleased, of course, and today the Empire State Building has buried these ancient rivalries beneath one hundred and two stories of steel and concrete, while the Waldorf and the Astoria remain united as one on Park Avenue.

For Caroline the contest did not end with Mary's departure for England and her own migration uptown. She had no more Astors to contend with, but it appeared that she must constantly defend herself against other women, all of them disgraceful climbers, who wanted to lead the Four Hundred. There was Mrs. Hermann Oelrichs, Alva Vanderbilt Belmont (O.H.P.'s wife) and Mrs. Stuyvesant Fish. Caroline rose above them, declaring grandly at one point: "Many women will rise to fill my place, but I hope my influence will be felt in one thing, and that is, in discountenancing the undignified methods employed by certain women to attract a following."

The certain undignified woman she meant was Mrs. Fish, who it must be admitted approached her social career more in the spirit of P. T. Barnum than as a defender of social dignity. Mrs. Fish's dinner parties were designed to be unforgettable. At one of them all the guests spoke baby talk. At another she introduced a live monkey that sat in the place usually reserved for Mrs. Astor. On occasion she distributed live white mice to lady guests as party favors (the ladies were scarcely enchanted, one might guess), or she would hire an entire circus troupe to perform.

These diversions could not dim Caroline's luster or shorten her rule by so much as a day. She carried on indomitably, bearing a weight of jewels and arrogance as clanking and ponderous as the chains of Marley's ghost. Her diamond tiara and stomacher were the caste marks she wore constantly. At her annual ball the guest list was all that stood between any family and oblivion, and her dinner parties determined what one hundred and fifty people might worship in the inner temple.

Before she died in 1908 at the age of seventy-seven, Caroline, *the* Mrs. Astor to the last, slipped away from the world she had dominated for so long. Mercifully, she did not know that her reign was over, that the only pushing rival she could not conquer was easing her gently out of the throne room. In a world of illusion, she was still Queen. Lloyd Morris, in his

Incredible New York, gives us a touching portrait of how it was for Caroline at the end: "Still erect, still bravely gowned and jeweled, she stood beneath her portrait—quite alone; greeting imaginary guests long dead, conversing cordially with phantoms of the most illustrious social eminence."

So it was that she died on an autumn day. Morris describes her funeral: "Chilly gusts were stripping the trees of Central Park. A rain of shriveled leaves fell on the great crowd waiting in silence along Fifth Avenue. The massive iron and glass portals of the Astor palace slowly opened. A flower-mantled coffin was borne out and deposited in its hearse. As the doors of the hearse closed, an epoch passed into history. Presently the crowd melted away."

Mary Vanderbilt had preceded her fourteen years before, and for William Waldorf that event was the beginning of a new era in his life, which he had begun to reconstruct in England, where he had founded the English branch of the House of Astor. After his wife died, he decided to do as he pleased, which was to indulge his taste for literature by becoming a publisher. He began by buying a newspaper, the *Pall Mall Observer,* changing its politics from Liberal to Conservative in the process, after which he bought a weekly organ, the *Pall Mall Budget,* and in time came to own the *Sunday Observer.* That was in 1911. No one could understand why he had bought the *Observer,* any more than they could understand why he sold all his journalistic properties three years later—thoughtfully, to his son, who in turn disposed of them to his own profit.

William Waldorf was so disillusioned with America that he was determined to be more British than the British. He became a subject in 1899, and in his periodicals attacked America with the fervor of a returned lecturer. Always a gnawing curiosity made him wonder what his abandoned countrymen really thought of him, and in an effort to find out, he circulated a false report of his own death. The exaggeration was discovered before there were any obituaries for him to read.

He began to chip away at the fortune his father had left him, as succeeding Astors were to do. Accumulation was over; deterioration had begun. He bought a string of stately homes, as though they were polo ponies: Cliveden, Hever Castle, Western House, Sorrento, and at last a $1,500,000 house for the Astor Estate—as Amory observes, "a house to house other houses." It cost him $10,000,000 alone to restore Hever Castle.

Along with the reckless expenditure of money, which would have shocked old John Jacob to his foundations, William Waldorf indulged himself in behavior which was odd enough to make him one of the "queer" Astors. He aspired to be recognized socially, yet he whimsically insulted important people. When he was made Baron Astor of Hever Castle in 1916, and a viscount a year later, he was denounced in the British press as a renegade American who had attained the peerage by supporting the party in power and collecting his reward. Naturally, William Waldorf was enraged, but his vain and irascible nature led him more and more into conflict with others until at last British society would have no more of it. They had been remarkably patient; now they shunned him. As he had withdrawn from America, William Waldorf drew away from the British at last, and died lonely and bitter in 1919.

He left three English Astors to carry on his name. Two were sons: Major Waldorf Astor, who had acquired his journals; and Captain John Jacob Astor V. The other was a daughter, Pauline, who had disgraced herself in her father's view by marrying a commoner, Colonel Herbert Spencer-Clay. The major, who never liked his father and thought the peerage was a bore, perhaps hastened the pater's death by marrying a woman who was not only remote from the nobility but an American divorcee. She was, as the world soon came to know, the remarkable Nancy Langhorne, a Virginia girl who was scarcely satisfied to be Lady Astor but became a controversial ornament of Parliament for twenty-five years. When she first walked through its august doors, the first of her sex to do so, Lloyd George recorded that he could not have been more shocked if she had walked into his bathroom.

Nancy made the Astor name more famous in England than William Waldorf could have dreamed, collecting about her person a folklore that has become a cherished part of Anglo-American relations. At various times she came out strongly against war, men, Russia, sin, even motherhood—"it's all tommyrot." It was inevitable that she should overshadow the other English Astors, even her brother-in-law, the captain, who had a distinguished career of his own as an aide to the Viceroy of India and as owner of the *Times,* for which he spent seven million dollars of Astor money in 1922. By that time he was a major, as a result of distinguished service in the First World War.

Before he died, William Waldorf had done what he could to preserve his accumulated eighty million dollars, all that remained of his inheritance, for the benefit of his sons. A good deal of his wealth was in London real estate, but he put his American property in trust for them, with the pious intention of avoiding inheritance taxes.

It is doubtful whether the English Astors added materially to the family fortune, but unquestionably they added prestige. According to Harvey O'Connor, no less than five of them were in Parliament in 1935: Waldorf, in the House of Lords; and in Commons, Nancy; their son, William Waldorf Astor II, his brother-in-law, Lord Willoughby de Eresby; and John Jacob V.

In the United States, however, it was a different story. The American Astors, by the turn of the century, were beginning to see the cumulative effect of wealth on people who had not earned it, did not have to work to preserve it, and who regarded it merely as the guarantor of position and privilege.

The Mrs. Astor's eldest child, Emily, married James J. Van Alen, but not before her father had insulted her future father-in-law, precipitating a challenge to a duel which was never fought. The second daughter carried on the peaceful family tradition of marrying Roosevelts, her choice being James Roosevelt. The youngest of the family, Caroline, became another marital statistic as Mrs. Orme Wilson, Jr. But the fourth daughter, Charlotte, precipitated the first, and perhaps in some ways the most lurid, scandal in a family history which was to have more than its share of them.

Charlotte made an auspicious debut; by any social standard, she was well launched. Shortly afterward she made a proper marriage to a proper society figure, James Coleman Drayton, a Philadelphian who maintained another residence in South Carolina, and for the next few years, to all appearances, she was a model matron, bearing four proper children at respectable intervals. But meanwhile, it appeared later, Charlotte was also dallying with a gentleman of impeccable reputation, a vice-president of Equitable Life and a member of the best clubs. His name was Hallett Alsop Borrowe, and to the astonishment of his friends, he turned out to be an utter cad. No gentleman, it was said over the aspic, would ever sell his mistress' letters to the newspapers. Equitable Life could survive the scandal—after all, it had survived Thomas Fortune Ryan and James Hazen Hyde and the other assaulters of its morality—but there was serious question whether

Borrowe could survive it. Charlotte's husband wanted to fight him in a duel (this kind of thing was rapidly taking on the aspect of a tradition in the Astor family), but although numerous challenges were made and accepted, the rivals were not seriously disposed to bloodletting and never met on the field of honor. Possibly disillusioned by this development, Charlotte got her divorce and married someone else. The divorce petition presented the novel argument that she had been deserted by her husband as the result of "cruel suspicion as to her marital fidelity."

Charlotte's brother, John Jacob IV, further confirmed society's suspicion that the Astor blood was thinning when he deliberately involved himself in an affair that was simply not acceptable. Taking over as head of the family at twenty-eight, the youngest of the Astors to achieve the throne room, he seemed to his fellow members of the Four Hundred even quieter and more normal than Charlotte had been at the beginning of her career. He liked to drive automobiles and sail, he enjoyed inventing things, he served in the Spanish-American War with enough distinction to become a colonel, and he moved quietly about the business of the estate and his social obligations. Moreover, he had married in 1891 a Philadelphia beauty, Ava Willing, who was perhaps the most glamorous figure in society at the time.

John Jacob IV was a quiet man, and the divorce he obtained from Ava in 1909 was as quiet as influence could make it. There was no scandal, but there was total astonishment among the Four Hundred. No one could begin to understand it. John shortly gave them something they could understand, however, when he presented to his guests at 840 Fifth Avenue a charming girl named Madeline Force, described in the newspapers as "a member of an old Brooklyn family." She was eighteen; he was forty-six. There was scandalized whispering and then an outright boycott. Society would not meet Miss Force, except for a few loyal Astor friends, nor would it sanction her marriage to the colonel the following year.

Concluding that it was best to wait and let time work for him, John took his bride to Europe for a year. There she became pregnant. In her fifth month, she sailed for home again with her husband on the *Titanic,* and in the ensuing tragedy John Jacob IV proved to be a better man than many of his critics. He succeeded in getting his wife into a lifeboat, then went back to the ship's kennels and tried to save his dog, refusing to take a lifejacket and jump. Struck by a falling object, so it was said, he died with $2,500 in his pockets, and with his death he brought to a close the era of the "old" Astors.

The new generation was represented, as so frequently in the Astor family, by two sharply contrasted personalities: John Jacob VI, rescued in embryo from the *Titanic* and born four months later to Madeline Force Astor; and Vincent, Ava Willing's son, who had been given into the custody of his father by the terms of the divorce. There was a third child, Alice, Ava's daughter, who remained with her mother. Among them, these three Astors have accounted for ten marriages.

John Jacob VI, who has sometimes confused Astor *aficionados* by calling himself John Jacob III, is a fully qualified member of café society, seen nearly as often in the newspapers as he is in the night clubs. He has summed up his own career in a singularly clear statement: "I have found that work interferes with pleasure." He has not, however, permitted anything to interfere with marriage.

In this context, he first came to public attention in the thirties when his engagement to Eileen Gillespie was broken on the eve of their wedding, followed by the announcement that he would wed, instead, one of the bridesmaids, Ellen ("Tuckie") French. There was a good deal of acrimony about the whole affair. Eileen returned her $100,000 engagement ring, but John Jacob VI went on making rude remarks about her family, until her mother, Mrs. Lawrence Gillespie, threatened to disclose his correspondence with her daughter if he did not stop. Perhaps remembering poor Charlotte's letters, he stopped, but not before he had remarked that one of the reasons he had broken the engagement was because the bride's parents wanted to go along on the honeymoon.

To the bridesmaid, Miss French, went the possessions Eileen might have owned—a million dollars' worth of them. Apparently John Jacob VI meant to encrust his intended with as many diamonds as *the* Mrs. Astor. Tuckie glittered with a $75,000 diamond ring and a $50,000 bracelet. She rode in another gift, a $15,000 automobile, and was invited to spend her summers in Chetwode, a $250,000 Newport cottage, still another affectionate memento from her bridegroom.

This romantic idyll lasted nine years. Divorced in 1943, John Jacob VI married Gertrude ("Trudie") Gretsch. The marriage was marred, on the surface at least, only by the appearance in court and the newspapers of an eighteen-year-old Philadelphia girl who asserted that Astor had been courting her for three years, and had some letters and a photograph to prove it. She and her mother did a slow-burning fadeout, however, without offering the proof, remarking that they had been treated badly.

In 1954, Astor went to Mexico and obtained a divorce from Trudie, after which he married a twenty-six-year-old ex-receptionist and cosmetic salesgirl. Trudie did not take kindly to this development. She declared that the Mexican divorce was granted without the benefit of her consent, and the implication was that Astor had become, among his other difficulties, a bigamist. It cost him $500,000 to console her, the same amount he had given Tuckie as a settlement.

Somehow John Jacob VI could not stay out of the newspapers. When it wasn't his marital troubles, it was some other domestic problem that provided the headline writers with such gems as, NURSE TELLS HOW ASTOR BEAT HER IN ROW OVER SON. John Jacob Astor Settles Out of Court for Beating Nurse, But She Still Would Like to Have Her Pressing Iron. The settlement in this case was presumed to have been three thousand dollars.

Meanwhile, his stepbrother, Vincent, had been leading an entirely different life. His three marriages—to Helen Dinsmore Huntington, Mary Cushing and Mary Brooke Russell—were overshadowed by his accomplishment in working his inheritance of $68,000,000 into a fortune estimated variously at between $100,000,000 and $200,000,000. In contrast to the pleasure-before-business philosophy of John Jacob VI, he asserted: "It is unreasonable to suppose that because a man is rich he is also useless." Vincent was known to his friends as "V.A.," while John was called "Jackaster," and even in the nicknames the difference between them was implicit.

A product of St. George's School and Harvard, which he did not complete, Vincent was in many ways like his father—tall, quiet, withdrawn, not an easy man to know. He belonged to the right clubs, forty-two of them, and he performed the other rituals of wealth, but his mind turned to social reform, an odd occupation for an Astor, and he became the first capitalist—or the first traitor to his class, as some would have put it—to support Franklin Delano Roosevelt and the New Deal. The President sometimes borrowed Vincent's magnificent yacht, the *Nourmahal,* and often entertained him and another Astor friend, Raymond Moley, the Columbia professor who was a member of the original brain trust.

When it became apparent to Moley that the President intended to shape the government according to his own rather than Moley's wishes, Vincent and his friend withdrew the *Nourmahal* and their counsel from public service. Moley yearned to keep on giving the nation the benefit of his advice, and Vincent gave him the means to do it by founding the magazine *Today*. Even this proved an inadequate vessel for Moley, and in 1937 *Today* became *Newsweek*, Astor holding a majority of stock in the new corporation.

In the first frantic months of *Newsweek*, when it was trying desperately to be a news magazine which did not look or read like *Time*, Moley was the Olympian overlord of the numerous executives, many of them future *Time* men, who were attempting to make a magazine that would be successful in spite of its management. Occasionally Vincent would appear at the *Newsweek* offices, then in the RKO Building on Sixth Avenue, and play the part of publisher for a week or two, throwing the editorial operation into more than its usual state of confusion. Then he would depart again, thoughtfully leaving behind him another transfusion of financial plasma to keep his fainting property from expiration.

Although *Newsweek* eventually prospered and gave Vincent no further cause for alarm before he got out of it, it did not make him happy. As he grew older he grew more melancholy—about his marriages, his various properties and his stepbrother. Perhaps his excellent hotel, the St. Regis, a jewel in the crown of New York's hostelries, gave him some pleasure, as it also provided haven for many of his friends when they came in from their country places or their far-flung mansions. But he found little to cheer him, and toward the end even his real estate investments, made in the grand Astor manner, did not turn out well.

The will he left when he died without an heir in 1959 reflected his profound disillusionment with the world. Two million went to his widow and the remainder to charities, principally the Vincent Astor Foundation. John Jacob VI was cut off without a penny, a matter about which he began immediately to argue legally. He had been in court only the year before, petitioning the august justices of the New York Supreme Court to decide who, if anyone, was legally married to him. In the case of his stepbrother's will, the issue was clearer, apparently.

In appealing for Vincent's money, John Jacob VI made honest confession that he was down to his last five million, all that remained of an original seventy-million inheritance. When this distressing circumstance was made known in the newspapers, the proprietor of a Brooklyn luncheonette and his customers organized a John Jacob Astor Pauper's Fund for his aid.

It was not enough. The man who had once complained that everybody thought he was worth ninety million when actually it was only thirty-three million was now facing the quite real danger that he might succeed in spending all, or nearly all, of his substantial fortune. The only good this ill wind might blow, it seemed, would be to keep him out of the papers at last, and relatively safe from pretty young women to whom the smell of money was far more potent than alcohol. Whether his son, William Astor II, or his daughter, Mary Jacquiline, would inherit anything except an insubstantial remnant of the great Astor fortune was problematical. As for the bulk of that fortune, in Vincent's disillusioned but prudent hands it had been safely foundationized.

Could an Astor ever face life with only five million dollars or less? Old John Jacob, the founder, believed it was possible. "A man who has a million dollars," he once remarked, "is as well off as if he were rich."

4

The Dodges of Detroit, and Elsewhere

On the Dodge family's coat of arms, which experts now say is a forgery, there is emblazoned a woman's breast, happily giving milk. If this is symbolic of anything in family history, it can only represent the wonderful invention of John and Horace Dodge, who began as nearly penniless bicycle mechanics, tinkering in a Niles, Michigan, shed, and in time produced a motorcar which turned on a veritable fountain of wealth that no one could seem to turn off or control. Their heirs and heiresses had to cope with a fortune of well over $146,000,000—which the auto business alone was worth when it was sold in 1925. Like the Fords, the Dodges were a family primarily of the twentieth century, but with its roots in the nineteenth.

One who knew the family well regards their life and times as a tragedy, with the fortune cast as a villain. For the founding Dodges who found themselves poor one year and rich the next, figuratively speaking, appeared to be able to withstand the pressures of unexpected wealth, but the successive sons and daughters found themselves more the prisoners of money and what it could buy than the masters and manipulators of a fortune.

It was a fortune amassed by the sheer business ability of the original accumulators. The Dodges built their bicycle business into a machine shop, and as soon as the automobile emerged as a serious rival of the old-fashioned wheel, they quickly adapted themselves to changing times and began to make parts for Ransom E. Olds, whose Oldsmobile was to become an American standard.

One of those who observed the rise of the Olds Motor Works with interest was a shrewd and well-to-do Detroit coal dealer, Alex Y. Malcolmson, who sensed from the beginning what the motor industry would become, and determined to invest in it the small fortune he had acquired. Malcolmson looked over the field and decided that Henry Ford was his man, although until that time Ford had done no more than produce the famed big red racer "999," which had been showing its wheels to every competitor, under the daring hands of Barney Oldfield. But Ford had other assets which made Malcolmson certain he had chosen correctly, and the two men began to plan the founding of the Ford Motor Company.

In organizing this giant of the twentieth-century industrial world, Malcolmson made several astute moves to assure its initial success, and one of them was to secure the Dodge brothers as primary suppliers, to build motors and certain other key parts. Malcolmson wanted the experience and management ability of the Dodge boys, as well as their excellent machine shop. To get it, he permitted them to retain ownership of the shop, John Dodge was made a director of the new company, and each brother got five per cent of the Ford shares. In return, the brothers severed all other connections and put their eggs in the capacious Ford basket. A month before the company was incorporated they began to retool their shop in preparation for the Ford-Wills car, and when it was produced they were in charge of actual construction.

Assembly was begun and nearly completed in their shop and the models were then loaded onto hay wagons, to be taken to the Ford plant on Mack Avenue in Detroit, where, during the first year at least, no more was done than to add tires and a few body touches.

With the success of the Model T, the Dodge brothers could have sat back, taken their ten per cent out of the business, and made a comfortable living. But they were both ambitious and talented men, and when the Ford plant started to do its own assembling they began to concentrate on making Ford parts. Their plant equipment was valued at between ten and fifteen million dollars by 1913. In doing business with the Ford Motor Company, they had also been careful to scale their prices as high as they thought Henry and his associates would stand. Once when a Ford executive accused them of making on a single part a profit of sixty cents each more than Ford would have had to permit any other supplier, John Dodge is said to have replied: "Hell, those things don't even cost sixty cents apiece."

Partly as a result of their own single-minded initiative, and partly for more complicated reasons, the Dodge boys were increasingly left outside the inner circle of the company as time went on. Horace did not care particularly about this exclusion, but John, a strong-minded man himself, found it intolerable. He was cast in the mold of the nineteenth-century accumulators—tough, aggressive, a sharp dealer and keen-witted. John told a Detroit newspaperman, about 1912: "I'm getting tired of being carried around in Henry Ford's vest pocket."

One reason for his impatience was the fact that the parts business was becoming highly competitive, and the Ford Motor Company was now dealing with several suppliers, playing them against each other. The Dodges, like these others, were wholly dependent for their Ford business on the annual contract which they signed with the company, a contract easily canceled by either side. John suspected that Ford might well cancel the Dodge contract, leaving him and Horace with a specialized shop that would be unable to fill orders for anyone else. The brothers determined to jump before they were pushed.

With twenty-five million dollars in cash to back them up, they reasoned that they, too, could start an automobile company. John resigned as a member of the Ford board of directors in 1913 and flamboyantly announced that he and Horace would make a car costing three or four hundred dollars more than the Ford. "Think," he added sarcastically, "of all the Ford owners who will someday want an automobile."

For a year and a half the brothers got away with it. They made a good car and sold it well; meanwhile, they continued to reap dividends from their Ford stock. Then, one day in 1916, Henry Ford and C. H. Wills, his chief engineer, visited the brothers and Henry announced that Ford Motor Company stockholders would no longer get their accustomed dividends but would have to share a fixed annual sum of $1,200,000; the remainder of the profits would be put back in the business.

"If you're going to adopt as radical a policy as that," John Dodge is reported to have protested, "why not buy out all the holders and then do just as you please?" Characteristically, Ford answered that he wanted no more shares than he already owned, and if minority stockholders like the Dodges didn't care for his limited annual dividend plan, they could take it or leave it.

If Ford thought he was going to intimidate the Dodges by this declaration, he underestimated John. The boys immediately filed a suit against him, petitioning the court to compel the issuance of reasonable dividends and to enjoin any expansion of the Ford interests until these dividends were paid. Aside from this legal move, John made no secret of the fact that he considered Ford's action an attempt to hamper and embarrass the Dodge Corporation. If Henry succeeded, the Dodge operation would certainly be less fluid, lacking the greater capital which Ford profits would provide. Beyond that, both Dodges considered that they had contributed to Ford's success and that their share of the profits, represented by their stock, would be threatened by such an arbitrary action as limiting the dividends. Indeed, under Ford's plan, they could hope to collect no more than $120,000 a year on their ten per cent, and they were well aware that the company's profits were running between thirty and sixty million at the time.

Thus the Dodges, in their suit, were in reality representing all the stockholders of the Ford Motor Company, who were facing a similar curtailment. A principle was at stake. Stockholders were being defied, in effect, by a corporation's management.

Defiance was exactly what Henry intended. He absolutely refused to buy out any of his former partners who were stockholders. When this idea was suggested to him on the stand by Elliott G. Stevenson, the Dodges' attorney, he snapped: "If you sit there until you are petrified, I wouldn't buy any Dodge brothers' stock, if that is what you are talking about. . . . I don't want any more stock."

For three years the case dragged on, until it finally reached the state Supreme Court, which ruled in February 1919 that Ford must declare at once a special dividend of nineteen million dollars, with five per cent interest dating from the time of a lower court decision, and it further enjoined Ford

from applying any limited dividends policies to its stockholders at any time in the future.

Apparently John Dodge and the other stockholders had
won, but Ford was too sharp for them. A month before the
Supreme Court's decision, he had astonished everyone by
stepping down from the presidency of the company, remaining on the board while his son Edsel was elected president.
A month after the decision he announced from California
that he intended to bring out a new Model T at a third or
half the price of the old one, and it would be manufactured
by an entirely new company in which he and Edsel would
be the only stockholders.

It was a maneuver of consummate shrewdness. By these
two moves Ford had discouraged any independents from
buying Ford stock, and he could now proceed to make his
own terms with Dodge and the other minority stockholders.
This he accomplished with great stealth, denying constantly
that he intended to buy any stock at all, and sending out purchasing agents who were pledged to the greatest secrecy, so
that the minority stockholders came to terms one by one
without even knowing they were selling to Ford. Only James
Couzens understood what was happening, and succeeded in
getting a thousand dollars a share more than the others. The
Dodges, like the rest, had to sell for about half what they
should have been able to obtain on the open market.

Still, for John and Horace Dodge it was not a bad deal.
Each of them got $12,500,000 and, added to the immense
profits of the Dodge Corporation, it made a sizable fortune
which has never been accurately estimated but must have
been well over $200,000,000, if the money of both men is
considered together.

John Dodge died in 1920, leaving to his heirs by the terms of
his will ten overcoats, eighteen suits, a hundred pieces of un-

derwear and one hundred and nine shirts, along with the usual benefactions. His brother died the same year. Their widows sold the business five years later, and part of the $146,000,000 it brought was added to the fortune with which the heirs were now blessed.

There appeared to be a plethora of heirs. Both Dodge brothers had married twice, and between them they had fathered seven children. John had married, first, a girl named Ivy Hawkins, who gave him John Duval, Winifred and Isabel; later he married his secretary, Matilda Rausch, who gave him Frances and Daniel. Horace had two children, Delphine and Horace, Jr., by his first wife, Anna, but no issue by his second wife, later Mrs. Hugh Dillman, who divorced her second husband in 1947 when she was seventy.

Oddly enough, it was the children of Horace, the quiet brother, who made the headlines and did more than all the others to help spend the great Dodge fortune. Delphine achieved some fame by marrying, as the first of her three husbands, Mrs. Edward T. Stotesbury's son, James H. R. Cromwell, who later became the husband of Doris Duke. Horace, Jr., achieved a more usual kind of newspaper immortality by marrying five times.

When one surveys the tangled history of the Dodge brothers' heirs, the contrast between the founders' canny accumulating of the fortune and the way it was squandered is depressing, although some might argue that it is only depressing in another way. Basically it is the story of Horace, Jr.'s and Delphine's dependence on their mother for money, which they used to marry and divorce, to buy love and to live high. John's children were less spectacular in their spending, but were sometimes ostentatious in other ways. When Frances made her Detroit debut in 1936 she wore a black orchid, achieved by the judicious use of paint. Anyone, it seemed, could wear a real orchid.

Of John's five children, only his son, John Duval, achieved much public notice. His brothers and sisters all inherited one fifth of their father's estate and promptly disappeared into the relative obscurity of the society pages, except for Isabel Dodge Sloane, whose race horses earned her a place on the sports pages as well.

John Duval's life, however, was marked by contention and violence from the beginning. His father had left his mother and the other children each a fifth of an estate valued at $36,892,588.41, including $1,049,288.68 in cash, but to the oldest son he had left only $150 a month income. That was because the boy had infuriated his father by eloping at twenty (in 1918) with his high school sweetheart and going off to Texas to be an auto mechanic. Old John, who had begun life as a mechanic himself, had social ambitions which he felt his son had thwarted, and cutting him off was his revenge.

As a result of this piece of senseless cruelty, John Duval's life became a series of public brawls and court suits in which he attempted to obtain his full inheritance. The family, partly out of sympathy and partly to keep him from constantly washing the Dodge linen in courtrooms, gave him $1,600,000 as a belated inheritance, but he ran through this substantial sum with an astounding celerity. He was a free-spending playboy, lost much of the money in real estate ventures, parted with more of it in equally unprofitable Detroit night club operations, and got rid of what remained in the designing of an automobile which proved to be highly unsuccessful.

John Duval was often in the headlines, and always he was in trouble. Sometimes it was drunken driving; once he ran down a child. Later, as his money began to thin out, the litigation was mostly civil court cases—suits involving furniture, jewelry, automobiles and unpaid hotel bills. He filed several unsuccessful suits to break his father's will. As he pursued his haphazard, aimless way through life it often appeared to John Duval's friends that he could not fail to come to a spectacular end, and he did not disappoint them. In the mid-forties he died one night in a drunken brawl involving his second wife, an attractive neighbor lady into whose bedroom window he had crawled, and the police, who mistook him for a prowler. At some point in the ensuing struggle he suffered a brain concussion and died. For a time there was a question whether he was the victim of a police rough-up, whether his fatal injury was the result of pub crawling earlier in the evening, or whether his wife had hit him with a bowl of ice cubes. It was officially, if arbitrarily, decided that he had accidentally banged his head on the floor of the police station.

Needless to say, he died penniless. His wife, an ex-secretary, was killed a few years later, in 1950, when she drove her car head on into a Florida East Coast freight train. In John Duval's case, the Dodge fortune ran into a blind alley: no heirs, no money.

Violence ran like a crimson thread through the Dodge family. John Duval's half brother, Daniel ("Danny") Dodge, caused a sensation in the papers in the thirties by marrying a telephone operator, and eleven days later created much larger headlines by drowning after a somewhat mysterious explosion wrecked his speedboat on Lake Erie. His bride was left with eight million dollars of Dodge money.

As noted, the others of John's children led relatively quiet lives. Isabel, who belonged to the very horsy set of Long Island, carried on in a most conventional way by becoming a leader of the Old Guard in Palm Beach and acquiring the customary pieces of real estate—a huge estate on Long Island, her Concha Marina cottage in Palm Beach, a Park Avenue apartment, farms in Virginia and South Carolina, and a hunting lodge in Scotland. Thus a good deal of Isabel's $5,000,000 share of Dodge money could be said to have been spent in a substantial Astor way. Furthermore, Isabel achieved the social prominence her father longed for by marrying into the Sloanes, an old New York family which had little in common with *nouveau riche* Detroit automobile families.

As for Matilda Dodge, John's widow, she took her Dodge money into another marriage as the wife of a Detroit lumber dealer, whom she met at a church function, and so another portion of Dodge money was safely immured.

Horace's widow, however, was far from being so conservative—except for holding the purse strings tightly when it came to the children, Horace, Jr., and Delphine. She married in 1926 an ex-actor and ex-secretary from Chesterfield, Ohio, named Hugh Dillman, who was several years her junior. The two reigned for many years as king and queen of Palm Beach society, entertaining such notables as the Duke and Duchess of Windsor. Mrs. Dillman was famous for her yacht, which was worth two million dollars, and for her Palm Beach cottage, Playa Riente, which she picked up for only $1,800,000. It had rare marble floors and centuries-old heavy wooden doors from Spain, valuable Sert murals, and a ballroom cantilevered over the ocean. The rug on the living-room floor was valued at $500,000. What remained of her fortune, and it was still a sum worth having, was passed on to the children and grandchildren.

Certainly a conservative matron like Mrs. Dillman, who liked to deplore the democratization of Palm Beach society, could have found little satisfaction in her children.

Delphine's first marriage, to James H. R. Cromwell, was only the first of her many attempts to find love. The handsome Jimmy, who was then making a serious effort to work in Wall Street, found her an unstable companion, given to unpredictable moods and conduct which could only be described as impulsive. He complained to his friends later that when he returned from a hard day in the Street he might find her entertaining fifty people he had never seen before, or else curled up alone with a bottle and not inclined to see anyone. Sometimes it seemed to the harassed Jimmy that he almost preferred Delphine's mother, a lady with whom he had a lasting friendship.

Neither of Delphine's other two marriages was to rich men, and there is the suspicion that she desperately tried to buy love. Failing that, it seems that she may have tried to give it away, judging by the several threatened alienation-of-affection suits aimed at her. The most celebrated of these occurred as the aftermath of a front-page affair she had with a crooner-pugilist from Belfast, so often defeated in the ring that he became known as the "Mild Irish Rose." The Rose's wife, described as a movie actress, made Delphine the defendant in a $2,000,000 suit, alleging, as the tabloids like to put it, love piracy—a social error with which Delphine was often charged.

This episode produced what may be a high-water mark in process serving. The beagle assigned to track down Delphine and serve her with the papers in the suit was a crafty and ingenious man. Attired correctly in an Inverness cape, tails and top hat, he crashed one of Delphine's parties, announcing himself as the Count de Kakiak, of Paris, and thereupon, emerging in the glitter and glory of high Dodge society, gave Delphine the bad news before he was thrown out.

Until she died in the forties, Delphine contrived to spend a good part of her share in the fortune, but she was a miser by comparison with her brother Horace. Four of his five marriages were reported to have cost him a million dollars each before he could extricate himself, and the fifth was said to have cost him a million to get into.

Horace, Sr., had a premonition, apparently, that his son would be an easy man with a dollar because his will gave Horace, Jr., only twenty-five hundred dollars income a year to spend. His protests to his mother persuaded her to raise the amount to twenty-five thousand, but that was scarcely enough to keep Horace alive, and after considerably more family discussion Horace and Delphine were made trustees of the estate, able to draw on the money they would eventually inherit anyway—but only with their mother's consent, which was not readily given.

Equipped with something more than a pittance, Horace began marrying. His first wife, whom he married in 1921, was a Detroit society girl, Lois Virginia Knowlson. The marriage lasted six years, during which two children, Horace III and Delphine, were born. A year after the divorce he married Muriel Sisman, another Detroit society figure, who also gave him two children, Diana and David, in their eleven years together.

While he was still married to Muriel, Horace, Jr., had become friendly, as the newspapers euphemistically phrased it, with Martha ("Mickey") Devine, a show girl and model in New York. His mother opposed the marriage, quite naturally, but she was finally won over, or lost interest, and Horace, Jr., married Mickey in 1940, after which it appeared that he himself lost interest, as the bride complained later. It was a stormy four years before Horace appeared in the divorce courts again, but he seemed not to have lost heart for the battle because he married, almost immediately, Clara Mae Tinsley, who proved to be still another short-term proposition.

A friend thought he knew why Horace had endured so

many matrimonial failures. "Horace," he explained, "is a hard man to get along with—he just plays too hard, and has all day and night to do it in. He never has to be anywhere at any time, and can't understand why anybody else should have to."

When he was fifty-four, described by a New York tabloid as a "middle-aged millionaire with a bad heart, lame leg, ravaged face and a tendency to mumble in his beer," Horace, Jr., met the love of his life, a sculptured piece of glamor named Gregg Sherwood, a former show girl and television actress, who was twenty-seven years his junior. Before his divorce from Clara Mae became final, Horace was conducting Gregg on a triumphal tour of Europe, in the summer of 1952, announcing their engagement.

Horace met Gregg and her ever present mother, Mrs. Helen Fjelstad, on the *Queen Mary* at Cherbourg, went on with them to Southampton, and then whisked them off to his stately home in England, a hundred-acre estate, St. Leonard's, at Windsor near the royal castle. St. Leonard's, which cost nearly two million dollars, had been in the Dodge family for a long time. Its main house had 103 rooms, some of them never visited by Horace, and its upkeep came to thirty thousand dollars a year. From this plush rookery, Horace and Gregg and her mother went on sorties to Paris and the Riviera, accompanied by Dodge's constant bodyguard, T. H. Parrish, a former government investigator, and several hangers-on.

For these strolling players, Horace took over two floors in one of the best Cannes hotels, where his own rooms cost him more than two hundred dollars a day. His intention, he said, was "to show Gregg what life with me would be like." Life, it seemed, would be a round of sunning, swimming, drinking, dancing and making short side trips, like running over to

Geneva for lunch in a chartered plane, at a cost of more than a thousand dollars.

At the engagement party itself, Horace presented Gregg with a diamond ring estimated variously as worth $10,000 and $100,000, but in any case a valuable piece of jewelry. Forty guests came to the party in special planes arriving from London, Paris and Rome. Another airplane brought in sixty pounds of Astrakhan caviar from behind the Iron Curtain, at five dollars an ounce. The party took place in the exclusive Cannes gambling spot whimsically called the Palm Beach Casino, which Horace had smothered in twelve hundred dozen red roses and five hundred dozen tuberoses for the occasion. On the horseshoe dinner table were spread a thousand giant orchids at fifteen dollars each. Mrs. Florence Sisman, of Detroit, Horace's former sister-in-law, agreed to act as hostess. For her trouble, and because it was her birthday, Horace gave her a $60,000 diamond solitaire. Mere guests got perfume and cigarette holders.

No one had a better time than Horace, Jr. While Gregg played with her ring, he was waltzing with Mrs. Sisman, although he had to be held up by two nurses, one on each side, because of a leg injury remaining from his flying days.

But the course of love did not run smoothly between Horace and Gregg, either before or after their marriage. Before, the trouble centered on Clara Mae's reluctance to give her husband a divorce—unless, that is, he agreed to a $3,000,000 settlement. Later there was a strange disagreement in Detroit when Horace had Gregg arrested, charging that she had stolen four cigarette lighters and a box of candy from him. She retaliated by writing a sexy newspaper series, coyly titled "How to Dodge Wolves," and "Wolves I Have Dodged." A sample of Gregg's style, presumably with astral help: "If you see an automobile magnate coming your way, dodge, girls! dodge! and I do mean dodge!"

Both as betrothed and as wife, Gregg displayed an inability to stay out of the newspapers equal to Horace, Jr.'s. At various times she was reported as assaulting the police, slapping a Spanish guitarist, fleeing from her Palm Beach home in an ambulance, and claiming that kidnapers were threatening to take her child. She seemed to be no help at all in curing her husband of his inability to produce ready cash. As late as 1959 he was being sued by irate jewelers and furriers for unpaid bills.

To the astonishment of some, Gregg once appeared in the role of Lady Bountiful, as founder and national director of a home for wayward girls in Palm Beach, to be known as Girls' Town, with the slogan, "The American girl with a future."

The distance between the Dodge brothers' bicycle shop and Palm Beach, not to mention Cannes, sometimes seems startling to students of American fortunes, who have followed the rise and decline of Dodge wealth with morbid interest. Yet the Dodge story was not untypical, particularly of the Middle Western families who made their money late and passed it on rather quickly to heirs unaccustomed to wealth and its more conventional uses.

There was a difference, clearly, between the Vanderbilts and the Dodges that had nothing to do with spending of itself. The difference was that between society and money, and the gulf has widened with the passing of the generations.

5

Tobacco Society: Dukes and Reynoldses,
with a Side Trip to Barbara Hutton

There was little in common between the Duke and Reynolds families except for the fact that their fortunes were founded on tobacco. James Buchanan Duke was a strong, exceptional man who used tobacco as the basis of a fortune grossing $156,000,000. Richard J. and William Neal Reynolds were brothers who accumulated a gross of $117,000,000 by unexceptionable means, and were themselves quiet Southern businessmen who enjoyed their money and scarcely made a dent in history.

It was the descendants of these men who became better known than their progenitors, albeit for the wrong reasons, and who demonstrated again that regardless of family background it is the inheritors, not the accumulators, to whom money is a mixed blessing, at best.

The Duke fortune was fashioned along traditional nineteenth-century lines, faithfully tracing the prescribed pattern. James Duke was born in 1856 on his father's modest farm near Durham, North Carolina, and grew up in the customary poverty. His mother died when he was still an infant; his father came stumbling home on foot from the Civil War with a half dollar in his pocket, and leading two blind mules.

There was nothing much remaining on the farm; the pillaging Union Army had seen to that. Poking around the ruins with their father, young James and his brother Benjamin found some leaf tobacco the Yankees had overlooked. They carried it into their log barn and pounded it out with hickory sticks, packaged it in containers labeled PRO BONO PUBLICO, and hitching the blind mules to a wagon, they traversed the dusty roads of southern North Carolina, selling their tobacco wherever they could.

James had already obtained a little schooling in a log house, but now, with the newly earned tobacco money, he contrived to go to the academy in Durham and later to a boarding school in Guilford County. By that time, rising from their poverty-stricken beginnings, the family had a small tobacco factory in operation, in which young James, only fourteen, was managing the Negro boys. Taking time off to go up to Poughkeepsie, he hurried through the curriculum of the Eastman Business College there, setting some kind of educational record in the process. At eighteen he was a member of W. Duke & Sons, and in business to stay.

The pivot point on which his fortunes turned came when legislation was enacted which reduced the government cigarette tax by two thirds. Two months before the law took effect, Duke astutely lowered the price of his cigarettes from ten cents to five cents a package, and began to advertise them in a manner unprecedented in the business. That brought on what came to be known as the "great tobacco war," a period of ruthless price cutting and competitive advertising which threatened every company involved in it with ruin. In a sense it was like a giant poker game, in which the player with sufficient guts and will power stood the best chance to win.

Duke had those qualities, besides an unlimited self-confidence and a powerhouse store of energy and ambition.

That was enough. At first the older companies in the field tried to buy him up. Then, when he refused, they left him to his own devices, confident that his business was too new to withstand the pressures of the war. But Duke persisted, carried the fighting to his enemies and finally in 1890 forced them to come together in the combination called the American Tobacco Company so that they would run no further risk of failing separately. Naturally, Duke was president of the new company. Virtually his first act was to begin organizing the plug manufacturers, who combined in 1898, with Duke as president and his friends controlling this combination as well. The friends included some New York and Philadelphia moneymen of formidable reputation: Oliver H. Payne, Peter A. B. Widener, Grant B. Schley, William C. Whitney, R. J. Reynolds and Thomas Fortune Ryan.

There followed the familiar nineteenth-century pyramiding—the American Snuff Company was formed in 1900, then successively the American Cigar Company, the American Stogie Company and United Cigar Stores—followed by the equally familiar Supreme Court decision, except that this time it was the justices' decision in another case (the Northern Securities Company) which led Duke and his associates to think twice and to dissolve, without being told, their Consolidated Tobacco Company, the holding company for their diverse interests.

Out of the complicated backing and filling came the enlarged and enriched American Tobacco Company, which at its peak was to control 150 factories, whose capitalization was more than $502,000,000. One wonders why James Duke, shrewd man that he was, imagined that the creation of this company would do any more than postpone the day when the Supreme Court would declare it the trust it so obviously had been designed to be. Yet evidently Duke could not see the obvious, because he fought the case through the courts for five years before the justices ordered the combine dissolved.

Duke had cannily not placed all his tobacco in one basket. He had begun the equally complicated process of buying light and power properties, which culminated in the formation of the Southern Power Company, and out of his profits in this endeavor he set up a trust fund which ultimately amounted to $100,000,000. This was the money, primarily, that he used in creating Duke University, known as Trinity College until that time. Duke insisted on the change of name. Other portions of it went to build hospitals in the two Carolinas, to help Methodist churches and clergymen, and to orphanages.

Duke liked to see himself memorialized. At his university, later often to be referred to unkindly as the country club of the South, his marble image reclines in the chapel and his bronze likeness stands boldly outside. The bronze statue depicts him holding a cigar in his hand—philanthropy enlightening the South.

He was, quite obviously, a self-made man, in the nineteenth-century image. He was also a maker of homilies, giving them a somewhat sardonic twist ("Nothing makes people happier than luxury") or turning them into rhetorical questions ("How can you be happy if you're not busy?").

This big, arrogant man was the typically successful businessman who finds himself lost in his relationships with people outside the business world, particularly women. He had no time for marriage until he was forty-eight, and then it turned out to be the kind of mistake he would never have made in business. He was married only a year to Mrs. Wil-

liam McCready, a forty-two-year-old New York divorcee, before he sued for divorce on grounds of adultery. But the first
Mrs. Duke was that lawyer's delight, a litigious woman, and
she kept her ex-husband involved in a series of court actions
until he died.

Having digested his mistake for three years, Duke married
again, a widow this time. Nanaline Holt Inman was something of a success story herself, having been brought up in
a Macon family impoverished by the death of her father
when she was in her teens. Nanaline had never forgotten
what it meant to a proud family when, suddenly, boarders
came to stay in the bedrooms of the house she had grown
up in, and her mother worked late at night making party
dresses which she and her sister had to deliver. These experiences shaped everything else that happened to Nanaline.
When she married, it was to a man who had made a respectable fortune in cotton, Walter Inman. Two years after his
death she was married to James Duke, possessor of one of
the great American fortunes.

That would have been security enough for most women,
but Nanaline could not forget. She was a cool, reserved lady,
once described by a friend as a "withholding personality,"
and what she withheld, among other things, was money. In
that she was like her husband. His forceful, lusty, almost exuberant nature did not prevent him from being a careful man
about money, perhaps as a result of recalling his own poverty.
His one indulgence in later life was his daughter, Doris, but
that influence was counterbalanced by Nanaline, who constantly impressed the value of money on her daughter. Both
parents made it absolutely clear to their tall, shy "Deedee,"
as she was called, that people were going to try to take her
money away from her, by various means, and their admonitions were heeded. Years later Doris remarked: "People

wouldn't have money long if they didn't ask how much things cost and then refuse to buy half of them."

Yet the pressures on Doris to spend her money were overwhelming. She was, to begin with, the second most famous heiress in the world. Her father died when she was thirteen, leaving her about $70,000,000, which the newspapers estimated all the way from $55,000,000 to $200,000,000, enough in any case to pin on her the names she hated: "Princess," "Golden Girl," "Richest Girl in the World."

Withdrawn, like her mother, and hating publicity, she was nevertheless a well-known figure in America, even as a child. "I wish I could go into a store and shop for things just as a girl," she once remarked wistfully. But she had to follow the rigid pattern laid down for her by her socially conscious mother: Brearley School, then a Newport debut in 1930 when she was eighteen, with three orchestras and four hundred guests; and, later in her debut year, a presentation at the Court of St. James's.

Even before she came out the newspapers were speculating about her endlessly. Since she refused to be interviewed, the society reporters had to be content with imaginative descriptions of her surroundings and daily life. But everything she did was news. As a subdeb, when she joined a dancing class at the Ritz-Carlton, it was a news story carried by the major press associations. At fourteen, page-one headlines announced: DORIS DUKE, HEIRESS, SPURNS BODYGUARDS IN SALT LAKE VISIT. Doris had taken a walk alone.

After the debut, and before her first marriage five years later, a glimpse into her life was offered the hungry society writers by her Inman half brother, who had given them an enchanting time with his own scandalous divorce action. Notoriety, said Inman, surrounded Doris. "Everywhere we go it's the same. She gets to see a few sights, go out to dinner a few times, and then her identity becomes known and we have to rush off somewhere else." They had to watch out constantly for gangsters and racketeers, he went on, "but that's not the worst of it. Cranks are the principal annoyance. Mail comes in by the bagful with all sorts of requests, because she is supposed to have so much money."

Did she handle her own money? the reporters asked. "Doris knows where every dollar of her money is, and what it's doing," Inman told them. But what about suitors? the reporters pursued. "No, not so much," Inman said. "The average eligible suitor doesn't want to appear to be a fortune hunter."

James H. R. Cromwell, heir to the Stotesbury millions, which was Morgan money, certainly did not appear to be a fortune hunter when the two met at Bar Harbor and fell in love "at first sight," as Jimmy put it. "I found a lonely repressed girl," he told a friend later, "and determined to make her happy."

Ah, poor little rich girl, people sighed, she has found her prince, and unless someone has tampered with the story line she will live happily ever after. Doris and Jimmy sailed away on a trip around the world (a wedding present from Nanaline), but as Jimmy asserted later, the honeymoon came to an end before the ship got to San Francisco. It was the beginning of eight years of backing and filling, charges and countercharges, intervals of apparent peace followed by new quarrels.

Whatever the rights and wrongs of the marriage, and the stories could scarcely be more conflicting, one thing was clear: it was a marriage that was costing Doris money, and it marked the beginning of a relative dissipation of James Duke's fortune. Perhaps Cromwell was right in his later assertion that some kind of sea change took place in his young wife (she was twenty-three, he was thirty-seven) on their

honeymoon cruise, converting her from a shy, withdrawn
girl to a free-spending, good-time woman.

Money, at least, appeared to be the principal consideration
when the divorce came at last in 1943. It was a tangled business in every respect. Charging desertion, Cromwell won a
limited decree in New Jersey, by the terms of which neither
of them could ever remarry, and at her death he was to be
entitled to half of her New Jersey property. Her lawyer made
no objection to the property disposition; the estate was running at a deficit of $300,000 a year, he said. Cromwell also
demanded that Doris set up a $7,000,000 trust fund for him,
the income to be used for philanthropic purposes. In reply,
Doris countered with a Reno divorce suit, charging extreme
cruelty and citing "constant demands for money." Answering
the suit, Cromwell named a "British Casanova" as his rival,
and charged further that when their daughter died twenty-
four hours after birth in Honolulu, Doris had maliciously
made him stay away from her so that he would lose face in
the eyes of the voters of New Jersey, where he was then running for the Senate, thus contributing to his defeat.

As the argument went on, Doris the stingy one, as some
had called her, began to emerge as Doris the spender, by her
own admission. It had cost her a million dollars, she said, to
build their dream house, Shangri-La, in Hawaii, a Moroccan-
Persian palace with two stone camels flanking the doorway
and a swimming pool with a hydraulic elevator springboard.
Moreover, Doris declared, she had given Cromwell a substantial allowance and contributed fifty thousand dollars to the
Democratic Party, to which her husband belonged, but he
had urged her to undertake in addition the costs of his appointment as minister to Canada, at which she had balked.
Life with Cromwell, she concluded, had cost her $700,000,
not counting Shangri-La.

In the end Cromwell won an absolute divorce in New Jersey in 1947. Meanwhile, Doris had happily operated a canteen for merchant seamen during the Second World War— "I'm happier now than I've ever been in my life," she said then—and after the war was over she had worked as a reporter for Hearst's International News Service in Rome and the Balkans, lingered for a time in Hawaii, and become a fashion editor in Paris for *Harper's Bazaar*.

In 1947, when Doris was divorced and thirty-five, there occurred the second major change in her life, when she joined the ranks of what Cleveland Amory has immortalized as Publiciety by marrying Porfirio Rubirosa, one-time son-in-law of Trujillo and a kind of *homme fatal*. But Doris had learned. Her lawyers were partners to the marriage, producing a document in advance of the ceremony which specified that Rubirosa was to have no claim on her wealth, although to soften the blow she did give him an airplane and a house in Paris after they were married, in which they lived while he acted as honorary chargé d'affaires for the Dominican Republic.

During the ceremony, which took place in Paris, Rubirosa was reported to have nonchalantly puffed on a cigarette. There were twenty-three presumably happy days on the Riviera, and then came trouble. It was reported that the State Department was about to pick up Doris' passport because of her marriage, as it had done once before in Rome because of her associations there.

A Washington informant told a New York paper that the trouble could be laid at the door of Rubirosa. "When Deedee married him," this informant said, "Ruby was brought into the limelight and given great publicity. Publicity was one thing he couldn't afford. He will probably be in all kinds of trouble now. People who in the past despaired of getting their money back will now try to get it back. People who opposed him, as Dominican exiles in France, Spain and the U.S., will fear, now that he has real money behind him, that he will be a greater menace in the future than he was in the past. They will take every means possible to stop him. The hubbub that all this will create may cause the State Department to act in the case of Deedee."

Another friend described Rubirosa as a man who had posed as a millionaire when, in fact, "he hasn't got $50 to his name today," and thus Doris had once more been betrayed by her generosity. "When she met Jimmy Cromwell," the friend went on, "she was an inexperienced girl and she spent plenty. Now, while she may not pay in money, thanks to a prenuptial contract which her friends insisted on—she may pay in heartache and disillusionment."

The payment came a year later with another divorce. Her subsequent career in the last decade has not, apparently, been a happy one, although continuing to be expensive. In 1954, Doris and a friend named Johnny Gomez, described as a jazz enthusiast, bought Rudolf Valentino's Hollywood mansion, Falcon's Lair. Two years earlier the newspapers reported that she had become a West Coast disciple of a bearded Hollywood yogi, who was said to look like Rasputin and talk like Billy Graham. As a disciple, it was said, Doris was known as "Gita."

"It's not Gita's fault that she has so much money," the yogi remarked consolingly, to which Miss Duke replied: "No, it was my father who made all of it. I just inherited it."

Whether she could make any real impression on the fortune, however, was open to question. The tabloids asserted that she had run up her inheritance to a staggering $300,000,-000, a figure which might well be doubted, although probably it had increased by the normal processes of investment.

If Doris did not have love, she unquestionably had possessions, and many of them were in the form of real estate. There was Shangri-La, in Hawaii, valued at a million; the 2200-acre estate in Somerville, New Jersey, operating at formidable cost; the cottage called Rough Point in Newport, once Frederick W. Vanderbilt's home, which her mother had persuaded her father to buy when Doris was ten; another estate, Lynnewood, near Charlotte, North Carolina; still another cottage at Antibes; a villa in Palm Beach; a house in Reno; an apartment in Paris; and a town house in New York.

The life of the "poor little rich girl" was remarkably parallel in many ways to that of the equally famous lady with only money to console her, Barbara Hutton.

Born in the same year, 1912, Miss Hutton was, in the public eye and in reality, both as poor and as rich as Doris. Once more, too, it was the story of the father rising from poverty and amassing a fortune so great that it could hardly be dissipated, even with effort. Frank Winfield Woolworth, Barbara's grandfather, was a farm boy who became an accumulator by capitalizing on other people's low incomes. Like James Duke, he followed a traditional path. He left the farm in Rodman, Jefferson County, New York, only to go to country schools and briefly to attend a business college in Watertown before he started out to make his fortune. Unlike Duke, however, he was not immediately successful, and indeed appeared to have remarkably little talent for making money.

Frank Woolworth's story, in its earlier phases, is almost Horatio Alger in reverse. Starting as clerk in a village grocery store, where he worked without wages for two years, he got his first real job in a Watertown store, where again he received no pay for a three months' trial period, at the end of which he was put on the pay roll at $3.50 a week and in two years was raised to $6.00 a week. He supported himself on that pittance and even saved a little.

Nevertheless, he seemed unable to get ahead. With a Watertown man who was anxious to try the new "ninety-nine-cent store" idea in merchandising, he went to Port Huron, Michigan, where he proved to be so inept a salesman that his salary was cut from $10 to $8.50 a week, and he had to go home again, ill and disconsolate. After a while he went back to his old job in Watertown. He couldn't forget, however, what was to him the fascinating idea of selling a large quantity of articles at a fixed price, and he persuaded his boss to try a counter in which all the goods were priced at five cents. The result was highly successful, but when he induced one of his employers to lend him $300 to try out the same idea in Utica for himself, he went broke in three months and had to close the store.

With the help of the same willing partner, he tried again with a store in Lancaster, Pennsylvania. This time he varied his five-cent stock by adding a ten-cent line, and so the fabled five-and-dime store was born, from which innumerable heroines of novels and motion pictures would struggle to better things.

It was characteristic of Woolworth that even with the formula for success in his possession, and proved, he still had trouble becoming a rich man. With the profits from his Lancaster store he took the logical next step and began to establish branches in other cities, but because he had not made a careful study of where to establish them, the first stores he operated in Philadelphia, Harrisburg, York, Pennsylvania, and Newark, New Jersey, were not profitable for some time. It was not until others in Buffalo, Erie, Scranton and similar cities tapped the low-income market that the Woolworth fortune began to rise. In the same year his granddaughter was born, he formed the F. W. Woolworth Company, gathering in all his current competition and standing alone temporarily as the only five-and-dime-chain merchant in the United States, a status symbolized by his 792-foot Woolworth Building, which fulfilled a dream he had nurtured since he was a small boy. By the time he died in 1919 he had a thousand stores in the United States and Canada, doing a volume of $107,000,000 annually.

Out of these riches Woolworth accumulated a fortune estimated at $65,000,000, but certainly more, all of which was left to his wife. They had had three daughters, one of whom, Edna, married a handsome young stockbroker named Franklyn Laws Hutton and gave him a daughter, Barbara, who eventually outranked Doris Duke as the world's most famous heiress and the poorest of poor little rich girls. Edna died under tragic and mysterious circumstances when Barbara was five years old, and until her grandfather's death the motherless child often visited him in New York and on Long Island.

Frank Woolworth had the pleasure of his granddaughter's company for only seven years before he died, but the relationship he bore her was curiously like that between James Duke and Doris. The two old men were much alike in background and, aside from their business personalities, were essentially simple, plain men who found themselves by virtue of their money living in a world of culture they could not understand. Both loved their little girls and were overindulgent with them. Barbara would visit her grandfather in his ornate house on Fifth Avenue, where she delighted in listening to the music that emanated from the great organ her tone-deaf relative had had constructed so that its music filtered to every corner of the house, emerging from the closets and even through hollow bedposts into his own bed. That was Woolworth's act of revenge for a childhood that had been deprived of music, for which he had an abiding love.

The mansion was an eerie place, echoing with music, inhabited by an aging millionaire whose mind was going and a wife whose reason had already gone. These two, with a nurse for one and a keeper for the other, entertained Barbara. Her grandmother Woolworth died when she was thirteen, and the fortune was left to Barbara and her two aunts, Mrs. James P. Donahue and Mrs. Charles McCann. Now began the unhappy career of the unhappy Miss Hutton.

It is a familiar story, following the pattern of Delphine Dodge, Doris Duke and a succession of lesser heiresses. There was the lonely, motherless girlhood, the extravagant debut (four orchestras as against Doris' three, and these included Rudy Vallee's, transported from California), the presentation at court, and then the night clubs, the private railroad car (both Doris and Barbara had one), the seeking of release through marriage, and after that the long succession of husbands and close friends. In Barbara's case the men began a little earlier, with "Prince" Alexis Mdivani, at fifteen, but the result was the same. Her marriage at twenty to Mdivani cost her a million dollars at the beginning (it was the prince's idea of an advance) and another two million in settlement at the end, but twenty-four hours after the divorce she was married again to another nobleman, this time a genuinely certified Danish count, Kurt Haugwitz-Reventlow.

That marriage cost her $4,500,000 for a magnificent Regent Park house, and would have cost her five million more if the count's demand, in return for which he would spare her "three years of hell with headlines," had been granted. More than the money, however, was the hurt caused by the hatred of people in depression America who picketed her hotel and mobbed her in theaters because she had become the symbol of rich irresponsibility in a time of poverty. They could not forget the headlines about her marriages and her extravagant use of money—for example, ten thousand dollars to fly an orchestra from London to Paris in 1934, one of the blackest years.

She could not endear herself to the public even by marrying Cary Grant, every girl's secret desire, although this time the inevitable divorce cost her nothing except another husband. Barbara apparently could not get over the infantile desire to marry into royalty. Her fourth was a Lithuanian prince, Igor Troubetzkoy, who was not only expensive but proved to be "the meanest man in the world," as Barbara put it when they were divorced. In 1953, Doris Duke passed on to her Porfirio Rubirosa, as their parallel paths, in effect, turned and merged. It was the shortest marriage of all, only seventy-two days, and at the end of it Barbara observed, "I feel as if I'd been hit over the head." Still staggering, she married a sixth husband, the German tennis star and another nobleman, Baron Gottfried von Cramm. Separated three years later, she was in the headlines once more with an attachment to a man twenty years younger, Philip Van Rensselaer, of an old New York family.

Cleveland Amory, who has given us the best and most complete account of Barbara's life and times, reported from the lips of Van Rensselaer one of the most cruelly penetrating summaries of Barbara Hutton's tragedy that anyone has uttered. "She gave me enormous sums of money," this young man said candidly. "She said I was a gentleman and I was meant to have lots of money. And anyway, she wasn't paying for me, she said, Grandpa Woolworth was."

As the Duke money grew in spite of Doris' inroads, so did the Hutton fortune increase. But its ultimate fragmentation seems inevitable; assuredly it will pass one day into the hands of another unhappy rich boy, Lance, Haugwitz-Reventlow's son, or perhaps part of it will be diverted for tax purposes into a foundation that might or might not prove to be beneficial to anyone except the owners of the wealth.

A less spectacular example of how hard-won fortunes suffer attrition and generate tragedy is the case of the Reynolds family, the other tobacco entrepreneurs. They were not unusual Southerners at the beginning, Hardin W. Reynolds and his wife Nancy, who had four sons. Two of these sons, Richard J. and William Neal, were the accumulators, founding their company in 1875 and building it carefully. Richard J., it appears, did little more than to give his name to the company, as far as public notice is concerned, before he died in 1946; actually, of course, he was the motive power behind the making of the fortune.

William Neal, his brother, died in 1951 at the age of eighty-eight, after a lifetime in which he mixed horses and philanthropy. The horses were trotters; his Mary Reynolds won the 1933 Hambletonian, an event known in racing as the "$40,000 stumble." William owned stables at Tanglewood Farms, his show place near Winston-Salem, and also had winter training quarters at Orlando, Florida. Philanthropically, he was a trustee of Duke University; gave money to the Kate G. Bitting Reynolds Hospital for Negroes (named after his wife) in Winston-Salem; gave $340,000 to support salaries at North Carolina Teachers' College; and $100,000 toward a new library in Winston-Salem. These benefactions were made during his lifetime; others, of the same conventional variety, were included in his will.

But the bulk of his fortune and that of his brother filtered down in the family; it had begun filtering before either of them was dead. Much of it came to Richard J.'s son, Zachary Smith Reynolds. Zachary, called Smith, was a moody, strange young man who seemed to understand that he had been born under an unlucky star. It is doubtful he thought himself cursed by wealth. In 1929, when he was eighteen, he met and married nineteen-year-old Anne Cannon, of the towel fortune, happily uniting tobacco and linen as well as two of the richest families in the South. They settled down at Reynolds, Smith's plantation outside Winston-Salem, which was so large that it had its own private church, post office, dairy, poultry yard, general store, artificial lake, stables and airplane.

It was the kind of cozy establishment in which a bride could be expected to feel at home, but it was only a year before Anne Cannon Reynolds left the plantation. The families kept the estrangement quiet until one night in 1930 when Tom Gay Coltrane, a prominent Southerner, was found dead under the garden hedge of a Dr. E. A. Misenheimer. An investigation disclosed that Anne had been with the dead man about ninety minutes before; they had left together from a party. During the inquest the secret that the Reynoldses and Cannons had tried to keep came into the open, although presumably it was already well known to many people.

Anne was not implicated in Coltrane's death. The inquest produced evidence that he had received threats against his life, and in any case the coroner returned a verdict of death as the result of heart failure and alcoholism. In 1931, Anne divorced Reynolds, again secretly, taking custody of their daughter, Anne Cannon Reynolds II.

Before the divorce was filed, Smith had met and fallen in love with Libby Holman, the great sultry-voiced torch singer of the late twenties and early thirties. As soon as the divorce was final they were married—once more, secretly. This secret was kept until a hot July night six months later when, in one of the most sensational news stories of the thirties, young

Reynolds was either murdered or committed suicide during a party at the plantation.

For a time newspaper readers forgot the crash and the depression, stopped cursing Mr. Hoover, and paid little attention to the rising fortunes of the governor of New York. They were following avidly the deliberate, drawling processes of Southern law as it delved, some thought with distaste, into the tragedy of the rich and influential Reynolds clan. People who knew Miss Holman only for her throaty renditions of "Moanin' Low" and "Body and Soul," which had made her and the songs famous, now learned that she was the daughter of a law professor, who herself had quit the study of law to sing in night clubs. Her secret marriage to Reynolds was, of course, disclosed in detail for the delectation of the tabloid audience, who were pleased to note, as an added fillip, that she was twenty-six and Reynolds only twenty.

Slowly the events of the fatal night unfolded. In the slang of the day it had been a "wild party," a not infrequent occurrence at Reynolds, which was often host to a hard-drinking show-business crowd from New York, many of them Miss Holman's friends. That night Libby and Smith had quarreled over what Smith thought were the attentions of his best friend, Ab Walker, to his secret bride. Walker had put an arm around her, it seemed, and Reynolds was jealous. At the end of the party, when the guests were leaving (it was then about one o'clock in the morning), a shot echoed from upstairs. Ab and Libby, hurrying to the second-floor sleeping porch, found Reynolds there, shot but still living. Libby knelt over him, sobbing, her gown darkening with her husband's blood. He was taken to the hospital and died there four hours later.

Certain puzzling circumstances appeared to demand an investigation, which was conducted with something less than vigor. The fatal weapon lay on the sleeping porch, but the police did not discover it until they had searched the place three times. At the hearing Miss Holman said she could remember nothing of the night's events. There appeared to be some confusion as to her whereabouts, and that of Walker, when the shooting occurred, and although the district attorney seemed to doubt whether he had a case, Libby was indicted for murder and Walker was charged with being an accessory. The preliminary hearing had already returned a verdict of suicide, notwithstanding that Smith, who had been shot through the right temple, was left-handed.

The case did not come to trial. Smith's uncle and head of the Reynolds clan, William Neal Reynolds, indicated gently in a letter to the solicitor that the family would like to drop the whole matter, and it was dropped. Libby Holman went on to further tragedies, the apparent suicide of her second husband, the actor Ralph Holmes; and the death of her son Christopher in a mountain-climbing accident.

Christopher had been the final Reynolds secret to be disclosed. Libby had been pregnant with him the night Smith was shot. He was born seven months after the event, and immediately a lawsuit started over disposition of the fortune Smith had left behind. After two years of litigation the court awarded Anne Cannon Reynolds II a substantial $9 million; Christopher was given $6 million; Libby got a token $750,000; Anne Cannon Reynolds got nothing. The remainder, which was the bulk of it, went to the Zachary Smith Reynolds Foundation.

Other Reynolds heirs are still extant. Smith's brother, Richard J. Reynolds, Jr., who has six children, early in 1961 got into the news as the result of a honeymoon with his fourth wife, a Ph.D. from West Germany, on his own island, Sapelo, off Georgia, an event which "shocked" his third wife, a Canadian socialite, who remarked that Richard J. had not yet been divorced from her.

Richard J., one of the liveliest of the Reynolds, and the most married, had taken his fourth wife, Annemarie Schmitt, aboard a ship in the South China Sea. In 1946, he had done his part to diminish the family fortune by paying one of the highest divorce settlements up to that time, a tidy three million dollars in cash and property valued at twice that much, to his first wife, Elizabeth Dillard Reynolds.

As for Anne Cannon Reynolds II, she took the nine million dollars the court gave her into a marriage, at eighteen, with her childhood sweetheart, Lloyd Patrick Tate, known as "Junebug," her riding master's son.

Dukes, Reynoldses and Woolworths were united by a common pattern which in the eyes of the public seemed only to prove the truism that money doesn't buy happiness, or, as some cynic observed, that wealth doesn't pay. In reality, however, they exemplified the theme that recurs again and again in the history of the accumulators and their descendants—the story of relatively moral, hard-working creators of wealth, and the inheritors who know not what to do with it.

$ **6** $

Royal Family: The Vanderbilts

If America has a royal family among the accumulators and their descendants, it surely must be the Vanderbilts, whose very name is a synonym in the language for wealth and everything it represents. Their history divides into two separate stories. One is the narrative of the family's fight for social supremacy through the use of its enormous fortune, and the second concerns how that fortune dwindled through sheer spending and the multiplication of heirs.

The contrast between these stories is familiar enough by now, but in the case of the Vanderbilts the spending has been on a scale probably unapproached by any other American family. Consider, for instance, the present Alfred Gwynne Vanderbilt's assertion that he has only $8,500,000 remaining of what he inherited, and Gloria Vanderbilt's inheritance in 1945 of $4,346,000, as contrasted with the $107,000,000 the original Commodore Vanderbilt left in 1877 and the $200,-000,000 left by his son, William H., eight years later. These are minimum figures. Total Vanderbilt wealth at the turn of the century approached $400,000,000. The most energetic spending, it would seem, could scarcely harm so enormous a fortune, yet the comparative pittances possessed by Alfred Gwynne and Gloria indicate not only how it has been split off into fragments by a growing number of heirs, but testify to the constant attrition of the most monumental accumulation of this world's goods ever compiled by one family, not to mention the additional high cost of numerous divorces and huge inheritance taxes.

The spending began with the Commodore himself, that simple man who nevertheless owned a yacht more than 270 feet long, weighing 2300 tons, with a ballroom half as long as the deck, rosewood saloons upholstered with green plush, and a marble dining room. But the Commodore could afford such luxuries, and so could his son, William Henry, who passed on a fortune twice the size of his father's when he died after dinner one evening in 1885, expiring of an apoplectic fit during a hot argument over the Baltimore & Ohio's right to enter New York, an altogether fitting end for a railroad man.

Contemplating the $200,000,000 William had now entrusted to future generations, a broker friend of the deceased observed: "The ordinary human mind fails to grasp the idea of such a vast amount of wealth. If converted into gold, it would have weighed five hundred tons, and it would have taken five hundred strong horses to draw it from the Grand Central Depot to the Sub-Treasury in Wall Street. If the first of the Vanderbilts had been a contemporary of old Adam, according to the Mosaic account, and had then started as president of a railroad through Palestine, with a salary of thirty thousand dollars a year, saving all this money and living perquisites, the situation being continued in the male line to the present day, the sum total of all the family savings thus accumulated would not amount to the fortune left by William H. Vanderbilt, unless this original thirty thousand dollars had been placed at compound interest, and that in a bank from which young Napoleons of finance had been strictly excluded."

The formidable task of managing this enormous wealth fell upon William's four sons, his four daughters each having been consigned ten million dollars in securities and a Fifth Avenue mansion. In entrusting his fortune to the four sons, William could not have picked four more diverse men. Cornelius II and William Kissam, the two oldest, who each got sixty million, were exact opposites: Cornelius was the hard worker and expander, William K. the society figure and sportsman. The two youngest, Frederick and George Washington, were more alike, but far different from both their brothers: George, a shy man who was in love with the land and cared little for the business world; and Frederick, equally in love with science, but a shrewd investor as well.

Cornelius II had been his grandfather's favorite. When he was only twenty-four the Commodore installed him as assistant treasurer of the New York & Harlem; in thirteen years he was vice-president, and six years after that became president. Old Cornelius thought so much of his namesake that he left him a special legacy of five million dollars, which one may be sure Cornelius invested wisely.

Tourists who visit Newport today and shuffle through the incredible $10,000,000 summer cottage, the Breakers, which Cornelius had built there in an astonishing two-year span may imagine that the owner of such opulence must have been the apotheosis of the idle rich. Except for his grandfather, however, Cornelius was the hardest worker in the Vanderbilt family, profoundly uninterested in society, and often the first one to arrive at work in his offices at the Grand Central Building. He took himself and his responsibilities with the utmost seriousness. The management of his business and of the estate showed it.

Outside business, he worked nearly as hard at philanthropy. Vanderbilt money began to drain off in a variety of directions. With three of his brothers, he added the Vanderbilt Clinic to the College of Physicians and Surgeons, and his sister, Mrs. William D. Sloane, presented a maternity hospital. Cornelius was also active in the affairs of several other New York hospitals and held trusteeships of Columbia University, the General Theological Seminary, and the Cathedral of St. John the Divine, among others. He made frequent gifts of art and money to the Metropolitan Museum, including Rosa Bonheur's "The Horse Fair," and served as life chairman of its executive committee. He founded the YMCA's Railroad Branch and gave it a fine clubhouse. In his own church, St. Bartholomew's, he was a warden. When one of his four sons died at Yale, where all of them were students, he gave the university a dormitory in the boy's memory, bringing the total of his Yale gifts to $1,500,000.

In his own right, Cornelius qualified as a conservator of wealth, but unfortunately he had a socially ambitious wife whose primary aim was to surpass her sister-in-law, the wife of William K., and in the struggle between these two women, not only to surpass each other but to establish the Vanderbilts firmly in society, the family fortune began to dissipate in an unbelievable display of ostentation.

The two women who fought to be *the* Mrs. Vanderbilt, and to emerge even higher in the social scale than *the* Mrs. Astor, were essentially small-town society girls who saw their opportunity, in the Vanderbilt fortune, to reach the highest pinnacle of the *haut monde*. Cornelius' wife, Alice Claypoole Gwynne, was a Cincinnati girl whose family was dominant in Queen City circles. Alva Smith, William K.'s wife, came from a Mobile, Alabama, cotton family, and in the Southern manner was a talking encyclopaedia of her family's history, which she believed to be far more distinguished than the Vanderbilts'.

There still exist two monuments to the spending orgy of these women: the summer places they built at Newport. More ephemeral were the $2,000,000 Gothic palace that William K. built for Alva on the northwest corner of Fifth Avenue and Fifty-third Street, the $5,000,000 palace which Cornelius immediately built for Alice on the west side of Fifth Avenue, between Fifty-seventh and Fifty-eighth streets; Cornelius' fast yacht, and *Alva*, William K.'s somewhat larger craft which, naturally, was faster. Almost beneath mention were such small items as the solid silver favors Alva gave away at her cotillions, only to be surpassed by Alice's golden favors.

The Newport cottages, rising amid the decaying splendors of the playground, are eloquent testimonials to the battle of the Vanderbilt girls. The Breakers, Alice's place, now operated as a tourist attraction for the benefit of the Newport Preservation Society, has seventy rooms designed around a baronial hall rising more than forty-five feet through two floors. Its ornamental fence once cost five thousand dollars a year to keep painted. The house is entered through a front door weighing seventy tons. Both fresh and salt water are piped to the bathrooms; the billiard room was done from top to bottom in pale green marble.

Marble House, Alva's place, was no less extravagant. The driveway was of white marble, and the white marble architecture of the cottage was modeled somewhat on the lines of the Temple of the Sun, at Baalbek, with pilasters and capitals.

Alva's supreme bid for the leadership of New York society

was her famous fancy dress ball, given on the evening of March 26, 1883. It was a $250,000 extravaganza which Henry Clews, one of the guests, described as follows: "The ball seemed to have the effect of leveling up among the social ranks of uppertendom, and placing the Vanderbilts at the top of the heap in what is recognized as good society in New York. So far as cost, richness of costume and newspaper celebrity were concerned, that ball had, perhaps, no equal in history. It may not have been quite so expensive as the feast of Alexander the Great at Babylon, some of the entertainments of Cleopatra to Augustus and Mark Antony, or a few of the magnificent banquets of Louis XIV, but when viewed from every essential standpoint, and taking into account our advanced civilization, I have no hesitation in saying that the Vanderbilt ball was superior to any of those grand historic displays of festivity and amusement."

Something of what Clews was talking about could be deduced from the New York *World's* careful estimate of what the ball actually cost, including $155,730 for costumes, $11,000 for flowers, $4000 for carriage hire, another $4000 for hairdressing, and an omnibus $65,270 for champagne, catering, music and other items.

The New York *Sun's* reporter described the spectacle: "Mrs. W. K. Vanderbilt's Ball was gorgeously accomplished with no interruption by dynamite. In lavishness of expenditure and brilliancy of dress, it far outdid any ball ever given in this city. It was a scene from Faery Land, Mother Goose, the Picture Galleries, the Courts and Camps of Europe, Audubon's Birds of America, Heathen Myths and Christian Legends, and even from Mr. Diedrich Knickerbocker's invaluable notes on the fashions in New York a long time ago. All the revelry of color involved in such a catalogue moved gleaming in a garden of flowers under bright lights to soft music from hidden instruments. It is only at a Fancy Dress Ball that men can make themselves really picturesque—and qualified voters, grave and gay, vied in artistic quality and cost as well with the lovely women who adorned the evening."

The only qualified voter of prominence who was not invited to this levee was Jay Gould, who was not acceptable to either the Vanderbilts or the Astors.

While one supposes William K. looked with indulgence upon his wife's spending, he was not likely to be lavish with his own desires, and indeed it was said that he gave only one Newport party in his own behalf, at which, according to *The New York Times*, "The masterpiece was a large owl on a perch, the bird being composed of seven hundred pieces of sugar and almonds. The eyes alone contained sixty pieces. A chain of confections in imitation of silver held the bird to his candid perch, the links of which were as nicely made as the links of a watch chain."

In spite of the Vanderbilt women's extravagance, Cornelius remained essentially a sound guardian of the family money, and passed a great deal of it down intact when he died of a cerebral hemorrhage, at fifty-five, in 1899. The eulogy which the rector of St. Bartholomew's, Dr. Greer, gave him in the *Outlook* was not entirely a conventional tribute to the church's most prominent vestryman and chief benefactor.

"Mr. Vanderbilt," said Dr. Greer, "was a rich man, with the emphasis on the *man*. That, to those who knew him well, and even to those who did not know him well, was his decisive characteristic. The value of his estate, great as it was, was not equal to the value of him. The man was more than his money. It did not own him; he owned it. Nor did he own it exclusively for himself; he owned it for others. His wealth was regarded by him, not simply as something personal, but as a great and sacred trust which it was his duty to administer, not with a lavish carelessness, but with a wise and discriminating conscientiousness, for the benefit of his fellow men. That was the way he looked upon business; and while, of course, he added very greatly to his own personal fortune by his wise and conservative business management, it was not the hope of personal enrichment that constituted the principal motive in it. He literally sacrificed his life in the administration of his great trust, for he not only gave money, but what was still better, he gave himself. . . ."

No doubt about it, Cornelius was the conscientious Vanderbilt, and some say it killed him, as Dr. Greer intimated. The result of his labors, aside from the benefactions of his will, was to give his sons and daughters substantial sums of money to carry into the twentieth century. Other than the $100,000,000 he left his brother, and the scant two per cent of the fortune that went to charity, the residue was left to the children. Alice got the New York house and The Breakers, and a trust fund of $7,000,000. Cornelius III, the oldest living son, whose marriage had alienated him from his father, was virtually cut off with a $1,000,000 trust and $500,000 outright, while his younger brother, Alfred Gwynne, was named as residuary legatee, with $42,575,000. Generously, and under no compulsion to do it, Alfred gave his brother another $6,000,000.

After this exchange the sons and daughters faced the new century with respectable fortunes: Cornelius III, about $7,500,000; Alfred Gwynne, $36,500,000; Reginald Claypoole, $6,250,000; Gertrude Vanderbilt Whitney, $7,250,000; and Gladys Moore Vanderbilt, $6,250,000. The fortune was splitting apart, but it was still substantial. Moreover, since the death of Cornelius' father, stock in the Vanderbilt railroad properties had appreciated $173,497,000.

The head of the family was now William K., whose Alva

had divorced him to marry Oliver H. P. Belmont. William
had been sharing the duties of the estate with his brother,
diligently and without enthusiasm. His interests were many,
but they were not business. As Frank Crowninshield described them, "Willie" was "the greatest supporter of sport,
opera, yachting, racing, art, architecture, coaching, and the
theater in American social annals."

Finding himself at the helm alone, he soon demonstrated
that he was no manager of large properties by permitting
direction of the New York Central to pass into the hands of
men who had long desired it, a combination of Rockefeller,
Morgan and Pennsylvania Railroad executives. But the Vanderbilt interests were much too vast to be dissipated by indifferent management alone. The fortune went on increasing
for a time, in spite of William K.'s relative inattention.

The world knew Willie as an international sportsman, an
owner of race horses in America and France, and a noted
yachtsman whose *Defender* sailed victoriously in the America's Cup races. He was often seen at the Metropolitan
Opera, in whose affairs he took an active part, and at the
theater. He continued the family philanthropies and its collecting, of which the Metropolitan was the constant benefactor. A good part of his money went into real estate. Besides
Marble House and his elaborate New York town house, he
owned an establishment on Long Island no less fantastic than
the Newport place. Idle Hour had 110 rooms and 45 bathrooms, but in spite of its frivolous name it was an austere
mansion, almost institutional, Jacobean with French touches.
A huge gargoyle reared up on its interior stone staircase, and
it was equipped with a cloister, a palm garden, huge barn-
like rooms, tapestries, fireplaces, fringed lamps, and high,
straight-backed Jacobean chairs. It was most recently occupied by the Royal Fraternity of Master Metaphysicians, who

renamed it Peace Haven and got themselves into the newspapers by announcing the adoption of a five-month-old baby girl whom they intended to make immortal.

William K., appropriately enough, began to die at the race track, on an April day in 1920. He suffered a heart attack at Auteuil, the fashionable French track, and three months later he was dead. His estate totaled $54,530,966.59, on which the inheritance tax was $1,934,571.73, the highest recorded up to that time in Suffolk County. And so another part of the Vanderbilt fortune began to break up.

There were the usual charitable bequests—$50,000 to St. Mark's Church, Islip, Long Island; $250,000 to Vanderbilt University; $1,005,000 worth of art to the Metropolitan Museum. William K.'s second wife, Anne Harriman Sands Rutherford, received what might have been Alva's portion, a surprising $109,196.47, besides a Paris town house and, for her lifetime, the Château of Le Quesnay. William K.'s three children were, of course, the principal legatees. Consuelo, who was reported to be the beneficiary of $15,000,000, with $1,000,000 each to her two sons just before her father died, by the terms of his will got the income from $2,500,000 and with her two brothers shared equally in $5,000,000 outright. Of the brothers, William K. II, known as "Willie K.," as distinct from his father "Willie," received $21,252,757.38, and Harold Stirling got $21,739,857.38, as well as Idle Hour.

The fortune filtered down even further under the terms of William K.'s will. His son, Willie K., had a son, William K. III, who was given $425,526, and his widow's two daughters by her former marriage each inherited $100,000.

Cornelius II and William K. had been the chief custodians of the family fortune, but their two younger brothers, although less well known to the public, were extremely substantial Vanderbilts in their own right. In fact, when Frederick Vanderbilt died at the age of eighty-two, in 1938, his talent for investing had made him the richest of the brothers. In a single checking account he was said to keep a more or less constant balance of $3,000,000. But "Uncle Fred," as he was known in the clan, committed an act of fiscal desecration so awful that every Vanderbilt shuddered when his will was opened. He had no children by his only wife, Louise Anthony Torrence, who had died before him, but there were several legitimate and expectant Vanderbilts about who might hope to get some of Uncle Fred's fortune of $76,838,530, the largest remaining individual fortune in the family. Instead, nearly all of it went to his wife's niece, Mrs. James Laurens Van Alen, familiarly known as "Daisy." There was small consolation in the fact that Mrs. Van Alen had to pay a staggering $41,272,109 in inheritance tax.

Thus, in their separate ways, three of the four sons of William H. had succeeded in fragmenting the family wealth—Cornelius II the least, perhaps, but Frederick the most by willing it right out of the family. The fourth son, George Washington, was so unlike the others that he deserves special mention. Not that he was a conserver of Vanderbilt money; in some ways, he was the grandest spender of the lot. But his values were different from the others', and he was curiously like the first President for whom he was named, in his distaste for public life and his steady desire to be no more than a breeder of fine stock, a scientific farmer.

George, shy and studious, never played more than a minor part in the management of the estate. He cared nothing about accumulating money, but he did know how to enjoy it. He bought 130,000 acres of magnificent land in western North Carolina, near Asheville, and on it built a $3,000,000 country home, probably the finest in America.

Unlike other rich men, who say, "Build it," and it is done,

George took a personal part in the construction, from plans to the building itself. To prepare for this task, he studied architecture, forestry and landscape gardening, so that he could work intelligently with the architect Richard Morris Hunt, whom he hired for the job.

The product was a work of art. Biltmore, as he called it, was a French château with the largest roof in America, set in an incredible estate which New York society admiringly termed "a barony." It employed more people than the entire United States Department of Agriculture, and within its gates were a hospital, a church, schools, shops for employees and a private railroad spur. Biltmore's cows were milk-producing champions, and its pedigreed hogs were better known than their owner. In the famous Biltmore Nursery, George raised trees and plants of the region, and through the great forest of his estate he constructed miles of roads and trails. The first superintendent of this forest was Gifford Pinchot, who departed in time for a better job as head of the United States Division of Forestry. Pinchot helped George found the Biltmore School of Forestry on the estate.

For the benefit of the many employees he acquired, the master of Biltmore planned and built a model village. He preferred to live on the estate himself, although he had three other residences: a house in Washington, the Fifth Avenue mansion where he had stayed with his widowed mother until her death in 1895, and a summer place in Bar Harbor. His mother had left him her house, but he had hurried down to Biltmore as soon as he could, and two years after the funeral married a young Newport girl, Edith Stuyvesant Dresser.

George was quite happy to putter about his Carolina barony, observing trees, birds and animals, actively directing operations on the huge estate, and researching in his library, which was an outstanding collection of nature books. By any standard he was a cultured man, speaking eight languages and able to read in several others. With the help of tutors, he studied French, German, Spanish, Italian, Hebrew, Sanskrit, and ancient and modern Greek.

The house that was the center of George's barony was perhaps the most elegant of all the Vanderbilt shelters. It was not as large, or as expensive, but it had character, of a kind, even if it exuded a certain arrogance. It had forty master bedrooms and several state chambers. There was a Court of Palms, decorated with fine statuary, and the Oak Drawing Room held a rare collection of engravings. Five Gobelin tapestries hung in the Banqueting Hall. There were Dürer etchings and a chess set that had belonged to Napoleon I in the Print Room. The walls of the Tapestry Gallery were covered with rich Flemish hangings, and the library's shelves were filled with 250,000 volumes.

His philanthropies lay in the direction of his interests. He built an entire library, now known as the Jackson Square Branch, and gave it to the New York Free Circulating Library, later the New York Public. He bought the Bloomingdale Asylum property for Columbia University, at a cost of $100,-000; Teachers' College rests on it today. In 1892 he donated an entire art gallery, a reproduction of the Galerie Georges Petit, to the American Fine Arts Society. George liked to do things that way—in packages. He even offered to sell most of his beloved forest land to the federal government as a forest reserve; after his death the offer was accepted.

When he died in Washington in 1914, of a heart attack following a successful appendectomy, George had a surprise in his will almost as astonishing as his brother Frederick's. Where Fred had simply willed his money out of the family, George had quite obviously spent most of his fortune and little remained of it. The allegation in *The New York Times* that it totaled $50,000,000 was a gross exaggeration. There was, of course, a $5,000,000 trust fund which he had been unable to touch during his lifetime, under the terms of his father's will. That went to his only child, Cornelia, then fourteen. Not included in the final accounting, either, were Biltmore and the Bar Harbor and Washington houses. What remained after these deductions was a total of only $1,314,-852.45, and after further deductions of $385,111.47, including $312,047.86 for debts, the net estate was a piddling $929,-740.98.

The answer to this comparative poverty was Biltmore. Into it George had poured his fortune's valuable railroad stocks, so that when he died his corporate stocks and bonds amounted to no more than $11,125. Fortunately for his wife, there was $1,000,000 in insurance, but it too was reduced to $640,822.61 by virtue of a mortgage. The three houses were passed on to her, however, and they must have been financially consoling. Edith, who was still young, soon sold all of the barony except for 12,500 acres (the forests were deeded as a national park) and not long afterward married Peter Goelet Gerry, United States senator from Rhode Island, after which she went to live in Washington.

Biltmore remained a problem. It lay huge and empty, expensive to maintain. Edith decided at last, in 1930, to open it to the public. All that remains of the barony today are herds of dairy cows which roam the unsold acres, and herds of tourists who tramp through the great house at two dollars each.

Cornelia, George's daughter, set an example that was now, unfortunately, to be followed by the children and grandchildren of the four brothers. In 1924 she married the Hon. John Francis Amherst Cecil, First Secretary of the British Legation in Washington, gave him two sons, and left him in

1934. Cecil got the two children, and Cornelia also happily made him general manager of Biltmore. Thus George's beloved estate passed out of Vanderbilt hands, so to speak.

Later, Cornelia became a Greenwich Village bohemian, was named as corespondent in a divorce suit brought by an artist's wife, and so joined the intricate design of marryings, divorces, scandals, remarryings, separations, more divorces and more scandals which makes later Vanderbilt history so complicated that only the most willing historian can make any sense out of it. This was particularly true of the William K. and Cornelius II branches of the family, where marital troubles persisted into the fifth generation.

Of William K.'s three children, his son Harold may have pleased him most. Harold, too, was a cup racer, a sportsman, a respectable figure in society, who limited himself to one marriage, to Gertrude Conaway, but he produced no children to carry on his good name. He may, however, have immortalized himself more than any other Vanderbilt by inventing contract bridge.

The second son, Willie K., was much more like his father, an energetic man interested in a variety of matters. In one respect he was different. Vanderbilts were traditionally horse lovers, but Willie K. was fascinated by that new invention, the automobile, and in 1904 backed America's first motorcar race, over 284 miles of dusty Long Island roads. This course was one he acquired himself at extraordinary expense, running from Flushing to Lake Ronkonkoma. Down this suburban track, then a rural retreat from growing Manhattan, were held the first Vanderbilt Cup races, which made automotive and sports history.

When the racing was over, Willie K. thoughtfully turned his speedway into the Long Island Motor Parkway, open to the public as a toll road. Users often saw the donor speeding by them as fast as his current automobile would travel, on the way to or from his Northport house. With the rising rate of taxes assessed against the roadway, Willie K. eventually declared he could no longer afford the luxury and turned it over to New York State—another indication of how far down the Vanderbilt fortune had been watered. It was not watered far enough, however, to prevent him from cruising about in his $2,500,000 yacht.

Willie K.'s marital affairs were comparatively quiet, for the Vanderbilts. He was married only twice, once to Virginia Graham ("Birdie") Fair, and later to Rose Lancaster Warburton. Both of his daughters, however, were much married, and it seemed as though the divorcing and remarrying were too often the subject of scandalous stories in the newspapers. His daughter Muriel was married three times; the other daughter, Consuelo II, had four husbands. Even his stepdaughter by the second marriage, Rosie Warburton, married twice. By this time, as Amory remarks, "It was becoming impossible to tell the Vanderbilts from anyone else," and with every marriage and divorce a little more Vanderbilt money was sluiced away from the main fortune.

All the marriages, however, on this side of the family at least, were overshadowed by that of Willie K.'s sister, Consuelo, William K.'s only daughter, who was involved in a truly historic international scandal through no fault of her own. The story of her marriage to the Duke of Marlborough is well known; Consuelo told it herself for an American magazine, but in the most dignified way.

The villain of this fantastic drama was Alva, and a plausible theory is that the motivation for her incredible deed stemmed from the duel with Alice to be *the* Mrs. Vanderbilt. Both had teen-age daughters about to make their debuts, and marriage to an international figure like the duke, a nobleman of royal lineage in the bargain, undoubtedly appeared to the indomitable Alva to be a coup which would put her permanently one up on Alice. In any event, it was one of the most sensational stories of the decade when, in 1895, the seventeen-year-old Consuelo married the duke after the haggling over terms of her dowry had been rehearsed in newspapers all over the world.

This story was as nothing, however, when the whole affair came to light in 1920 with Consuelo's divorce, and she was depicted as a weeping, agonized girl who had been "sold" against her will by her mother. Alva confessed to the Rota, the Catholic Ecclesiastical Court: "I forced my daughter to marry the duke. I always had absolute influence over her. When I gave an order, nobody discussed it." The frightened Consuelo, it appeared, had tried to elope with her true love, Winthrop Rutherford, a young society bachelor, but her mother kept her prisoner in a guarded room, warning her that if she continued to rebel, poor Alva would be likely to have a heart attack, a prediction backed up by the Vanderbilt physician.

The duke, who appears to have been as much upset as the unhappy bride, told the Rota that twenty days after the ceremony Consuelo confessed honestly: "I have married you only because I have been forced by my mother to do so." In spite of the circumstances, the marriage lasted longer than most Vanderbilt ventures, and Consuelo bore the duke two sons before she divorced him and married, happily, Jacques Balsan, a French sportsman and society figure. The duke was also married again, to Gladys Deacon, a rich girlhood friend of Consuelo's, but that venture too ended in divorce.

There was considerable attrition of the Vanderbilt fortune in the Marlborough affair. Not only did it cost Alva $2,500,-000 to make the marriage, but it was Vanderbilt money that renovated the duke's stately home, Blenheim, where Winston Churchill was born. Consuelo also built a huge London town house known as Sunderland House, which was later sold to the Astors. Like some other Vanderbilt houses, Blenheim has in these latter days of decline become a tourist attraction and charges admission to view its splendors.

If there were more than enough troubles on William K.'s side of the family, as related here, his brother Cornelius II had an ever flowing Pandora's box of them, attributable to the fact that he had more children, and therefore more opportunities. As against William's three, Cornelius had seven. Five of these and *their* children had accounted for thirty-five marriages at the last addition, a counting which may not be accurate by any means and is likely to err on the side of understatement.

Somehow the troubles seemed to begin with Cornelius III and his marriage to Grace Wilson, who was destined to become the last of the peerless Vanderbilt social leaders. The quarrel that arose between father and son over this marriage embittered their relationship, and after Cornelius II died in 1899, his widow would not speak to her daughter-in-law for eleven years.

It is difficult, in retrospect, to see why there was so much objection to the match. Grace was a popular and pretty member of New York society. Her father, Richard T. Wilson, had been a Tennessee boy who laid the foundations of his fortune in an utterly traditional way by supplying the Confederate Army with blankets. One of his daughters had married Ogden Goelet, a respected New York name; his son was married to Carrie Astor, *the* Mrs. Astor's daughter. The family had, indeed, married so well that they were known as the "matchmaking Wilsons." The match Grace wanted to make from the beginning was to marry a Vanderbilt, and it may have been the obviousness of her intention that irritated old Cornelius II.

The newspapers were delighted with the struggle for Cornelius III. They called the marriage a "nine-day wonder" when it occurred in 1896, and hinted that the Vanderbilts did "not approve of what they have considered too evident a disposition on her [Grace's] part to receive the intentions of their son." There was a later scandal when an anonymous letter writer circulated a missive which claimed the young Vanderbilts "had" to get married, and that Grace had formerly been involved in a romance with a church vestryman.

After the marriage young Vanderbilt was never again permitted to see his father, and when the old man died four years later he left his son only $1,500,000, as has been noted, and only the generosity of his brother Alfred in restoring $6,000,000 gave Cornelius III a respectable fortune to work on. Even at that there was a coolness between the two brothers, possibly because Alfred had originally agreed to part with more of his $42,575,000 inheritance, or because Cornelius had expected he would.

Once established as a Vanderbilt, however, Grace overshadowed them all and within four years was not only *the* Mrs. Vanderbilt but unofficially the queen of American society, over which she reigned from 1900 until 1953, when she died at the age of eighty-three. A formidable *grande dame*, she chased titles and crowned heads on her yachts; entertained them at home; spent from $200,000 to $300,000 a year on parties; and on Sundays, at her home, the famous Vanderbilt palace at 640 Fifth Avenue, she entertained hundreds of guests at tea. There were fifty or sixty guests every day at Grace's house, distributed through luncheon, tea and dinner. At Christmastime a thousand people milled through her door.

Like the other great Vanderbilt women, Grace had a cottage at Newport, called Beaulieu, enormous and drafty as the others were, furnished with unbelievable opulence. Unlike the other cottages, however, this one was leased, rather than built by the young Vanderbilts. There she hired the casts of hit Broadway shows to entertain her guests, and gave such historic parties as the Fête des Roses, and the Oriental Ball, which was held in a tent costing $900, put together by electricians and carpenters who presented her with a bill for $11,800, and at which the costumes for the guests alone cost $5000. The New York *American,* always an authority in such matters, called it "the most extravagant affair of its kind ever seen in Newport."

At home on Fifth Avenue, Grace lived in a splendor probably never approached by any of the accumulators or their families. The ballroom of 640, which her husband inherited from his father, was a replica of the one in the palace at Versailles, resplendent in red velvet hangings, mirrors, cream-and-gold woodwork, and parquet floors. Often a thousand guests whirled before the mirrors in this room. Near it was the dining room, with a table capable of seating sixty people, adorned with centerpieces costing from fifty to seventy-five dollars and five golden fruit bowls, filled with out-of-season hothouse fruits which might cost two hundred dollars for a single dinner. There was also plenty of candy to be found. Grace liked candy, and her bill for these confections was often three hundred dollars a month. Her idea of economy was to rent bath towels and potted gloxinias. To serve the guests and herself, Mrs. Vanderbilt employed as many as thirty servants at a time.

To escape the perpetual socializing that went on in the house, Grace's husband took to slipping away by means of an elevator behind a secret panel, which whisked him to his private quarters. Sometimes it was necessary to go farther, and then he went for cruises on one of his yachts. It was

Cornelius III's belief that there were no material differences between the foyer of 640 and Grand Central Station.

His daughter, another Grace, also took a dim view of her mother's non-stop social career: "Mother has become a waltzing mouse," she remarked. "It's a sad thing for us in that we've never had a *real* home with mother and we just have to play a game most of the time in order to keep her from absorbing all our lives."

The cost of it all was a heavy drain on the Vanderbilt money. Signing checks one morning which totaled eighty thousand dollars, Grace casually asked her secretary, "Do I have this much money?" She did, and there was a good deal left over—enough to make it possible for her husband to keep a yacht that cost him seven thousand dollars a month, whether it moved away from the pier or not.

Grace's son, Cornelius Vanderbilt, Jr. (really Cornelius IV), who has written of her and other members of the family, recalled in his *Queen of the Golden Age* how he returned to 640 Fifth in 1918 after his mother had refurbished the place so it would not look like "the black hole of Calcutta," as she called it.

"Crossing the marble foyer," he related, "I passed through a pair of towering bronze doors, blazing with gold leaf, and into the great hall which stretched up four full stories. Beautiful seventeenth-century Brussels tapestries lined the galleries, and green palms; nothing else detracted attention from the chaste, clean lines of the Caen-marble walls and columns crowned with alabaster. In the center of this great hall stood an immense vase, eight feet tall, on a bronze pedestal. It was fashioned entirely of the green semi-precious stone malachite; its twin stood in the St. Petersburg palace of the Czar Nicholas. . . . In the picture gallery with its dark red tapestry walls and crystal chandeliers hung the Millets, and Meissoniers and Corots collected by my great-grandfather, as well as other paintings purchased by my parents. . . . The house was so lavishly conceived that when movie producers were looking for some house elaborate enough to copy for Rhett Butler's mansion in *Gone With the Wind,* they chose old photographs of 640."

At 640 and elsewhere, Grace entertained the greatest names of America, Europe and England: King Albert of Belgium, the Queen of Spain, the King of Siam, the Crown Prince of Norway, Lord and Lady Mountbatten, the Duke of Kent, Calvin Coolidge, Herbert Hoover, Winston Churchill and on and on, through an endless list. She had, at the summit, gone to tea with the King and Queen of England.

A sympathetic relative once remarked to Cornelius, Jr.: "Your mother succeeded against the heaviest odds in becoming the person she most wanted to be. Her life was dedicated to being the topflight hostess of her era. If she trampled a few people attaining her goal, it was no more than any other entirely successful person does, and from my point of view, the result was worth it."

Grace, who was not even a Vanderbilt by blood, got the publicity in her era, as her husband was meanwhile living a quiet life. Except for his yachting, he could most often be found at his office, working hard, as he had done since he was sixteen years old. Like his father and grandfather, he was often at his desk before anyone else arrived. His business interests were primarily railroads, but he also successfully ventured into hotels by building the Vanderbilt.

Another quiet Vanderbilt was Gertrude, Cornelius II's fourth child, who made a career for herself as a sculptress, married Harry Payne Whitney and restored some dignity to the family. Her children were Cornelius Vanderbilt Whitney, Flora and Barbara.

When charm was passed around Cornelius' children, it was his fifth child, Alfred Gwynne Vanderbilt I, who got most of it. As head of the house, after his brother's quarrel with his father over Grace, he was content to let Cornelius III sit in the Grand Central Building and manage things while he devoted himself to his horses, automobiles, yachts and two marriages. The first of these, to Elsie French, cost him ten million dollars and a divorce trial which linked him with the handsome wife of the Cuban attaché in Washington, Mrs. Agnes O'Brien Ruiz, who later committed suicide. By contrast, his second marriage to Margaret Emerson McKim, was as near perfection as the marital state admits, so that it was all the more tragic when he went down with the *Lusitania* in 1915, gallant to the last as he gave his lifebelt to a woman, although he could not swim, and instructing his valet to save himself. One who saw him at the final moment reported: "He stood there, the personification of sportsmanlike coolness. In my eyes he was the figure of a gentleman waiting for a train."

Alfred had a son, William Henry Vanderbilt III, by his first wife and two sons, Alfred Gwynne Vanderbilt II and George Washington Vanderbilt III, by his second. It was his namesake who became one of the well-known Vanderbilts in our own time, inheriting his father's charm as well as a watered-down part of the family fortune. He also inherited his father's distaste for business; an accountant handled his estate, and he was said never to have been inside his office. The public has known him primarily as an owner of racing stables and successful horses, carrying on another Vanderbilt tradition. Sometimes it seems as though Alfred II's whole life has been devoted to horses, since he made his first bet (on the Preakness) when he was only eleven years old. Alfred II does not bet today, asserting that it is beyond his means on an income he estimates at a quarter of a million annually. He does spend a great part of the time at the track, however, and as one magazine writer put it, he "has an immensely good time based on a fine appreciation of the fact that some horses can run faster than others."

Alfred Gwynne I's other sons have had what might be called varied careers. William Henry Vanderbilt III, the oldest, became governor of Rhode Island; George Washington III devoted his time to exploration and big-game hunting. It is only in their marital lives that they have followed Vanderbilt tradition. The governor first married Emily Davies, who divorced him, had two more marriages and divorces, then committed suicide. Anne Colby, a West Orange, New Jersey, girl, was the governor's second wife. His brother George also married twice, and both marriages ended in divorce.

Cornelius II's sixth child was "Reggie" Vanderbilt, another family symbol in the public consciousness because of the publicity, mostly unfortunate, which surrounded his life of gambling, drinking and driving fast automobiles. Shortly after his much-publicized marriage to his second wife, Gloria Morgan, the drinking became a serious problem, and probably led to his death in Newport. It was the child of this marriage, Gloria Vanderbilt, who became still another "poor little rich girl" in the public prints, first by reason of a highly sensational custody fight between her mother and her aunt, Gertrude Vanderbilt Whitney, in which the aunt attempted to prove the mother incompetent to bring up her own child. Of this disturbed childhood, Gloria once said: "Every time I was hurt or lonely as a child, I wished I had a father living, and a mother who loved me and loved him. Rich children can be lonely, very lonely."

After the aunt was awarded custody, a compromise was reached by which young Gloria lived with Gertrude five days a week and her mother two. Thus divided, she was launched upon a life which has since become public property through her marriages, first to Pat DiCicco; then, at twenty, to sixty-three-year-old Leopold Stokowski; and finally to the young television and movie director, Sidney Lumet, a lower East Side boy who could scarcely have been farther from Gloria's milieu.

So one comes to the last of Cornelius II's seven children. (Two, William Henry, who died while he was at Yale, and Alice Gwynne, never married.) Gladys, the seventh child, was probably the least known and in many ways the best representative of what this royal family in American society might have become. A true gentlewoman, she married in 1908 a Hungarian nobleman, Count Laszlo Széchényi, later Hungarian Minister to Washington before he died in 1938. The couple had five daughters. Gladys did not remarry after her husband's death but went to live, for at least part of the year, at the Breakers, in a top-floor apartment where she could see the tourists without being seen. From that viewpoint she once pronounced the epitaph of the Vanderbilt family: "I guess when all is said and done, the people who should have set the standard, didn't."

One Vanderbilt who agrees, cheerfully, with that estimate is *the* Mrs. Vanderbilt's son, Cornelius, Jr., a shrewd and observant chronicler of his family's lives and times in the course of writing seven novels and nine books of non-fiction. "Neil" first collected schools, seven of them, and after that wives, six in all. A newspaperman working on nine papers, a roving correspondent, lecturer and business entrepreneur, he wrote himself out of the Social Register with such articles as "How My Cousin, the Duchess, Was Sold to Marlborough" and what was perhaps the best known of his books, *Farewell to Fifth Avenue*. Of the Vanderbilt troubles he has remarked:

"Any man who bears a name that is a household word in America has his share of troubles. I think marriage for them is more difficult than the general public believes. If you are John Jones, no one cares what you do or how you do it. But I often pity other men whose family names are as well known as mine."

Thus the Vanderbilt line reaches what must be nearly its end, as blood and money alike are diluted by numerous marriages and divorces, most of them costly in one way or another, and as inheritance taxes, increasing from generation to generation, whittle down principal.

In the end, of course, it comes down to the difficulty of living with great wealth, once it is accumulated. There are two contrasting viewpoints on this subject among Vanderbilts, which in a way sum up the family's history. Here, first, is William K., Cornelius II's brother, speaking: "My life was never destined to be quite happy. It was laid out along lines which I could foresee almost from earliest childhood. It has left me with nothing to hope for, with nothing definite to see or strive for. Inherited wealth is a real handicap to happiness. It is as certain death to ambition as cocaine is to morality. If a man makes money, no matter how much, he finds a certain happiness in its possession, for in the desire to increase his business, he has a constant use for it. But the man who inherits it has none of that. The first satisfaction, and the greatest, that of building the foundation of a fortune, is denied him."

There speak the Vanderbilt men, who were, more often than not, realists about the immense sums of money for which they bore responsibility, regardless of whether they took it seriously. But listen to the Vanderbilt women for the negating factor in the uses of wealth. William K.'s sister-in-law, Alice, Cornelius II's wife, was having luncheon one day at the old Ambassador Hotel with her son, Reggie, and his new second wife, Gloria Morgan, when she inquired of the not so freshly minted bridegroom: "Has Gloria received her pearls yet?" He would love to give pearls to Gloria, Reggie answered, but he could not afford the kind he thought were worthy of his bride.

"Please bring me a pair of scissors," Alice commanded the maître d', and when they were produced, she cut off about a third of her own pearls, or roughly $70,000 worth, from the ropes of them that hung around her neck.

"There you are, Gloria," said Alice fondly. "All Vanderbilt women have pearls."

A Bouquet of Eastern Inheritors: Ryans, Goulds, Stotesburys, Belmonts and Wideners

Whenever the voice of isolation speaks from the Middle West or the South, seeking to blame the ills of the nation upon some agency large enough to bear the largest of them, the phrase "Eastern wealth" ranks easily with "Wall Street" as the most popular. The supposition in these circles is that a sinister conspiracy exists among Eastern millionaires to undermine the American way of life, morally and politically.

This popular image appears to be declining, as the conviction grows that chicanery in the manipulation of money is not governed by geographical distribution. There were accumulators in Chicago and California, for example, who got their wealth by means no more unblemished than those who frequented Wall Street.

When it comes to morality of the conventional kind, however, the East remains unjustly the symbol of sin. The modicum of truth in the conception rests on the fact that the socially prominent families of the East, inheriting from the accumulators, have been so much divorced, so much involved in scandal, that the idea of decadence is easily believed by those whose only information comes from newspapers and magazines.

We have seen thus far how this idea is perpetuated by the great family dynasties, whose names are familiar to everyone, but it remains to examine the somewhat less well known families. A sampling of them indicates that the pattern is the same, and of course there is no reason why it should be different. There is always the hardheaded accumulator, followed by those who dissipate the fortune, and unfortunately the good inheritors are always overshadowed by the bad ones, except in certain conspicuous instances, which belong to another part of this book.

The first flower in the present bouquet is that fragrant manipulator, Thomas Fortune Ryan, and his descendants. As we have seen, he attempted to atone for his sins by giving $20,000,000 of his $200,000,000 to the Catholic Church, so it can be said that a substantial part of his ill-gotten wealth was turned to good works. In gratitude, Pope Pius X made the first Mrs. Ryan a Countess of the Holy Roman Empire.

Ryan was a good Catholic, in spite of his innumerable iniquities, and he would never have ended his first marriage by divorce, unhappy though it was, but his wife died in 1917, an invalid during her last years, and Ryan was free to marry again, although he was then sixty-six years old. He waited only twelve days to do it, a haste which his oldest son Allan termed "one of the most disrespectful, disgraceful and indecent things I've ever heard of." That remark cost him his inheritance. When his father died in 1928, he left Allan two black pearl shirt studs, which was altogether characteristic of Tom Ryan's sense of humor.

The remainder of the estate was carved up into fifty-four pieces. Twelve of them went to the widow, Mary Townsend Nicoll Lord Cuyler, Ryan's twice-divorced second wife, member of one of the oldest New York families. Twelve shares also went to each of the surviving sons, John Barry and

A lonely little girl at a charity circus, Gloria Vanderbilt buys a ticket for the sideshow. Woman at the left is her governess. The entertainment was part of a lawn party given at Greentree, Mrs. Payne Whitney's Long Island estate.

A shy, awkward, fourteen-year-old Doris Duke poses with her mother, Mrs. James B. Duke.

TOP: *The Fifth Avenue mansion of Cornelius Vanderbilt II, between Fifty-seventh and Fifty-eighth streets, a splendid example of late nineteenth-century Rich Men's Baroque. It cost $5,000,000.*

BOTTOM: *William K. Vanderbilt's residence at the corner of Fifth Avenue and Fifty-third Street. Costing only $2,000,000, its exterior was less ornate than Cornelius II's home, but inside it was pure Vanderbilt.*

Look-alikes of the late nine-teenth century: Vincent Astor strolls with his father, John Jacob Astor, who was later lost on the Titanic.

Mrs. Cornelius Vanderbilt, the Mrs. Vanderbilt (right center) poses with her daughter Gladys, the Countess Laszlo Széchényi, and two of Gladys's five daugh-ters, Nadine and Sylvia. Woman at the left is unidentified.

Fifi Widener, as a dashing society girl of seventeen, at the time of her elopement with a University of Pennsylvania sophomore, Carter R. Leidy, over the strenuous opposition of her father, Joseph E. Widener, son of Peter A. B. Widener, Philadelphia butcher's boy who founded the family fortune.

The Rockefeller brothers, from left to right: Winthrop, Laurance, John D. III, David and Nelson.

*Henry Ford (right) and his son
Edsel. In background is the
fifteen millionth Ford.*

*Horace E. Dodge, whose father
and uncle founded the motorcar
fortune, tunes up the motor of
one of his many speedboats, a
favorite hobby. Parted from one
of his wives when this picture
was taken, he vowed to pursue
her around the world in this
high-powered craft.*

A glamour girl of the twenties, celebrated as the original torch singer, Libby Holman is shown here at the time she was indicted by a grand jury in the mysterious death of her husband, Zachary Smith Reynolds, heir to the tobacco fortune, in North Carolina. The case never came to trial.

The weariness of a life spent in the vain pursuit of love is evident in the still lovely face of Barbara "Babs" Hutton, arriving in New York on the Conte di Savoia.

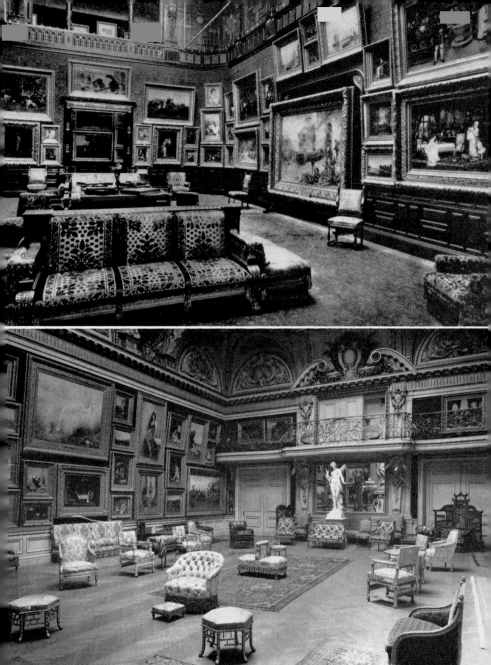

TOP: *Art gallery in the home of William H. Vanderbilt, on Fifth Avenue. It was widely regarded as among the best private collections in America.*

BOTTOM: *A rival to the Vanderbilt collection was the art gallery of Mrs. John Jacob Astor, in her Fifth Avenue mansion, frequented by other collectors and rich connoisseurs.*

Mrs. Horace E. Dodge, widow of the founder of the motorcar fortune, poses proudly, the epitome of Detroit automobile society, with her husband's product.

One of the better known playgirls of the twenties, Delphine Dodge, the motor heiress, sits at the wheel of her speedboat Nuisance, shortly before she drove it in the Gold Cup Regatta at Manhasset. She was then married to James H. R. Cromwell, son of Mrs. Edward B. Stotesbury.

Clendenin. Eight were put in trust for Allan's six children. Five more went to the children of two deceased sons, William Kane and Joseph, whose son, Joseph Jr., became the owner of the Canadian ski resort, Mont Tremblant, and later died under mysterious circumstances which suggested suicide.

There were other characteristic touches in Ryan's will, providing further proof of the inner contempt he always appeared to hold for other people, and his general bitterness toward the world he had used so badly. Any heir who questioned a benefaction, he provided, would lose whatever had been willed to him. Charities were to get nothing, because, the will argued, "in my lifetime I have contributed largely to religious, charitable and educational causes." The stipulation about protests did not prevent John Barry and Clendenin from coming to the aid of their disinherited brother Allan, as Alfred Gwynne Vanderbilt had done for Cornelius II. They gave Allan fifty thousand dollars a year for life.

Enemies of Ryan, of whom he had a multitude, could have made out a good case for the lasting effects of bad blood in recording what happened to his heirs. It was disintegration on a grand scale, calculated to prove that Eastern money was the lifeblood of evil.

Allan, who had deplored his father's conduct, scarcely improved upon it. His operations in Wall Street, perhaps in emulation of his father, resulted only in bankruptcy and expulsion from the Stock Exchange. His first marriage ended in a messy court battle involving another man, and it was followed by a divorce in 1925. His second marriage, to a Montreal girl, was disrupted in 1933 by a $100,000 suit instituted by his housemaid, who claimed that he had involved her forcibly in a backstairs romance.

Allan's six children fared better, possibly because there was so little Ryan money on their side of the family. They did well in business, as gentlemen farmers, and in politics. One son, Barry, became a professional trainer of race horses. Divorces, however, continued to be as prominent a Ryan trait as it had been for the Vanderbilts. Allan, Jr., was married four times, each time to a name distinguished in society.

John Barry, Sr. (Allan, Sr.'s brother), lived a somewhat incredible life, apparently dividing his time between creating poetry and children. The poems were published under his pseudonym, Barrie Vail. The children, fifteen in all, were by courtesy of Nan Morgan, John's wife; the ten who lived were equally divided between the sexes. These children appeared on occasion in the newspapers. One of the girls, Adele, was involved in a $500,000 breach-of-promise suit in 1930. A boy, Thomas Fortune Ryan II, was frequently in the headlines before he died in 1955, mostly through his marriages to two divorcees. Another son, John Barry, Jr., became a reporter and later married Otto Kahn's daughter Margaret; their children, the fourth generation, also married well.

The third son of the original Ryan, Clendenin, was marked by tragedy from the start, when his partnership in a brokerage firm with Allan involved him in his brother's troubles. Later he married and fathered four children, but in 1923 a show girl propelled him into the headlines by suing for five hundred dollars, for what she was pleased to call "room rent." Clendenin lived in the old Ryan home, a five-story gray pile, and there in 1939 he put his head into a gas fireplace and committed suicide. By a most gruesome coincidence, his son Clendenin repeated this act in 1957, also leaving behind four children. Like his father, Clendenin, Jr., was a lonely man who could not seem to find any lasting satisfactions in his life, notwithstanding that he had charm, money and intelligence.

Jay Gould, as cold and unscrupulous as the original Ryan, left behind him another set of inheritors who had a difficult time with the wealth that came to them. Gould and Ryan were both virtually friendless men, and seemed not to care. Their descendants were not always easy to live with, but they cared. Many of the Goulds, particularly, were the kind of men and women who appear to have a natural affinity for the kind of living most likely to create publicity. No one can be certain how much money they had to spend. Jay Gould's fortune was estimated to exceed $200,000,000 at his death, but later estimates placed it nearer $100,000,000—in either case, more than enough to live on handsomely for several generations.

Gould's widow, Helen, was an exemplary woman who spoiled her six children and unquestionably, although certainly not realizing it, prepared them for the selfish, wasted lives they were to lead. So ingrown were they that the younger sons sued the oldest for $50,000,000, a suit that dragged on for eleven years.

Most of the children lived conventional society lives, belonging to the clubs from which their father had been barred, living in a variety of ornate houses, pursuing the sporting life, and indulging in the usual marrying and divorcing. Among them they possessed a whole fleet of yachts, five in all, and one boat, Howard Gould's *Niagara*, was the largest American-built craft up to that time.

A daughter, Helen, named for her mother, had a magnificent Hudson Valley home whose swimming pool boasted a life guard. It was Helen who adopted, rather late in life, four orphans, one of whom had been retrieved from the steps of St. Patrick's Cathedral. The Goulds never did things in a small way. Yet, paradoxically, in the midst of luxury they were quite capable of petty economies, as in Helen's fifty-cent monthly allowances to her orphans, for which they had to account. There was little to account, because Mother Gould made her charges deduct forty cents a month for church and Sunday school collections.

The Goulds shunned a college education, as William H. Vanderbilt's sons had done (only Frederick went to college), and this particular piece of snobbery may well have cost the family fortune heavily. For George Gould, taking over the estate reins at twenty-eight when his father died, found himself without adequate preparation in a world that was beginning to change rapidly, and before the First World War came to change it even more he had lost all of the railroads his father had acquired, legally or illegally. In the meantime he was living a life of splendor in Georgian Court, his Lakewood, New Jersey, home which was considered to be one of the finest shelters in America. Meanwhile, too, he was not only siring seven children by Edith Kingdon, the actress he had taken as his wife in 1886, but fathered three others illegitimately by another actress, a circumstance he acknowledged in his will.

Like the Vanderbilts and Astors, the Goulds also married into royalty. Anna, the second daughter of the founding father, first married a count, and then his cousin, a duke. The Gould men, for their part, appeared to be fond of actresses. Besides George's two ventures, his brother Howard married one whom he later accused of adultery with a national hero, Buffalo Bill, who until that time had enjoyed a peerless home-and-family reputation.

Before he died in 1956, Frank Jay Gould contrived to set a standard that none of his fellow inheritors was likely to surpass. In his forty-room mansion, presided over by his eighteen-year-old wife, he was the master of twenty servants and the owner of an incredible collection of diamonds. He rode, when the weather was foul, in his own block-long riding hall, and often he appeared in one or another of his twenty-seven clubs. The obituary phrase, "a prominent clubman," could have been invented for Frank Gould.

Nevertheless he found time for girls, another Gould pre-occupation, and displayed the family predilection for actresses, wooing two of them while he was still married to his first wife, a process that may have been confusing since one of them had his wife's maiden name. But when she divorced him, the papers accused him of misconduct with two entirely different girls. Undaunted, he married one of the actresses, the one with the similar name. She, too, divorced him, after they had retired to live on the French Riviera, and he married a third time, a French newspaper editor's daughter.

When he was not otherwise occupied, Frank Jay Gould spent a good deal of his time in litigation. He sued his brother George in 1916, charging that he had mismanaged the estate, and got him fired as executor in 1919, after which he carried on the suit against Edwin, another brother, who succeeded him. The result of this marathon was satisfactory, if one discounts the four million dollars in legal fees it cost to get the settlement, because Frank Jay, Howard and two of the sisters emerged with fifty million.

The money came in handy for Frank, who was compelled to defend himself in court thirteen times, from 1918 to 1929, against suits instituted by his second wife. Cleveland Amory, who has recounted in detail this and other family histories in his *Who Killed Society?*, records of the Gould litigations: "All in all, from the time of World War I to 1960, when a Gould wife was in the process of suing *Town and Country* for its story on Frank Jay Gould—there was scarcely a single

year in which at least one member of the Gould Family was
not engaged in a highly publicized lawsuit."

Yet it must be added that Frank Jay Gould illustrates once
more the paradox of the inheritor who helps dissipate a great
fortune, often in a scandalous manner, but still through his
philanthropies contributes much to the cultural life of the
nation. Jay Gould's sons and daughters, unlike their father,
were liberal in their giving, and Frank Gould in particular
gave to the higher education for which he and his brothers
had so little use. His benefactions to New York University
totaled more than six million dollars, accounting for many
of the fine new buildings on its Bronx campus, and for good
measure he threw in a handsome estate on the Hudson which
he is said never to have seen.

Less publicized than the Goulds and Ryans, the Stotes-
burys of Philadelphia have also contributed an object lesson
in how to run through a fortune. Their story properly begins
with the second Mrs. Stotesbury, Lucretia Roberts Cromwell,
who was married first to Oliver Eaton Cromwell, a lawyer
and broker who was well to do but not rich in any substantial
sense. There was money in the family, however, a modest
fortune compiled by Oliver's grandfather, John Cromwell,
and passed on down in trust to Oliver's children, Jimmy,
Tony and Louise.

After Cromwell died in 1911, it took his widow only a year
to make what she later described facetiously as "the best and
most profitable financial transaction I ever completed." There
was more than an element of truth in the joke, for the wid-
ower she married, Edward T. Stotesbury, was a Morgan
partner who had already made one of the country's large
fortunes. He was sixty-three at the time; Eva, as his bride was
called, was twenty years younger. His own daughters were

grown and he welcomed the three stepchildren as though
they were his own; in fact, they were thereafter referred to
as "the stepchildren of E. T. Stotesbury, the Philadelphia
multimillionaire."

The wedding took place at the Cromwell summer place in
New Hampshire (Oliver also had homes in Rye, New York,
and Washington, D.C.), and it was attended by the President
and Mrs. William Howard Taft and the J. P. Morgans. Eva
wore a white velvet gown trimmed with bands of Russian
sable and old English point lace. For her going-away dress,
she appeared in gray silk covered by a long Russian sable
coat, lined with white satin brocade and lace frills. The bride
was given away by her son Tony, then in his early twenties.
Her wedding present from the bridegroom was three million
dollars and a fantastic collection of jewels, among them numerous strands of pearls and a diamond tiara. Eva wore so
many of these ornaments on her Palm Beach honeymoon
that it was necessary for a detective to accompany her everywhere except to the bridal chamber.

While the happy couple were in Palm Beach, Stotesbury
began happily to buy the ocean and lake frontage on which he
planned to build a winter palace for Eva. When it was completed and named El Mirasol, it impressed even the other
millionaire residents, who were accustomed to splendor, with
its lovely gardens, private zoo and a charming teahouse.

Then, with the honeymoon over, the new Mrs. Stotesbury
got down to the serious business of dominating Philadelphia
society and spending her husband's money. Her first public
appearance, a month later at the opera, was a sensation. She
wore a dress of white satin under silver net and crystal span-
gles, and she seemed to be virtually encased in diamonds
about her hair, ears and neck. They took on a special radiance
viewed against her purple velvet cloak. Like a jeweler dis-

playing the pride of his collection, Stotesbury sat at the rear of the box, obviously the happiest man in Philadelphia.

At the $2,000,000 Stotesbury mansion, Whitemarsh Hall, with its superbly landscaped grounds and 147 rooms, Eva later gave a succession of brilliant parties, each one costing $5000 or more, which delighted Philadelphians but annoyed WCTU members, who complained about the "smoking, liquor and expense."

Whitemarsh was virtually a small principality in itself. It had a power plant, telephone exchange, ice plant, movie theater, laundry, tailor shop, ballroom, library and art gallery. There was even a special house on the grounds built for Eva's father, James Henry Roberts, a Chicago corporation lawyer who came to live with his daughter after he retired.

Here, in unexampled luxury, Eva's three children grew up, with predictable results. Louise first married a Baltimore man, Walter L. Brooks. Her fond stepfather installed the couple in a $1,000,000 mansion, Rainbow Hill, which he built for them at Green Spring Valley, Maryland. They lived in it two years before the divorce. Louise then achieved a reflected fame by marrying Douglas MacArthur, a rising Army career man, and was known for years after her divorce as "the first Mrs. MacArthur." Later she married a movie actor, Lionel Atwill, but was no more successful with this venture.

Tony Cromwell, who had seriously considered working before his mother became a Stotesbury, also began to marry, an interest he shared with poetry and mountain climbing. His first marriage, in 1915, was to a Philadelphia society girl, Hope Beale. After he had tried unsuccessfully to get a Paris divorce a few years later, Hope saved him the trouble by getting one in Philadelphia, retaining custody of her son. In 1927, Tony married a Drexel granddaughter, Katherine Dahlgren Emmet. During this period he was getting a variable allowance from his mother, $36,000 a year until his second marriage, when it was increased to $48,000, but cut again to $20,000 after the crash had heavily reduced the Stotesbury fortune. The marriage to Miss Emmet ended in a separation suit, in which Katherine charged that Tony had abandoned her and their daughter Camilla for another woman, in so flagrant a manner that "Mr. Stotesbury had occasion in my presence to reprimand my husband for his conduct."

The youngest Cromwell, Jimmy, was a much more serious young man than his brother. He attended the Wharton School of Finance at the University of Pennsylvania on his annual allowance of $6000, and at twenty-three married Delphine Dodge, with results already described, and went to work as a vice-president of the Peerless Motor Car Co. in Cleveland, where he is credited with selling Dodge Motors for a figure estimated all the way from $145,000,000 to $160,000,000, in any case collecting a fat commission to add to his inheritance.

Jimmy was not the businessman his stepfather was, however, although it must be said that few men were. He got into Florida real estate with his mother and other investors, but when the bubble burst in 1925, Mrs. Stotesbury was $1,250,000 poorer and Jimmy was bereft of his Cromwell inheritance, the money he had saved from his stepfather's gifts, and everything earned in earlier businesses. Worse, the real estate firm which had been the vehicle for his Florida speculations was in bankruptcy to the tune of $6,000,000, and there were numerous suits filed by stockholders.

For a time Jimmy lived in Malmaison, the teahouse at El Mirasol, which his mother had redone for him. Then he married Doris Duke and embarked on the tortured marital life already narrated. Besides his ventures into politics and diplomacy, he worked for a time in an advertising firm and wrote three books: *Sound Money, The Voice of Young America* and *In Defense of Capitalism.*

When Edward T. Stotesbury died in May 1938, his will contained a painful surprise for Mrs. Stotesbury. The man who had boasted in August 1929, at the age of eighty, that he was worth $100,000,000 had left a personal estate of only $10,434,948, from which federal and state taxes amounting to about $5,000,000 had to be deducted. There was, of course, valuable real estate in addition: the Philadelphia palace, and the summer and winter homes in Florida and Maine.

Where had all the money gone? The crash had taken a great deal of it; a socially ambitious wife and expensive stepchildren had taken the rest.

To Mrs. Stotesbury, her position from that moment was one of poverty, and she began a slow decline. Her income, according to the will, was to be derived from $100,000 given to her outright, and the income from the $5,000,000 residual estate, out of which must come the maintenance for Whitemarsh Hall, the remainder to be shared with Stotesbury's daughter by his first marriage and her three children.

There was no alternative; Mrs. Stotesbury had to reduce her scale of living. Tony was first to feel the effects of the new regime when she cut his allowance to $6000 a year. She began to sell the Stotesbury properties, first the Palm Beach lake frontage, for $165,000; then two hundred feet of ocean frontage for $100,000. No one wanted to buy El Mirasol itself. Whitemarsh Hall was even harder to dispose of, but Mrs. Stotesbury had no other choice than to move out of it; the upkeep would have been suicidal.

For a time she lived in New Jersey, but early in the forties she moved to Washington, D.C., where she took up residence in another marble palace on fashionable Foxcroft Road. The newspapers reported that she had bought this house from her former daughter-in-law, Delphine Dodge, but Jimmy told a friend at the time that in reality the place had been rented from Delphine's mother. In any event, Mrs. Stotesbury went into virtual seclusion there and continued the decline that ended in her death in 1946. One who visited the place a few years before she died would have found it hard to understand her depression in the midst of so much splendor, but it must have seemed to her a far cry from the glories of Whitemarsh Hall.

Thus the Stotesbury fortune came to a virtual end, as a fortune. When the government had collected its money, the descendants could no longer be considered rich by the standards of most rich men. The fortune had made a long journey from the time Edward T. Stotesbury took his first job, at the age of twelve, while he was living in a walkup over a Philadelphia drugstore. He went into the banking business with the elder Drexel at a salary of $16.60 a month, was given a Christmas present of $200 from the firm after he had worked for it fourteen months, and with this money, carefully saved, he started toward his $200,000,000. The peak was 1929—after that, the long downhill road.

It must not be supposed, however, that the making-spending sequence was invariable. Sometimes an accumulator began spending while he was still alive, in a manner that would set a brisk example for anyone who came after him. Such a man was August Belmont, the New York banker and diplomat, who also departed from tradition by being born to a wealthy father in the Rhenish Palatinate. Able to choose whatever he wanted to do, he chose the one office in which to begin work (without pay) where he had the best opportunity to become, ultimately, a very rich man. This was the office of the Rothschilds, in Frankfurt-am-Main.

The Rothschilds could see that their fourteen-year-old office boy had talents far beyond sweeping the floors, and they took him in hand, sending him first to their branch office in Naples, allowing him to carry on negotiations with the Papal Court, and then transferring him to Havana. While he was on the way to Cuba he heard aboard ship of the panic of 1837, and, already thinking like a financier, he determined to take advantage of the financial chaos he knew must be prevailing in New York. Transacting the Rothschilds' Havana business as rapidly as possible, he sent in his resignation, took the first boat to New York, and went into business for himself.

From the small Wall Street office in which he began, Belmont moved rapidly toward his ultimate goal, the establishment of a great banking house, August Belmont & Co. Nothing even slightly impeded his progress except a duel he fought in 1841 at Elkton, Indiana, "over a subject too trite to be mentioned." It left him with a permanent limp. He was soon one of the leading bankers in America.

The rise of the Belmonts from nothing to the top level of society, and their long fall back again, took a century and $100,000,000. August, who founded the fortune, also had a hand in spending it. He was a short, heavy, aggressive man who was not widely loved. Short-tempered and arrogant, he did not look or act the part of a society figure at first, but it developed that Belmont knew how to enjoy money as well as make it. He liked horses and women, not necessarily in that order, and he had a fondness for society strange in a man of his peculiar nature. He memorialized himself among the rich of his day by helping to found the first polo club in this country, the Westchester Polo Club.

But it was some time before society accepted him, just as it was reluctant to accept the original John Jacob Astor and the founding Cornelius Vanderbilt, both August Belmont's contemporaries. He succeeded at last by marrying into it, so to speak, winning the beautiful Caroline Slidell Perry, daughter of Commodore Matthew G. Perry, whose family had been one of the ornaments of society for generations. With Caroline's eager help, he entered the carefully guarded portals. Soon the best families were being entertained at his home on the northeast corner of Fifth Avenue and Eighteenth Street, at the rear of which was New York's first private art gallery, built to house his growing collection.

In this house were born August's three sons, August, Jr., Oliver Hazard Perry Belmont, and Perry Belmont. His pride in them was equaled only by his satisfaction in being president of the American Jockey Club, in recognition of his fine stable and his constant work to improve the breed.

Of the three sons, it was August, Jr., who appeared to be most like his father, with a head for business but an expensive penchant for maintaining social prestige. August, Sr., and Caroline had spent a great deal to establish themselves; August, Jr., and his first wife, Bessie Hamilton Morgan, daughter of Governor Morgan of New York, spent even more to maintain their position. At least a hint of what this maintenance must have cost is contained in the list of things August, Jr., had named for him. There was, for example, the old Belmont Hotel, which stood on Forty-second Street, opposite Grand Central Terminal. Belmont Park, on Long Island, one of the finest race tracks in America, is a testimonial to the fortune he spent on horses alone. The only thing Augie did not achieve was to get a New York telephone exchange named after him, in the manner of the Beekmans, Barclays,

Rhinelanders and Schuylers. Other than that, however, the list was a lengthy one, and every item on it meant money.

August, Jr.'s first wife died in 1898, and for his second wife he took one of the beauties of the New York stage, Eleanor Robson, an accomplished actress. Miss Robson appeared to have no social ambitions. She lived quietly while her husband went on to greater notoriety and unwelcome publicity in his efforts to control the New York subway system, after he had founded the Interborough Rapid Transit. No one knew how much this and other ventures had cost him, but when his will was probated in 1924 the news was even worse than it had been in "Uncle Fred" Vanderbilt's document. Social prestige and the subway struggle had cost the better part of the Belmont fortune. The Cape Cod Canal was the principal asset remaining.

Again, as in the Stotesbury case, one could reasonably ask, Where had the money gone? Aside from what was lost in business, substantial in itself, most of it appeared to have gone into high living. There were a few parcels of real estate to show for it: a mansion on Madison Avenue, a country estate in Hempstead, Long Island, and a Newport cottage, By-the-Sea. The rest was financial silence.

It is not surprising, therefore, that August, Jr.'s three sons lived quiet lives, and in the third generation the grandchildren virtually disappeared from society. Not one of them could be called rich.

August, Sr.'s other two sons did somewhat better in managing the inheritance left them by their father. Perry, the Beau Brummell of his day, stirred up one of the major society scandals at the turn of the century by falling in love with the dashing Jessie Robbins Sloane, whose father was the Robbins of McKesson and Robbins, the drug firm. Jessie was unhappily married to Henry T. Sloane, who nevertheless loved his pretty wife and gave her everything—except, apparently, whatever it was that Perry, a handsome and gallant figure himself, offered her. The two saw each other so openly that the Sloanes and Perry were referred to as the "triangle." Sloane forbade his wife to see Belmont, but it did no good. He threatened her with divorce and disgrace, and she refused to believe him.

Then, in 1899, the storm broke and society had a major divorce scandal to talk about. Jessie did not even bother to contest the suit. On the day Sloane got his decree she married Perry in Greenwich, Connecticut.

This outcome divided society into warring camps, one contending that Sloane was stuffy, the other that nothing better could be expected of August, Sr.'s son. The latter view was so predominant that the Belmonts retreated to Paris for a time. When they came back, it was not to hostile New York, but to Washington, D.C., where they built themselves a fine house. But they never quite recovered from the ostracism. Washington was only slightly more friendly than New York, and as Perry's fortune, too, began to dwindle, the Belmonts were to be seen less prominently. After Jessie died in France, in 1935, Perry ended life as he began it, in his clubs and living the gay life of Newport. He died in 1947, at ninety-seven.

As for Oliver Hazard Perry, August, Sr.'s third son, his first marriage, to Sarah Swan Whitney, ended so disastrously that after Sarah's remarriage she would not permit her ex-husband's name to be mentioned in her presence. By that time Oliver had a great deal more to think about, because in 1896 he had married William K. Vanderbilt's ex-wife, Alva, who was five years older, at forty-six already a veteran of the Vanderbilt wars, still *the* Mrs. Vanderbilt even though she had a new name, and the acknowledged leader of society.

Alva had brought from her first marriage not only the largest alimony ever granted in America up to that time, but also the Vanderbilt cottage in Newport, Marble House, where she continued to reign as though nothing had happened. Acting more or less as a prince consort was extremely wearing for Oliver, who suddenly found himself traveling at a perilous social pace. He died in 1908, but Alva the indomitable was eighty before she died in Paris, in 1933.

Oliver left no children from this marriage, and only a daughter by the first one. Perry died childless. Only August II's children and grandchildren were left to face the melancholy fact that the Belmont fortune, along with much of its social position, had all but disappeared.

For a final examination of Eastern wealth, it may be instructive to consider the family of Peter Arrell Brown Widener, as an example of the ultimate loneliness of riches. There is a story, perhaps apocryphal, of Peter A. B. Widener II, who as a young boy once came to visit his namesake and the accumulator of the $100,000,000 Widener fortune. While his grandfather talked to him, the boy glanced about at the old man's extraordinary art collection, later valued at $18,-000,000 to $50,000,000, and now in the National Gallery.

"Grandfather, what's to become of these pictures and things when I grow up?" he inquired.

Old Peter looked about with pride at "these things"—a priceless Mazarin tapestry, Rembrandts and Van Dycks, Cellini jewels. "When I die, they'll belong to your father," he answered.

"What will Father do with them?" young Peter persisted.

"Would you like him to give them to you?"

The boy was horrified. "Oh no!" he answered quickly. "Please, Grandfather, I don't want them. They make me too lonely. When I grow up I want to be with people. I don't want to live with pictures and be lonely!"

History does not record what Grandfather Widener answered, but it may be he remembered his own rise to wealth and power and wondered what on earth the child could mean. For Peter A. B. Widener was never a lonely man, whatever else he may have been. Philadelphia born, he had left high school halfway through and gone to work as a butcher's boy, an occupation he pursued for some time.

The pursuit was highly profitable during the Civil War, when Widener followed a well-worn path trod by the accumulators and secured a government supply contract, this one to furnish mutton to federal troops in and near Philadelphia. That operation resulted in a $50,000 profit, which he invested legitimately in a chain of meat stores, and with far less virtue in the street railway system of Philadelphia, which was fully as corrupt there as it was in Chicago and New York.

Politics and street railways were a natural alliance, and so it was no surprise that Widener's subsidiary career as a Republican politician, particularly as city treasurer, proved to be extremely profitable and led to his acquiring total control of the city's traction lines, which were merged as the Philadelphia Traction Company. Since metropolitan transportation lines appeared to have a distinct affinity for each other, it was not difficult either for Widener to get himself involved in both Chicago and New York, where he came to the financial aid of Thomas Fortune Ryan and William C. Whitney. He was also active in United States Steel, the International Mercantile Marine Company and the American Tobacco Company.

Aside from business, this forceful, plausible man found his enjoyment in collecting art, which he housed in his splendid home, Lynnewood Hall, in an exclusive Philadelphia suburb, Elkins Park. Here were the treasures his grandson wanted none of, and much more besides—Chinese porcelains, probably the finest collection in the country; bronzes, tapestries, statuary, chinaware, old furniture. The place also had a splendid library whose books, unlike most of the other accumulators, Peter Widener often read. His grandson, Harry Elkins Widener, was a noted collector of rare books who had been launched in collecting by no less an authority than A. S. W. Rosenbach. When he went down with the *Titanic* he was clutching a 1598 edition of Bacon's essays. Harry's mother, also a lover of books, was the donor of Harvard's Widener Library.

Widener believed in sharing his wealth. Certainly his children would have had a much larger fortune to inherit if he had not given more than eleven million dollars to institutions and organizations. In memory of his wife, Hannah Josephine Dunton, and their son Harry he built and endowed the Widener Memorial Industrial Training School for Crippled Children; his Broad Street house, where he lived before Lynnewood Hall was built, he gave to the city as a branch of the Philadelphia Free Library.

But in spite of these good works Peter A. B. Widener was not acepted by Philadelphia society. He had lingered too long in the meat market, and Broad Street was on the wrong side of the traction tracks. It may have been, too, that the accumulated odor of street railway franchises, wafting from New York and Chicago and mingling in the turgid Philadelphia air, had assaulted the tilted noses resident along the Main Line.

The brunt of this snobbery was borne by Widener's grandchildren. Two of his three sons had died young; the third, Joseph E., took what he supposed was a rightful place in society, and consolidated it by marrying a Philadelphia belle of excellent family, Ella H. Pancoast Herberton.

Ella's first husband, William H. Herberton, had died on their honeymoon, and shortly afterward she married Joseph Widener, to become a reigning hostess in Philadelphia, Newport and New York before she died in 1929. As a great beauty and a member of one of Philadelphia's oldest families, she considered her position unassailable. Her marriage to the butcher boy's son demonstrated that it wasn't. The knowledge came through her children, Josephine, called "Fifi," and Peter A. B. II.

As all good Main Liners know, the Assembly Ball was for years the true test of blood. The ins were invited; the outs were not. To be excluded was equivalent to being cast into the seventh circle of the special hell reserved for ineligible Philadelphians. Ella, who was highly eligible, quite naturally expected that her daughter would be no less eligible. But as the time came, when Fifi was seventeen and ready to go, no invitation was forthcoming.

Consternation prevailed in the Widener mansion, then anger set in. As Fifi's brother remarked, "It made Father's blood boil." Joseph, too, had given substantial sums for the betterment of Philadelphia; consequently, when he was asked at the time of the snub to give something more, he told the askers that if his daughter wasn't eligible for the Assembly his pocketbook wasn't eligible for their enterprises.

At that, observing their mistake, the Assembly entrepreneurs sent Fifi a bid but, rigid to the last, it was a bid with insulting restrictions. Ella was not invited to chaperon her daughter, as was the custom, and Fifi was invited as an "out-of-town guest," rather than as a Philadelphian. It testifies to the power of the Assembly Ball that Fifi decided to go anyway, with her brother Peter as escort.

Peter was far angrier about the snub than any of the other Wideners. A serious boy, without pretenses, he had just returned from service in the First World War, where he had been a lieutenant in the Sanitary Corps and learned something about the democracy for which he had helped to make the world safe. He went to the ball in a black humor. As he came down the receiving line with his sister, Peter abruptly boiled over, remarking loudly to one of the hosts in the line: "I know we're not wanted here, and I wouldn't be here if I weren't escorting my sister."

Eyebrows elevated and audible gasps were heard. Fifi and Peter moved onto the dance floor, but they stayed only a short time and then, to the further shock of the guests, they did the unthinkable and walked out on the Assembly Ball.

Whether or not this incident was responsible, Fifi immediately set out on a life of further social crime which could only have made the Philadelphia old guard nod heads and say, "I told you so." She developed a more than passing interest in a nineteen-year-old freshman at the University of Pennsylvania, Carter Randolph Leidy, and to break up this highly unsuitable romance, her mother banished her to Worcester, Massachusetts, for a time, guarded by a governess, a maid and two detectives.

Seeking to divert the newspapers and the gossips from this maneuver, Ella invited hundreds of guests to a great ball at Lynnewood Hall, which someone once described as looking like the United States Mint with fountains. The affair was to be in honor of her daughter, but at that point Fifi disgraced herself entirely by eluding her guards and eloping with young Leidy. The invitations, of course, had to be canceled. She compounded the felony by settling down with Leidy in a plain little house in Berwick, while he took a job as a factory worker at $2.50 a day. They were rather a gay young couple, the newspapers noted, appearing occasionally in court for such offenses as speeding or carrying off red traffic lanterns.

Eventually the Wideners relented and the Leidys repented, so that the couple began to live in an increasingly Widener style and eventually moved to New York, where they had a daughter, Joan, and were finally divorced in 1926. After the divorce Fifi married a bond salesman named Milton C. Holdon. When Ella died in 1929, Fifi became the beneficiary of $1,000,000 in gilt-edged securities, as well as another $500,000 worth of jewelry, including a $250,000 string of pearls, a $125,000 emerald and diamond necklace, and a $17,000 diamond chain. Her father added another $1,000,000 to her private fortune by presenting her with an Italian palace in Palm Beach, whose residents could go to their private beach by means of a tunnel dug under South Ocean Boulevard. This inheritance was quite in keeping with Fifi's wedding to Holdon, a grand affair held at Lynnewood Hall in the huge Rembrandt Room, on whose walls were hung no less than sixteen Dutch masters.

Wealth apparently made Fifi restless. After frequent quarrels with Holdon, fully reported in the newspapers, she divorced him in 1932 and immediately after married Aksel Wichfeld, an attaché of the Danish Embassy, who had just divorced one of the Swift heiresses, a fabulous society spender herself, who died broke.

When her father died in 1943, the remainder of the Widener fortune passed on to Fifi and her brother, and both subsequently slipped into comparative obscurity. Disillusioned with humanity, Peter turned to thoroughbred racing, a sport in which he became a prominent figure, serving at one time as president of Hialeah Race Track; his father had once been principal owner of Belmont Park. He lived quietly and came to hate the loneliness and snobbishness of great wealth. The depth of his feeling he expressed in an autobiography, *Without Drums*, published in 1940, eight years before his death at fifty-three.

His aim in writing the book, said Peter, was "to set myself up as a horrible example of what an empty existence it is to be the son of great wealth, sheltered from reality and surrounded by a sea of snobbery."

It could have been an epitaph for the inheritors who were also spenders.

$ 8 $

Last of the Big Spenders:
William Randolph Hearst

All other spenders are overshadowed by the large bulk of William Randolph Hearst, whose spending was on such a magnificent scale that it is unlikely ever again to be equaled, much less surpassed. By comparison, the Texas oil moguls with their airplanes and Neiman-Marcus charge accounts are children playing with toys. Some of them are richer than Hearst ever was, but they do not have the extraordinary talent for spending money that made Hearst not only the last but the best of the big spenders.

In death, as he was in life, Hearst remains a contradiction. He was a man who cannot be neatly catalogued, for purposes of this book or any other. In one sense, he was a true inheritor of a nineteenth-century fortune, having been materially aided by the eight million dollars left to him by his mother, all that remained of the eighteen million dollars his father had accumulated. George Hearst, the father, may have been only a minor accumulator of the past century, but the legacy he left his son was not inconsiderable. Besides the money that came down through his wife's will, he left to W.R. a quantity of mining, land and industrial properties which never stopped pouring out wealth. Before he died, furthermore, George enabled his son to start out in the newspaper business with the decrepit San Francisco *Examiner*, which George Hearst had bought for political purposes.

Young Hearst, therefore, was an inheritor even before his father died. He started out rich, and with his later inheritance as a base, he dwarfed his father as an accumulator in his own right, pyramiding the profits from his newspaper, magazine and radio empire until, in the end, he amassed a staggering $400,000,000.

With this money he became the most fantastic spender of them all, and yet he was a conservator and expander in another sense, since he took a relatively small fortune and expanded it into a great one through sheer ability. It was the prime contradiction of Hearst's bewildering life that spending and conserving ran a neck-and-neck race in his career, with spending gaining the upper hand until it nearly brought his expanding empire down around his ears.

Thus Hearst was one of the overlappers between the centuries, and he was also such a varied man that he could have fitted into several categories of accumulating and inheriting. One category, however, would not accommodate him. Hearst had little or no sense of social responsibility, and only an insignificant portion of his money was ever dedicated to the welfare of humanity. He had virtually no concern for the common good; his chief interest in other people was whether they bought his newspapers or made money for him. The idea of Carnegie and Rockefeller that possession of wealth carried with it a responsibility to society was alien to him.

His accumulating was remarkable in itself. When one remembers that Hearst's personal expenses for nearly thirty years totaled fifteen million dollars annually, it remains one of the financial miracles of the century that the Hearst fortune not only survived the worst financial beating of all but actually increased until his death. It may well be that, leaving the Ford and Rockefeller monies aside, the Hearst wealth remains as nearly intact, as closely held within a family, and therefore relatively unfragmented, as any American fortune.

George Hearst, Willie's father, did not begin as a poor man. He was raised on his father's Missouri plantation, where he enjoyed the pleasures of Southern ante-bellum society and might have lingered with them if the California gold strike of '49 had not stirred his adventurous blood and sent him west in 1850. At first his luck was indifferent, but in 1859, prospecting in what was then called the Washoe Diggings, now in Nevada, he succeeded in buying for $450 a half interest in a gold mine, whose owner, Alvah Gould, thought it a dud and believed he had euchred the California buyers out of their money. What George had bought, in reality, was half of the Gould and Curry mine, as it was later called, which proved to be the second richest silver property in the whole Comstock Lode. While he was at it, George also acquired, for a few hundred dollars more, a sixth interest in the Ophir, which unquestionably *was* the richest of Comstock mines.

Nearly overnight, George Hearst was a millionaire. He went back to the Missouri plantation long enough to woo and marry a wealthy neighbor's daughter, Phebe Apperson, twenty-two years younger, took her on a honeymoon to New York, then sailed with her for San Francisco. There he installed Phebe in the Lick House, most elegant of the city's hotels, until she became pregnant, after which for reasons unknown he moved to the Stevenson House, a respectable family hostelry at California and Montgomery streets. In these modest circumstances William Randolph Hearst was born on April 29, 1863. As soon as possible, the whole family was installed in a large brick house on Rincon Hill.

During the year the infant Hearst entered the world, to be called "Sonny" by his fond parents, the Ophir mine disgorged nearly four million dollars worth of silver, and the Gould and Curry gave up almost as much. It seemed that everything George Hearst touched turned to wealth. With a partner he bought the Ontario mine in Utah, which immediately began paying about a million dollars annually, and would continue to do so for a long time. Then followed the others, that were to be famous in mining history: the Homestake, in South Dakota, where Hearst and his partners founded the town of Lead; next the Anaconda copper mine, in which he had a third interest; and finally, venturing farther afield, other mines in Chile, Peru and Mexico.

Along with the mines came land properties in George Hearst's rapidly developing empire. He had a one-third interest in a 250,000-acre cattle ranch in New Mexico; 25,000 acres near Phoenix; 4500 acres south of San Francisco; a thousand square miles in three states of Mexico and another 900,000 acres in the state of Chihuahua; and 75,000 acres between the California coast and the Santa Lucia Mountains, halfway to Los Angeles from San Francisco, where the towers of San Simeon would one day rise on the Enchanted Hill.

George was shrewd enough to get much of this immensely valuable property for next to nothing. He got his acres in the Mexican states of Vera Cruz, Campeche and Yucatan for nothing at all in cash, given free title by the government to whatever lands he wanted in return for surveying them, since the Mexican government had no surveyor of its own. He secured the Chihuahua acreage for only forty cents an acre, because it had been denuded of settlers, who were frightened by the raids of Geronimo, the notorious Apache. Hearst learned secretly that Geronimo had been captured, and before the news got out that the Chihuahua country was again habitable he made his deal.

These ventures in mining and real estate were the solid base of the eighteen million dollars George left to Phebe when he died in March 1891. He left nothing at all to young Willie, not because he did not trust him, as was said later by Hearst's enemies, but because it was family custom, and Phebe had managed his money shrewdly while he was alive. That Willie himself understood and accepted the situation with good will is evident in the letter he wrote to his mother at the time she informed him he was to be her sole heir. He wrote affectionately: "My father never did a better thing than when he made the will he did. I have admired him for it and have been happy to concur in it, and I have never told you how many times I have been advised by fools and scoundrels otherwise. That is the kind of thing for our own kind of people, and I hope to so live that you will have as much confidence in me as my father had in you. . . ."

Young Hearst was devoted to his mother, who was an entirely admirable woman, but he need not have worried about abusing her confidence. Willie was the major interest in her life, distantly followed by art and philanthropy, and there was almost nothing he could have done to shatter the illusion of near idolatry in which she invested him from the time he was a small boy.

The part of her husband's fortune that Phebe spent in her lifetime was largely for good works, particularly in education. The University of California benefited substantially from her philanthropy, along with dozens of other educational and cultural institutions, and beyond these, she paid the college expenses of hundreds of deserving young girls. The splendid art collection she gathered, at considerable expense, became the basis of her son's stupendous collection after her death. But it was the son himself who was her chief philanthropy, the most beloved ornament in her collection.

As a custodian of money, his mother's and his own, Hearst's attitude was perhaps most accurately expressed by John Francis Neylan, his chief counsel for years and one of the men he had to thank for preserving a substantial portion of his wealth. Testifying in a stockholders' suit brought against Hearst in 1940, Mr. Neylan made a declaration so candid that it startled the courtroom.

"Money as such bores him," Neylan said. "His idea of money is that it is something to do something with. He is a builder. He wants to build buildings. He wants to build magazines. He wants to develop ranches. He builds hotels in New York. His idea is to build, build, build all the time. I have said it repeatedly that in his make-up there is just almost a blank space in relation to money."

That attitude, plus the fluidity of his fortune, made Hearst the most extraordinary capitalist of our time. He was at once inheritor, accumulator and spender. *Fortune* magazine might declare truly that "the core of the Hearst empire is accumulation," but it was equally true that he was not an investor. Money, to him, was only a means of buying things. When he bought newspapers or magazines it was quite simply because he wanted them; whether or not they were good investments was secondary. If these properties were in trouble, Hearst poured in money as long as he had the fluid capital to do it in the effort to make them profitable; if they continued to fail, he held on until circumstances compelled him to sell.

In the closing years of the nineteenth century, when he was establishing himself in the newspaper business with the San Francisco *Examiner* and the New York *Journal*, Hearst spent a million dollars a year on his journalistic enterprises.

By the turn of the century he had contrived to run through eight million, and he owed money to so many creditors that collectors were always lying in wait outside the *Journal* offices to serve him with subpoenas. Hearst enjoyed the game of eluding them by sending out decoys dressed to resemble him, who hid themselves in their cloaks and grabbed the summonses before they rolled off in the publisher's waiting carriage. It was 1904 before his newspaper properties began to turn the corner and make money. They had produced a substantial fortune by 1919, when Phebe died and left him eight million more.

By 1922, Hearst had risen to the top of the publishing heap. He owned twenty newspapers, Universal Service, International News Service, King Features, the *American Weekly*, a string of magazines in New York and London, a newsreel company, and a motion picture company. His operating capital was in the millions. By 1935, after severe vicissitudes to be described later, the empire was still highly profitable, although it had been drastically trimmed around the edges.

Meanwhile, the mining properties and his real estate were pouring in wealth, which compensated for his losses and went on building the fortune even when the fluid portion of it had been siphoned off to a nearly disastrous level by Hearst's spending. In 1928 the great Homestake mine was paying $5.86 a share; in 1930, in the aftermath of the crash, it paid $8.00; and in 1932, at the bottom of the depression, it had risen to $10.60. As the result of a suit by an investment trust, in which it was disclosed that Homestake had valued its property at only $5,000,000 or less, when the figure should properly have been at least $86,000,000, the dividends jumped from $30 to $44 a share in the mid-thirties.

Hearst's other properties also flourished and paid dividends

—the American Metals Company, with its assets of more than $77,000,000, and the Cerro do Pasco Copper Company, whose assets were $40,000,000. His Mexican lands were producing varieties of wealth, from the valuable hardwood forests in Vera Cruz to the Campeche ranch from which came five per cent of all the chicle imported into America. The acres that had neither chicle nor timber nor agricultural products turned out to be rich in oil. Thus, unlike many other American fortunes, the Hearst wealth had its roots in sources which went on increasing in value and pumping money into the till.

This was a major factor in making increasingly solvent a man who could drop from two to seven million dollars in a single side venture, motion pictures. Most of Hearst's spending, however, was concentrated in real estate and collecting. He was a man who liked to live well, and certainly few men in history have been better housed, beginning with the luxurious apartment he occupied during his inglorious Harvard days.

Moving out to San Francisco, at the beginning of his career, he lived in a variety of city apartments and houses, but he spent his first housing money on rehabilitating the stock farm George Hearst had begun near Pleasonton, across the Bay. W.R. took the old-fashioned ranch and converted it into a charming country place, which he called El Rancho del Oso. There he rode and swam and entertained his friends. Phebe retired there in her last years, changing its name to La Hacienda del Poco de la Verona, honoring a five-ton wellhead Hearst had bought in Verona in 1892. So that her son might be near her, and bring his own growing family of sons, she built a fourteen-room outbuilding which she called the Boys' House. This astonishing structure had thirteen bedrooms on the second floor, to house grandchildren, nurses, tutors and governesses. An enormous playroom occupied the entire ground floor, filled with every conceivable device which might entertain a growing boy.

Eventually Hearst put California's sunshine behind him for a long time, and devoted himself to New York, where he established the headquarters of his empire. He lived first in the Hoffman House, one of the lush hotels of the period, but a mere suite could not contain him and he shortly acquired the entire third floor of another hotel, the Worth House, on Twenty-fifth Street. He remade it in the image of his California home, with beamed ceilings and tiled floors, furnishing it with choice items from his burgeoning collection of art works—mantels, furniture and tapestries.

The Worth House was sold and marked for demolition while Hearst was away on one of his trips to Europe, compelling the young publisher to buy his first New York real estate, a four-story brownstone at 123 Lexington Avenue, a building so modest by California standards that Hearst referred to it disdainfully as a shanty, despite the fact that it was both historic and elegant, in the manner of the period. Chester Alan Arthur had been sworn in as President of the United States in its formal living room, and died there five years later in the master bedroom on the second floor.

Hearst had scant respect for history. He replaced the President's deathbed with a Parisian couch, and hung deer antlers as chandeliers in the oak-paneled dining room, mingling them incongruously with collections of Delft and old glass. These odd mixtures were everywhere in the house: German armor and Egyptian mummy cases, French art works and a rosewood pianola mingled indiscriminately. To this house Hearst brought his wife, Millicent, when they were married in 1903.

A few years later, in 1907, Hearst moved uptown to one of the city's best apartment houses, the Clarendon, at the corner of Riverside Drive and Eighty-sixth Street. The move was occasioned not by his growing family—one son born and another on the way—but by the uncontrolled growth of his collections, which were bursting out at the seams. To accommodate both them and the family, he leased the three top floors, containing thirty rooms. Still, in a half dozen years, there was not enough room for Hearst art, and he proposed to knock out a few walls and ceilings to make more space. When the owner objected to such a drastic alteration, Hearst simply bought the whole building for $900,000. Then he proceeded to knock out floors and ceilings in his usual style, creating a five-floor-and-penthouse showcase for his works of art.

The center of this establishment was an enormous Gothic hall, with stone walls, housing his armor collection. On another floor was a Georgian library and a well-equipped art gallery, stocked with a small museum full of pictures. At Christmastime Hearst played Santa Claus and startled his five sons by seeming to emerge from the cavernous recesses of the huge Gothic fireplace, appraised as one of the most beautiful in the world. There was plenty of space, too, for Millicent's entertaining; one of the sixty rooms could accommodate 250 people at a party. This property remained in Hearst's possession until 1938, when it was returned to the Mutual Life Insurance Company, which held the $525,000 mortgage Hearst had taken out at the time he bought it.

Hearst had smaller retreats in New York and Los Angeles— a studio apartment in the Beaux Arts building on Sixth Avenue and an apartment in the Warwick Hotel, in New York; an entire floor in the Ambassador Hotel at Los Angeles. There were various other undisclosed snuggeries on both coasts, maintained in the interest of the privacy it was so difficult for Hearst to find.

From these relatively modest beginnings, Hearst graduated to palaces. One was at Sands Point, Long Island, a place he bought in 1929 and lived in almost not at all. Called St. Joan, it had once belonged to August Belmont, an old political friend of Hearst's, and it occupied thirteen acres on the shore of Long Island Sound. The house was a rambling French stone château, with Gothic towers, resembling a miniature barony. Its special glory was a real lighthouse, guiding mariners on the Sound. Inside the château was the customary great hall with fireplace to match, and carloads of furniture of every period from early Louis to early American. The owners' suites, however, were entirely French: Louis XVI for Millicent (by that time a wife in name only), and Empire for W.R.

The lighthouse was furnished authentically in early American, a kind of circular Williamsburg, where Hearst spent much of his time opening boxes with a hatchet and pulling out treasures for his collection sent from everywhere in the world. But it was not long before neither Millicent nor her husband had any inclination to visit St. Joan, and in 1943 the Dime Savings Bank, its mortgage holder, sold the place.

Far more beloved by Hearst was his second castle, a real one this time, a medieval gem in Wales known as St. Donat's, steeped in nine hundred years of tradition. Its atmosphere was that of the Middle Ages, the period Hearst loved most. He had bought St. Donat's sight unseen after falling in love with a picture of one room in it, shown to him by a New York art collector. When he saw the place at last, three years later, he was so enchanted that he refused to sit down and eat until he had made a thorough inspection, although he had not arrived until ten o'clock at night. He prowled around the cobwebby dungeons and dismal passages with a lantern, dirty but utterly happy.

Nevertheless, he was not entirely pleased with his acquisition. He was unhappy to observe that it lacked plumbing, and he ordered this repaired at once in a tone so demanding that the castle was soon equipped with so many baths that some of them were never turned on.

What St. Donat's did not lack was quantity. It had 135 rooms, and they cried out for furnishings, of which Hearst had what was probably the world's largest supply. In three years it was a collector's paradise, a museum worth coming miles to see. It had an extravagant collection of Elizabethan silver, and a fantastic red bedroom occupied by the owner himself. Its red-paneled walls were covered in places by lacquered cabinets, and its furniture was upholstered in red. The bed had belonged to Charles I, and a carved silver panel at the foot recorded that here the unhappy king had tossed on the night before the Battle of Naseby in 1645.

On the rare occasions when he was in residence at St. Donat's, Hearst blended a strange mixture of English and California country life in the daily routine of the castle. Meals were in the English style: mutton and hothouse fruits at luncheon; tea in the library, with the hot water brought in a George II teakettle worth as much as a whole tea plantation, and served from a Chamberlain Worcester tea service; mutton again at dinner, or a joint of beef, with $250,000 worth of silver on the table and a pair of Cellini cups flanking the centerpiece.

In other respects, life was pure California: cards and charades in the evening; tennis, swimming and riding in the afternoon. A large swimming pool had been installed almost at once. The ruler of the castle achieved a particularly Hearstian touch with the moat, in which he laid a velvety sward and staked out a croquet court.

St. Donat's was one of the first victims of the war Hearst

opposed so bitterly. The British government requisitioned it early in 1940, and Hearst never saw it again.

California, however, was Hearst's real home, and it was only natural that when he reached the climax of his accumulating, of both art and money, he should build there. It was also logical that what he built should be stupefying, in direct proportion to the size of his fortune and his art collection. Few other words would be adequate to characterize Marion Davies' Santa Monica "beach house," the fabulous San Simeon, and Wyntoon.

By this time his romance with Miss Davies, the blond movie actress, had become a model of faithfulness and devotion, as it was for three decades. Hearst had closed off any further discussion of it forever with his flat statement: "I'm not saying it's right. I'm saying that it *is*." The houses in which he now shared his life with her reflected both his personality and hers, but Marion's was badly overshadowed. In her Santa Monica beach house, for example, which a magazine writer once described as a "white-pillared manse, huge as a railway terminal," there were the usual appurtenances of California beach life, although on a grander scale than most others enjoyed, but there were also Rembrandts and Holbeins on the walls, mingled with portraits of Marion in her various motion picture roles. These were later removed to her Beverly Hills house.

But the beach house was much more Marion's than Hearst's, neither castle nor museum but a sunny, light, informal place. There was a Hearstian touch in Marion's bedroom, an enormous room facing the ocean; it had a bathroom at each end. When Hearst was in residence, the evidence of his presence was the traveling corps of secretaries and telegraphers who followed him about. The Great Collector himself occupied his time swimming, playing tennis and watching motion pictures. He spent less time there after the thirties, and in 1948 it was sold to new owners who converted it into a hotel.

San Simeon has been so often described that it needs no elaboration here, except to characterize it as the act of a man drunk with power and money. Hearst, who was familiar with both and had been from his early days, saw San Simeon in a different way, as a carefully planned, deliberate attempt to create a shrine to beauty. Unconsciously, he seemed to be trying to concentrate there all the meaning he had been able to find in his complicated life. It had sentimental associations, too, because it was the site where his father had built a small cabin on what he called Camp Hill. The family had spent summers there, "roughing it," a practice Hearst continued with Millicent and his sons during the early years of his marriage. That was the reason Hearst always called San Simeon "the ranch," even after the site became the Enchanted Hill and the $20,000,000 ultimate in rich men's houses rose on it. The boyhood illusion was further preserved with the paper napkins, catsup bottles, fruits, jellies and condiments which appeared in the "long, noble, high" refectory, the pride of Hearst's collection, where his constant flow of guests ate in baronial splendor.

Even in the days of San Simeon's legitimate status as a camp, there was a substantial difference between George Hearst's idea of "roughing it" and his son's. The father knew what a rough life was like, and camping out with him was primitive. When Willie took over Camp Hill, however, he brought an enormous portable main tent, about the size of a circus sideshow canvas, and ringed it with three smaller tents, each one with four rooms and bath, for his entourage of servants, tutors, nurses and chauffeurs. There were movies every night after dinner, a lifetime habit of Hearst's, and the familiar paper napkins and condiments were spread on a solid oak dining table of heroic proportions and cost.

Beginning in 1919, under Hearst's direction and with the help of an architect, Julia Morgan, a small army of workmen began to carve out San Simeon from the rocky mountaintop which crested the 275,000 acres of Hearst's property. Like the original tent camp, it contained three guest houses and a main house, but all four were Spanish palaces. The guesthouses were La Casa del Mar, which faced the Pacific; La Casa del Sol, pointing its spires toward the sun; and La Casa del Monte, facing the Santa Lucia Mountains. The big house, La Casa Grande, surmounted them. All the houses were connected by Italian gardens, luxuriant with flowers, filled with the sound of cool fountains, and adorned with statuary from Greece and Rome.

Hearst's own quarters were at the top of La Casa Grande, a two-bedroom suite, looking at the sea from one and the mountains from the other, with a sitting room between. A private carved-wood elevator transported Hearst from this eyrie to other rooms in the house—his medieval Gothic study, the cloisters, the library, and on the ground floor the great Assembly Hall, where his guests gathered for dinner, awaiting his appearance. Inevitably there were motion pictures after dinner, in a 200-seat theater hung with crimson Italian brocatelle.

None of the other accumulators ever enjoyed such elaborate luxury. Most of the single items in his agglomeration could have been matched, but the great houses of Newport, New York, Palm Beach and elsewhere could not begin to match San Simeon. It had its own airport and private train, an enormous white marble swimming pool, excellent tennis courts, a zoo with wild animals, a salt-water pool in a private gymnasium (it alone cost nearly a million dollars), and magnificent objects of art everywhere, including those that were stored in two acres of cellar beneath the main house and those still unpacked from a row of cases which stretched for a block outside.

Hearst's guests shared this luxury on an unprecedented scale. The steady supply of visitors found themselves equipped with horses, cars, valets, maids, large suites, each with two bedrooms and a sitting room, clothes for every occasion, picnics forty miles away but still on the ranch, where servants and a portable field kitchen prepared elaborate barbecues, and telephones everywhere. San Simeon's switchboard was in touch with the whole world. There were always at least fifty or sixty visitors at the castle.

The second busiest private telephone exchange in California was McCloud 3OK3, the nerve center of Hearst's remote northern California estate, Wyntoon, which Miss Davies, who did not care for it, referred to disrespectfully as "Spittoon." More isolated than San Simeon, it nevertheless housed thirty to sixty guests more or less constantly, some of whom never met each other. Where San Simeon reached its population density on weekends, Wyntoon was like a perpetual house party.

Its character, too, was different, because of its natural setting in pine forest and rugged northern mountain country. Instead of Italian fountains, the music of the McCloud River charmed Hearst and his guests. But the sports were the same—tennis, swimming, riding and croquet, a game Hearst loved next to tennis. The swimming pool was a gem in itself, heated and nestled in a grove of majestic pines, cedars and firs.

At Wyntoon, Hearst removed himself somewhat from his guests. He lived in what looked like a Bavarian village, centered around a huge, pine-paneled Alpine lodge, large enough to house sixty people comfortably. It was equipped with the customary movie theater. The guests lived a half mile down the river, in luxurious but removed accommodations. The mood at Wyntoon was vaguely Germanic. The main residence was called Bear House; a sturdy bronze fisherwoman, brought over from Salzburg, stood guard before it, and Hearst often emerged from it wearing a Tyrolean hat. The other buildings surrounding Bear House were known as Fairy House and Cinderella House. Again, these names derived from sentimental childhood associations. Wyntoon had originally been a rustic retreat for his mother. When it was destroyed by fire after her death, he built the new Wyntoon on the ruins. As in the case of San Simeon, it was a blending of childhood memories with latter-day luxury. As always, too, it was a place to house his collections. There he brought to his forest museum the things that seemed appropriate, items like cuckoo clocks and German medieval art; in all, three carloads of art objects were brought up the mountainside before financial adversities in 1937 cut off the flow.

The real estate and the collections always went together, and it would be difficult to say which was the greater drain on the Hearst fortune. The cost of the collecting can be figured with some accuracy, however, if round numbers are accepted as accurate. Hearst spent a million dollars on his art collection every year for fifty years. At the end of that time he had accumulated about twenty thousand different items, worth all told somewhat more than fifty million dollars, since there were a few years when his collecting bill was nearer two million. His acquisitions in those flush periods represented a quarter of the entire sales of objects of art in the world.

In sheer quantity alone, Hearst's accumulating bordered on the incredible. It was displayed in houses around the globe, from St. Donat's to Bronx warehouses covering several city blocks, and in four other warehouses in California, in addition to the lavish permanent displays in Santa Monica, San Simeon and Wyntoon. When half of it was sold at Gimbel's in New York, in 1941, the giant sale spread over three and a half acres in the store.

The people who believed that it was all quantity and without quality were contradicted by the art experts, who knew that, of the 504 separate categories in Hearst's collection, twenty were outstandingly good and five were the best to be found among private collections. These included his silver, Gothic tapestries, armor, English furniture and Hispano-Mooresque pottery. One of the things that interested him least was rugs, yet at one point he had the finest Navajo rug collection in the West.

The decision to dispose of his collections was carried out in as spectacular a way as the accumulating of them. In 1937, Hearst was at a critical point in his fortunes and decided to liquidate from a half to two thirds of his holdings, with the idea of avoiding inheritance taxes and building up cash reserves, which he needed badly at that juncture. For the first time in fifty years he stopped buying and began to sell. When his art was appraised at approximately fifty million, it could be seen that he had far surpassed other collectors like Mellon, whose accumulation had been worth only nineteen million, or Widener's, worth about the same figure.

Hearst's collection of old English silver was sold at Sotheby's in London, shortly after his decision; naturally, the pieces brought only fractions of what they had cost him. But it was the sale at Gimbel's in February 1941 that attracted most attention—100,000 persons in the first week, who bought a half million dollars' worth of art. The real prizes, of course, were sold to collectors and dealers in New York and London auction rooms. John D. Rockefeller, Jr., Marshall Field and other rich collectors bought some of the rarer pieces as museum gifts.

Ten years later there was renewed selling, with a series of sales at the Parke-Bernet Galleries in New York, which included some of Miss Davies' treasures from the Beverly Hills house. The prize of the lot was the Cellini cup, one of the rarest English silver items in the world, once the property, among other owners, of J. P. Morgan. Hearst had paid more than $30,000 for it; the purchaser was Clendenin Ryan, Thomas Fortune's grandson, who bought it for $10,500.

Aside from his homes, Hearst spent large quantities of money on other kinds of real estate, and entertained grandiose dreams of transforming parts of New York City, particularly Columbus Circle, which he hoped to have renamed for himself and then to have it serve as the starting point for a kind of Hearst Boulevard, which would run from the Circle across on Fifty-seventh Street to the East River. In attempting to create this real estate empire during the booming twenties, he and his associates bought from thirty to forty million dollars' worth of properties, excluding his newspaper plants. By the time he died, these holdings had been reduced by the depression and thirteen years of reorganization and liquidation to a few parcels, hard to pick out from the protective camouflage of dummy corporations. All that remained of the Hearst empire, in fact, were newspaper properties, ranches, mines and timber acreages.

The fortune had taken a beating, worse than any other accumulation had been called upon to endure. How, then, could it survive, pass through a period of near disaster, and still remain at or near the $400,000,000 mark? The first and major reason was that Hearst's fortune had a long start in the pre-income-tax era. Another reason was that it reached its peak before the depression, and skillful management saved it thereafter. The nineteenth-century accumulators were not so lucky. They had no income tax, but the frequent financial panics of the century were extremely hard on accumulations of wealth.

Hearst would never have been in any financial trouble at all if he had not made one mistake, which proved to be nearly fatal. In the early twenties, when expansion was a religion in America, the lord of San Simeon spent thirty-five million dollars on his art collections and bought six more newspaper properties he did not need. That led to his first financial crisis, in 1924. The crisis was mitigated, by degrees, but it did not end until 1943, when he finally paid off in full the sixty-five million dollars' worth of bonds he began to float in 1924 to provide himself with working capital. Hearst himself guaranteed these bonds. It was his personal lawyer and intimate adviser, John Francis Neylan, a San Francisco attorney, who managed Hearst's affairs so that the publisher could make good on his guarantee. The key to his client's difficulties was well expressed by Burton Crane, in analyzing the situation for *The New York Times* after Hearst's death. "The attempt to hold on to everything for the sake of mere size proved unsuccessful," Crane remarked succinctly.

The climax to Hearst's troubles came in early 1937, when he tried to bail himself out by filing registration statements with the Securities and Exchange Commission for slightly more than thirty-five million dollars' worth of debentures on behalf of Hearst Publications and Hearst Magazines. Under SEC regulations, the Hearst issues were required to be placed on exhibition for twenty days before sale. During this period the agency was deluged with protests—from Paul Kern, Civil Service Commissioner of New York City; in a brief filed by the Labor Research Association; and even one from the American Legion, which until then had loved Hearst dearly.

Taken aback, Hearst deferred the issues and consulted in New York with an old friend, Clarence John Shearn, who had been one of his lawyers since 1900. The result of their conversation was a total capitulation on Hearst's part. The New York *American* was suspended, as the first move. Then, four days later, it was announced that Shearn had been made sole voting trustee for the next ten years of the ninety-five per cent of common stock Hearst owned in American Newspapers, Inc. Hearst retained the right to his earnings and to editorial control; the proposed debentures were withdrawn. This could only mean that Hearst had turned over the management of his finances to Shearn, and indirectly to the Chase Bank, which he also represented. Hearst was now to be an employee of his own publications, with his salary cut from $5,000,000 a year to $100,000 as head of Hearst Consolidated.

Shearn did what Hearst could not do: he sold, leased and merged Hearst properties. The initial moves he made in disposing of newspapers and services saved $5,000,000 a year; soon after, seven radio stations were sold for $1,215,000. Between 1937 and 1939, Shearn and his fellow executioners, a committee of seven Hearst executives, accounted for six newspapers sold or scrapped, one news service and one magazine sold or scrapped, and radio stations cut from ten to three.

There were more troubles and more selling, in a welter of stockholders' suits and rapid manipulations of the shuddering Hearst empire. The Ritz Tower was sold. The auctions of Hearst art took place. But when it was over Hearst still owned twenty daily newspapers, fifteen Sunday newspapers, twelve magazines, several minor movie interests, three radio stations, King Features, the *American Weekly*, his mines and assorted properties of varying value.

Other rehabilitators came to Hearst's aid. One was John W. Hanes, a Wall Street banker, former Undersecretary of

the Treasury and SEC Commissioner. His task was to simplify
the tangled mass of Hearst corporations. Clearing out the
furniture from one room in his home, he began to make little
stacks of papers, one for each corporation. When he finished,
he found that there were ninety-four corporations, each ow-
ing one another and any bank that would lend them money,
a total debt of $126,000,000. It took Hanes five years to do
what had to be done, but in the end he had reduced the
ninety-four to about a dozen. He hoped to do better eventually and shave the number to four. Hanes had also paid off
all but $4,000,000 of the bank loans.

By 1944, Hearst was able to resume control of his empire
in most respects. He found it reduced, but still the most substantial operation of its kind in the world, and from 1945 onward its separate parts all made money. One indication of
the general prosperity was that Hearst's salary was listed
among the ten highest in the United States in the years just
before his death. In 1946 it was $233,333, and in the follow-
ing year it was $300,000.

The worst that could have happened if there had been no
Neylan and Shearn, no management miracles, no rejuvenation, would have been a collapse, staggering to contemplate,
that would have reduced a large number of people to comparative poverty, but one that would have left Hearst in such
straitened circumstances that he would have been compelled
to subsist on a bare five or six million dollars.

When he died, in August 1951, and his body had been spir-
ited out of Miss Davies' house in Beverly Hills, to be given a
circumspect family funeral under Millicent's direction in San
Francisco, the 125 pages which constituted his will were filed
for probate in Superior Court only a few hours after he died.
The lawyers explained that haste was necessary to insure the
continuity of his empire's operation.

On the surface, the will contained no difficulties. Its chief provisions were to set up three trusts. One, for his wife, was to contain $6,000,000 worth of Hearst Corporation preferred, the income from this sum to be hers, besides an outright bequest of $1,500,000 cash to pay the taxes that would be due on the stock. The second trust was for the benefit of his five sons, and contained enough additional preferred stock in the corporation to provide an annual income of $150,000 which the sons might add to their already high incomes as Hearst executives. Into this trust also went a hundred shares of Hearst Corporation common, probably a controlling interest.

The remainder, a residuary trust, was to be for the usual "charitable, scientific, educational and public purposes." Hearst directed that a memorial be built to his "beloved mother" which would contain at least part of his art treasures, "for the public enjoyment." He directed further that the beneficiaries of this trust should be the Los Angeles Museum, which had already been given more than three million dollars' worth of art from his collection; the University of California, also a beneficiary while he was still alive; and the California Charities Foundation, a philanthropic organization he had set up previously. Into this foundation were to go the proceeds from the furniture, paintings, statuary and objects of art from Wyntoon, San Simeon and St. Donat's. His sons were named trustees of all three trusts.

There was a typical Hearst clause in the will, the mark of a true accumulator: "I request my executors and trustees . . . not to part with the ownership or control of any newspaper, magazine, feature service, news service, photographic service or periodical, either directly or by sale, or by exchange of the capital stock . . . unless it shall, in their opinion, be necessary or prudent to do so."

The most confusing part of the will, however, was its nine

codicils, running to sixty-eight pages of the manuscript. All but three were revoked in the final wording, but their effect was, first of all, to change an original trust arrangement which would have provided a single family trust in which Mrs. Hearst and the five sons would have shared. The first codicil would have given Marion the Beverly Hills home, but it was canceled by one dated a year later, meaning simply that she had been given the home under another arrangement. It was the provisions for Marion, not contained in the will or its codicils, which precipitated a legal quarrel that for a time threatened to turn the Hearst private life into a courtroom drama.

A trust fund dated November 5, 1950, had given Marion a lifetime income from 30,000 shares of Hearst Corporation preferred, the principal to revert to the sons upon her death. This was acceptable enough, but a few days after Hearst's death attorneys presented to his executors a document which more than made up for Marion's omission from the will. It was a voting trust agreement, stipulating that Miss Davies was to have sole voting power in the Hearst Corporation. The agreement pooled her 30,000 shares of preferred with the 170,000 shares owned by Hearst.

There was an immediate and peremptory response from the executors: "This document was never executed and therefore might just as well never have existed." On second thought, however, it was apparent that if a fight ensued the document might stand up in court. It had been the last of Hearst's shrewd acts and, as the estate lawyers undoubtedly thought, the shrewdest.

The executors were in an embarrassing position. They could not attack the voting agreement with public dignity by charging W.R. with incompetency, or by claiming undue influence. They could only hope to find a technical flaw.

Obviously a compromise was called for. John Hanes, who had done so much to straighten out Hearst's tangled affairs, was consulted and examined the voting trust agreement with trust specialists. He gave his opinion that the agreement was not testamentary in nature, and therefore was not covered by the laws concerning wills; it could not be attacked, he believed, except on grounds of incompetency. No one seriously believed that the executors would go so far as to discredit the Chief's good name.

While the outcome was awaited with anticipation in some quarters and dismay in others, the lawyers shuttled back and forth among the fifteen individuals and the representatives of two corporations who had to agree on a compromise. It was finally effected, and a joint announcement designed to pour oil in every direction was issued. The meat of it was contained in two paragraphs:

"Miss Davies has relinquished all rights she may have to act as voting trustee for the stock of the Hearst Corporation for the reason, among others, that there is question as to when her right to act as voting trustee thereunder would commence. This question would have to be clarified by long court proceedings which all parties deemed unnecessary and undesirable.

"Although a great deal of Miss Davies' time is devoted to her private interests and her numerous activities in charitable enterprises, through which she has become well known and well loved, the most prominent of which is the Marion Davies Foundation's children's clinic which has served approximately 12,000 children a year for the last fifteen years, Miss Davies will continue to render services in her capacity as official consultant and adviser to the Hearst Corporation and the newspapers and magazines which it publishes. Such services will include advice on motion picture and other amusement activities."

On the night her nephew, Charles Lederer, telephoned the news of the agreement to her, Marion was entertaining a few friends in the green-walled powder room at Beverly Hills, talking amiably while her future was being settled in the law offices. She had not met with any of W.R.'s sons or executives, nor had she even heard from them personally. Momentarily she must have felt isolated. Even the Los Angeles Hearst papers, which had been delivered every day by messenger while the old man was alive, had stopped abruptly on the day he died.

As she listened to Lederer on the telephone, Marion began to cry softly. "Thank God it's all over," she said. "Thank you, Charlie, thank you. I'm so happy it's over, so happy."

Hanging up, she went back to the easy chair and sprawled out in it. "Well, I've sold my power for a dollar a year," she said. "Maybe I was wrong, but it's all over."

Where had the power gone—and the money? Here the case of Hearst was different from those of the other accumulators. Multiple marriages and divorces had not fragmented his estate. He had left Marion a millionaire through gifts during his lifetime. His wife had always been well provided for, and the will left her a rich woman. The foundation took care of much of his art treasury. San Simeon became, some time after his death, a state historical monument, open in part to a ceaseless stream of awestruck tourists.

But the estate was in sound and thriving properties, managed by shrewd and able men. It could not be split up by his five sons except by extraordinary means, hardly worth speculating about. Among these inheritors, there were the usual many divorces but a surprising willingness to carry on in the image of the father—as newspaper entrepreneurs, that is. No human being could have perpetuated Hearst's unique image. One son, John, died after a particularly sad life. William Randolph, Jr., became publisher of the New York *Journal-American* and won a Pulitzer prize. His brothers, George and the twins David and Randolph, all came to be Hearst newspaper executives. As inheritors, the Hearst sons were satisfactory, by and large. Shadowed by the overpowering figure of their father, they nevertheless showed no hesitation about taking up the reins, even though the reins were also in the firm hands of several Hearst veterans who were taking no chances on valuable properties being lost.

While Hearst was alive, the sons displayed a normal reaction to what might have been considered their father's unusual domestic life. As youngsters they accepted Marion, without quite knowing what to call her, but as time went on it appears they drifted away from the ménage at San Simeon, and when their father died it was Mrs. Hearst to whom they turned, conspiring to put on the final appearance of family respectability.

William Randolph, Jr., became head of the family after his father's death, and for a time it appeared that this amiable, well-mannered inheritor preferred the night clubs and café society to the tough business of newspapering. But he devoted more and more time to the empire his father had left behind, which was helpful because it required, and still does, judicious management. Pruning and paring have been the order of the day, but Bill, Jr., has shown a willingness and an ability that could hardly have come to the surface while his father was alive.

Nothing or no one could have competed with Hearst; he was unique, in his remarkable blending of inheriting, accumulating and spending. W.R. was a man who put money in its place. He even managed to take some of it with him. His casket was the best that money could buy; it may have cost twenty thousand dollars.

Long before Hearst died, the era of the spenders had come to an end. It was a gaudy era, and provided endless columns of news, gossip and Sunday copy for the delectation of people who wanted to believe that all of society was like the scandalous goings-on retailed in the pages of Hearst's Sunday papers. The spenders may not have been the most important part of American inheritance, but they were indubitably the most interesting, as sin is always the winner in a contest for attention with virtue. The Rockefeller and Ford inheritors have done an impressive amount of good as inheritors, as we shall see, but the Dodges, the later Astors, the tobacco heirs, and the modern Vanderbilts are much more fun to read about.

The spending inheritors were selfish, and gay, and tragic, and often silly, but they had a flair about them. Whatever they did, they appealed to less fortunate Americans who saw them, no doubt, as people who were doing the things they would like to do themselves, much as they might deplore their manners and morals. History may record the solid accomplishments of the conservators and expanders, and the distributors of wealth for the benefit of mankind, but it is the spenders who will be remembered by an envious, even admiring, public.

$ *Three* $

CONSERVATORS AND

EXPANDERS

$ 9 $

The Great Conservators: Du Ponts

In any accounting of accumulators and inheritors, the Du Pont family of Delaware must stand apart from the others, as Hearst does, because they are unique among the rich families of America in several respects. They are, beyond any doubt, the greatest industrial family in America, and while their getting and spending may have followed basic patterns, the way of life they followed was so distinctively their own that they removed themselves from the main stream of American society and stood alone. The industry they founded was closely held within the family; Du Ponts tended to marry other Du Ponts for some time. When they married, they did not build cottages at Newport or Bar Harbor, but what they did build was truly representative of the family. In sum, they developed a technique of conservation that was truly their own.

Perhaps because it is a French family, an aura of romance surrounds the Du Ponts. Their history has been often recounted, but it may be useful to review some aspects of it here by way of contrast to the other families of great wealth. The contrast is often a sharp one.

"No privilege exists that is not inseparably bound to a duty," said the family founder, Pierre Samuel du Pont de Nemours, whom Thomas Jefferson called "the ablest man in France," a scholar and economist who translated Ariosto, advocated financial reforms, and wrote *A Philosophy of the Universe* while he was in jail during the French Revolution. None of the other accumulators in this country sprang from such stock, nor did they have the benefit of such further patriarchal admonitions as the first Pierre's: "May each generation of your descendants strive unceasingly to make the next generation better than his own." One hears Andrew Mellon's father's chill voice: "It's only greenhorns who enlist."

The manner of the family's establishment in America was in keeping with its nature. Victor Marie, Pierre's oldest son, came first as the tall, handsome attaché to the first French Legation, later serving as consul in Charleston and consul-general in Philadelphia. His brother, Eleuthère Irénée, was that combination so often found in genius, the romanticist inside the scientist. Irénée was a chemist of some note in a powder laboratory, but he was also capable, at twenty, of fighting two duels with a rival for the hand of his sixteen-year-old sweetheart, and successfully opposing his father, who did not favor the match.

Pierre's business having been suppressed during the French Revolution, the whole family decided to come to America and make a new start. Pierre, the patriarch; Victor and his wife and two children; Irénée, his wife and three children all set sail for America late in 1799, arriving off Newport on New Year's Day, 1800, shivering with cold and hungry, but ready to found the mighty industrial dynasty which today bears their name.

The means by which they contemplated establishing themselves in the New World were expressive of their personalities. Old Pierre, a political moderate, sought to found a colony he planned to call Pontiana, to which French refugees from anarchy might come. He went so far as to sell shares in it to Lafayette, Beaumarchais, Talleyrand and Rousseau, and talked of organizing a land company for his colony in the James River valley of Western Virginia, where he expected the colonists to farm, and to make pottery and glass. Jefferson attempted to talk him out of this idea, but it is said the fateful incident that not only ended the plan but created the family vocation was sheer chance. Irénée ran out of powder during a hunt and had to buy more to finish the day. The young powder expert thought the American product he purchased was priced too high for its poor quality, and conceived the idea of going into powder making.

That was an idea President Jefferson could approve, and he did after a conference with Irénée, suggesting that the plant be situated near Washington. Irénée, who was an excellent businessman along with his other attributes, surveyed the Washington terrain and found it worthless for his purposes. He bought a 95-acre farm on the Brandywine River, near Wilmington, and there, settling down with his family in a log cabin, he began building his powder mills. The colonization company his father had formed provided two thirds of his capital; his reward for directing the project was to be $1800 a year and a third of the profits. Victor joined him in the enterprise after a time.

It was a severe struggle, far worse in many respects than the establishment of most other industrial fortunes. Irénée, a tireless worker, had a constant battle with debt. Self-effacing, retiring, he had to fight against one reversal after another as the business strained to survive its first years. He saw his father die, the victim of a devastating fire which the old man helped to fight all night. In 1818 there occurred the first of many shattering explosions, and this time the victim was his wife, whose injuries made her an invalid for the rest of her life, and whom he tenderly nursed. Even his beloved brother, Victor, died, and Irénée was left alone.

When the Du Ponts are attacked as munitions makers who made their money out of war and suffering, it is often said that the War of 1812 gave them a start toward their blood-stained profits. Yet the War of 1812 might have had a different outcome if it had not been for Irénée Du Pont's mills. Veterans of the Revolution could recall how their cause was nearly lost at more than one point for lack of powder. Certainly the 750,000 pounds of gunpowder which the Du Ponts supplied from 1812 to 1814—and it was powder of high quality—was one of the decisive factors in that strange war fought over half a continent and decided by a naval battle on a lake.

It was true enough that the Du Ponts profited from the war, thereby saving the company, since they had been compelled to borrow and take every risk to expand the mills sufficiently to meet government orders. Their gross sales for 1811 had amounted to only $45,000, but in 1812, the first year of the war, the figure was $148,597.

Irénée's contemporaries surely did not think of him as a robber baron or a "merchant of death." At the time of his death from cholera in 1834, the Delaware *State Journal* observed that when the people learned "the loss of one so esteemed and so loved, each seemed to feel it a blow inflicted upon himself."

Three sons assumed the work and the small fortune that Irénée had left them. Alfred, the oldest son, took his responsibilities with the utmost seriousness. When he was only twelve, he knew the mills from one end to the other, understood the making of powder as well as anyone, and could call every workman in the establishment by name. When his father died, Alfred and his brothers, Henry and Alexis, came together to form the first partnership in the history of the company. It was three years after Irénée's death before this remarkable agreement was drawn up by Alfred Victor, who was then thirty-nine, and certainly no more unusual document has been seen in business history.

Under the new agreement the company was to have no officers. As eldest son, Alfred was senior partner—"a position much like that of the Old Man of tribal societies," one biographer put it. The property of the partners was to be communal, even the several hundred acres of property surrounding the mills. If a partner married, the others were to build him a house in which he could live rent free. Carriages and horses came from company-owned stables, whenever they were necessary. No partner was to draw a salary, but they could finance their personal needs from a cashbox, and each one was credited with his share of the profits. The brothers employed a single clerk in the office, who performed all the duties of bookkeeping and payrolling.

It was an agreement, strange though it might be, that proved satisfactory for sixty-two years. Probably no one else but Du Ponts could have made it work. One family characteristic that made it workable was the steady supply of able sons from generation to generation, and the admirable ability of Du Pont daughters to marry men who would be useful to the company.

Alfred retired as senior partner in 1850. His place was taken at once by the next oldest son, Henry, but it seemed as though the succession would be interrupted when, soon after Henry assumed control, young Alexis, the third brother, only forty-one, was killed in one of the explosions that periodically rocked the plant. But just as Alfred's oldest son, Irénée II, was ready to enter the partnership when his father retired, so now was his second son, Lammot, prepared to follow Alexis into the company.

The Civil War, coming upon the company at this juncture, again meant a tremendous boost in its production and its profits. Again the Du Ponts differed from most of the other accumulators, however. They not only provided a good part of the powder, but they sent some family representatives to fight. Henry's son, Henry Algernon, had gone to West Point and graduated at the head of his class, after which he plunged into the war with such enthusiasm and talent for battle that his Army career became one brevet after another for gallantry, until he achieved at last the Congressional Medal of Honor for extraordinary heroism at the Battle of Cedar Creek.

Another Du Pont hero in the war was Victor's son, Samuel Francis du Pont, one of the few family members who ever made a career outside it. This tall, handsome man exchanged a certain career in the company for an equally certain one in the Navy. He served brilliantly in the Mexican War, helped make the study that founded the Naval Academy and became its first superintendent, and as a commodore in the Civil War was in charge of naval operations south of the boundary between the Carolinas. He captured Port Royal, a Confederate stronghold, after five hours of bombardment, for which he was made a rear admiral. Then Admiral Du Pont went from one victory to another until he suffered a defeat in trying to reduce Fort Sumter and capture Charleston. Although it shared the responsibility for this loss, the Navy Department thereafter treated the admiral shabbily, notwithstanding that he immediately compensated for his defeat by capturing one of the war's principal naval prizes, the Confederate ironclad *Atlanta*. Admiral Du Pont asked to be relieved of his command, smarting under the Navy's treatment, and died soon after Appomattox. In 1882 a grateful Congress, seeking to give him belated but rightful honor, decreed that the intersection of two Washington streets should be named Du Pont Circle. Befitting its aristocratic name, the Circle became a fashionable place to live.

The other Du Ponts sometimes felt as though they, too, were living at the front. Confederate saboteurs were constantly trying to blow up the works, and succeeded in setting off several explosions, which killed a total of forty men. The sabotage was recognition by the enemy that the Du Ponts were a powerful factor on the Union side, as they had been in the War of 1812. The powder they made was of excellent quality, better than any their competitors were producing; it could be guaranteed to go off, which was more than could be said for some other merchants' products. Four million pounds of Du Pont explosives went into the struggle, yet the company was often short of fluid capital because the hard-pressed government could not always pay its bills.

Again, when the war was over, the Du Ponts heard themselves called accumulators of blood money, but no critic was heard to speculate on the outcome of the war if the company had not produced its four million pounds. In any case, the brothers and sons paid little attention to criticism; they were too busy providing explosives for an expanding nation that was building railroads, digging for gold and silver, clearing land for homesteads, and trying hard to exterminate buffalo, passenger pigeons and Indians. Du Pont profits increased with all this expansion, under the careful guidance of the senior partner, old Henry.

The thirty-nine years of Henry's reign were perhaps the most remarkable of any corporate management in the history of American business. Henry ran what might well be called a tight ship. There were never more than four men and a boy on his office staff during the entire period, and Henry answered all of his own correspondence with a quill pen—six thousand letters annually. His memory was phenomenal; he knew the name of every man on the payroll. More important, he carried on what had become a Du Pont tradition— the maintenance of an unusually close relationship between the family and its workers. While labor leaders might scoff at it, the fact was that through the worst times of industrial unrest at the end of the century, and after, there was a rapport between management and men not to be found in any other American company, with possibly one or two exceptions.

In 1880 the company opened up a new source of revenue as the result of young Lammot du Pont's ability as a chemist, and his skill in persuading old Henry that a new explosive called dynamite was the coming thing in blasting powder. Henry was reluctant, but early in 1880 the Repauno Chemical Company, a subsidiary, was organized with Lammot as president. The product was dynamite. In two years the plant was making 2000 pounds of it every day. Two years later a ton of it exploded at the Repauno Company, killing Lammot and five other people. Another young Du Pont, William, took his place and Repauno went on.

Smokeless powder was the next door the partners opened to further wealth, and while they were developing it they began to buy up competitors, large and small, until by 1899 they were operating a trust which controlled ninety-five per cent of gunpowder and ninety per cent of blasting powder made in America. Du Pont had grown to be a giant, in a land of giants.

Henry du Pont died at last in 1889, on his seventy-seventh birthday, after fifty-five years in business. Eugene, oldest member of the third generation, succeeded him. By this time the business of marrying cousins had begun to complicate family succession. As Marquis James, one of the family biographers, has noted, the Du Pont genealogy from 1800 to 1936 would fill a sheet thirty-six by thirty-eight inches, and it would be "as crisscrossed by matings of cousins as that of a European reigning house." Old Henry had been alarmed by this development, and at one point had tried to forbid them, the penalty being removal from the company. But the family failing was too prevalent. Eugene, who succeeded him, had married a cousin, and William, who followed Eugene, divorced one cousin to marry another.

Those family members who agreed with Henry that too many cousins in the Du Pont mix was not a good thing pointed to William's domestic troubles, the first such family discord to be aired publicly in the century the family had been in America. They considered it proof of the possible degeneration of the tribe. Eugene, as new head of the house, did what he could by announcing William's retirement from the company, and the appointment of Ethel du Pont's husband, Hamilton Barksdale, in his place. But it was no use. Cousin marryings went on, and in time the divorces came too.

One marriage outside the family that appeared doomed at the beginning of the courtship was the love of old Henry's nephew, Lammot, for Mary Belin, who was a quarter Jewish. But Henry, who remembered that Mary's grandfather had worked for the company in its early days, approved the match and no one else in the family dared protest. It was one of the happiest of Du Pont marriages, producing five sons, including three company presidents.

While Eugene du Pont was at the helm, the company became a corporation. Henry Algernon had urged the move when Henry died, arguing that the affairs of the concern had become much too complicated for the simple partnership under which it was operating. But there was little enthusiasm for the idea at first among the other family members, and it took a decade of discussion before Du Pont was chartered as a Delaware corporation in 1899.

Under Eugene's reign, too, the company developed a shock-proof explosive for big guns, bought out eleven other firms making competing products, and went on pyramiding the empire both at home and abroad, where cartel arrangements were made with European manufacturers of explosives.

With Eugene's death in 1902, an era came to a close in Du Pont history. It was as though a dividing line had been drawn between accumulators and inheritors, after a century of compiling the fortune and establishing it officially as one of the most powerful in America. Paradoxically, it appeared that the vigor of the line had run out. Francis G. and Alexis I., Eugene's brothers, were not in good health, nor was Charles I., the company treasurer. Colonel Henry, the Civil War hero and one of the ablest men in the family, was completely involved with politics. There were reasons why other Du Ponts were not eligible to take over direction of the family and the company.

In this crisis, the older members of the family concluded with regret that their best course was to sell the company to their largest competitor, Laflin and Rand. But now the family produced, as it always seemed to do, a new Du Pont to carry on. He was Alfred Irénée, the thirty-eight-year-old eldest son of the eldest son of the company's founder, a black-powder man who was working in the mill at the time, and had neither business experience nor large sums of cash. Nevertheless, it was Alfred who, at the crucial meeting of the board of directors, first moved that the company be sold to the highest bidder, and then quietly offered to buy it himself for twelve million dollars. No wonder that his offer, according to a company historian, "occasioned some surprise."

Where would he get the money? Alfred didn't say, but he asked for a week to raise it. The other directors, reluctant to see the company pass out of the family, agreed. Alfred turned at once to two of his cousins, Pierre and Thomas Coleman, and suggested that the three of them buy the company and rehabilitate it.

The key figure in this maneuver was Coleman. Alfred knew the technical side of the business, how to make powder; Pierre, a small, neat man, was a splendidly conservative manager; but Coleman, a huge figure of a man, six feet four and weighing two hundred and twenty pounds, was a born organizer and promoter, an outsize man with outsize ambitions and appetites. He knew nothing whatever about powder making, but he knew a good business deal when he saw one and the idea of buying the Du Pont company fascinated him. The price of his participation, he told Alfred, was a free hand in managing the corporation and a larger share of the acquired stock. They agreed.

Coleman's life until that moment had scarcely been without incident. The restless son of a restless father who had thought powder making a dull occupation, he had gone to two universities, Urbana (Ohio) and Massachusetts Institute of Technology, but had cared for neither and left M.I.T. to go back to Kentucky, where the family had settled, to work in his father's and uncle's coal mines. The owner's son was indistinguishable from the other workers. He worked shoulder to shoulder with them, played with them, fought with them, got drunk with them, and even joined the union—if the Knights of Labor could be called one. In time he could not avoid being made mine superintendent, but once in power, he proceeded to make Central City a model mining town, in total contrast to the shabby, miserable communities in other coal areas.

If Coleman showed his Du Pont ancestry in any way at all, it was to marry a cousin. Otherwise he continued to be restless, where all the others were stable. He gave up the coal business for steel and went to manage the Lorain Steel Mills, in Johnstown, but he brought in his cousin Pierre to run the plant while he went off to form a new company which would build streetcar lines in New Jersey, upstate New York and Alabama. He was successful in this venture, too, with Pierre as a conservative partner who was a nice counterbalance to Coleman's exuberance. Both men had a valuable ally in Pierre's secretary, young John Jacob Raskob, who had a brilliant mind and was devoted to his boss.

Obviously, Coleman was the Du Pont whom Alfred needed to keep the company in the family, and he had no objection to permitting him to take the leading role. His confidence was justified by what happened next, as Coleman executed one of the most extraordinary deals in business history. In little less than a month, and with an investment of only seven hundred dollars of his own money, he became president of the Du Pont Corporation and its largest stockholder as well, with $4,320,000 worth of shares in his name. One would have to go back to the exploits of Ryan and Gould to match that accomplishment.

Coleman had approached his task by taking an inventory of the Du Pont business, which showed it to be worth twice as much as the $12,000,000 Alfred had bid. As an inducement to later concessions, Coleman raised Alfred's offer to $15,-360,000, with the stipulation that payment would be made in a new company's securities rather than cash, thus removing the principal obstacle to the deal. Coleman, Alfred and Pierre would have to pay $2100 for twenty-one incorporators' shares in the new company they would form, which would then dissolve the old one and acquire its assets, after which payment would be made with $12,000,000 in four per cent purchase-money notes and $3,360,000 in stock. Notes and stock would go to the stockholders of the old company; the 86,400 shares remaining, worth $8,640,000, were to be divided among the three buyers as promoters' profits.

The new management took over from the presumably still dazed old one on March 1, 1902, with Coleman installed as president, Pierre as treasurer, and Alfred in charge of production. Raskob came in as Pierre's assistant. It was the kind of division of labor Alfred had envisioned and desired. He could supervise the product, being the only one of the three who understood powder making thoroughly, while Pierre watched the money and Coleman devoted his time and talents to making the company the United States Steel of the powder business.

Again, Coleman lived up to expectations. Laflin and Rand, instead of emerging as the happy buyers of the old company, found themselves absorbed by the new one in 1902, for four million dollars. Another two million absorbed the Moosic Powder Company, and in the following year a super holding company was formed, capitalized at fifty million. Stewart Holbrook summarizes three years of progress under Coleman and his cousins as follows: ". . . the Du Pont industrial empire had acquired more than one hundred corporations. It was making one hundred per cent of all military powders; and approximately seventy per cent of all other explosives consumed in the United States. The net returns of the company in 1904 were four million dollars. . . ."

At the peak of this astonishing success, a crisis of another kind struck the Du Ponts and split the family wide apart. The cause was the second divorce in the clan. Alfred, who was celebrated as one of the most stubborn, determined Du Ponts, decided to divorce his old-family, Bostonian wife, Bessie, and marry his secretary's wife, Alicia Bradford, who was his cousin. If he had announced he was going to change his name the news could hardly have caused more consternation. "The family will never stand for this," Coleman told him, and he was right. Although he had never given the time of day to tribal conventions before, Coleman suggested that Alfred sell his stock and remove himself physically from Delaware.

Instead, Alfred chose to fight, which was entirely in keeping with his character. Coleman would have no more to do with him, and Pierre, after hesitating for a while in his conservative way, sided with Coleman at last, leaving Alfred alone in the family. Other Du Ponts shunned him, too, and a whispering campaign of a scandalous kind began to be heard in Delaware, which Alfred acknowledged with bitterness by instituting a slander suit against his wife's aunt and her friend Mrs. Mary Thompson, the social leader of Wilmington.

It was a break that could not be repaired. Nor was it helped by the secondary scandal which erupted when Alfred's oldest daughter was sued for divorce by her husband, who charged adultery on the honeymoon. The charges were dropped only after Alfred's wife uttered her famous threat to "rip the hinges from many Delaware closets, Du Pont cabinets among them." The suit was amended thereafter to desertion.

While the family was divided irreparably from a social standpoint, it was still capable of standing together against outside attack, as it demonstrated when the inevitable antitrust suit was filed against it. After four years of litigation, the Circuit Court of Appeals found for the government, but it was a hollow victory for Teddy Roosevelt, who had counted on it as a major triumph for trust-busting. Du Pont had dissolved sixty corporations in the process of building its empire, and it was obviously impossible to restore this jigsaw puzzle to its component parts. The only alternative was for government and company to work out some plan of reorganization that would at least make a gesture in the direction of anti-monopoly. It was a tiny gesture, in the end. A small part of the company's assets were distributed among two new powder companies, Hercules and Atlas. Moreover, another government stipulation, that Du Pont should keep the entire smokeless powder business, tipped the final balance in the company's favor, with the First World War in the offing.

There was still no sign of victory for either side in the great moral war, however. For his Alicia, Alfred built an overpowering estate, Nemours, of white marble, with seventy-seven rooms and three hundred landscaped acres, enclosed by a nine-foot wall which Alfred remarked was intended "to keep out intruders, mainly of the name Du Pont." Only two Du Ponts, it was said, ever tried to pass the barrier, out of the hundreds of Alfred's kinfolk.

Nemours was surpassed among the twenty or so other Du Pont estates, most of them equal to anything the Astors or Vanderbilts possessed, only by Winterthur, in Christiana Hundred, New Castle County, Delaware. This historic castle, with its more than one hundred rooms, had been built by James Bidermann, the first Du Pont in-law, whose wife was the daughter of the original Irénée, but it was owned later by Henry du Pont, and Henry Francis, who lived in it until 1950. It is now one of the finest museums in the country, displaying in room after room perhaps the best collection of Americana extant.

Castles might keep the Du Ponts in their back yards socially, but the feud could not help erupting in the board room as time went on. Coleman and Pierre were determined that they would eventually move Alfred out of the company, but what also appeared to be happening was Pierre's gradual emergence as actual head of the corporation, from his position as chairman of the executive committee, while Coleman, as might be expected, moved on to other interests in his restless fashion. Both Alfred and Pierre, oddly enough, were alarmed from time to time by these excursions of Coleman's. It was the only thing they had in common after 1911, when Pierre, by an adroit maneuver labeled as "closer consolidation of authority in the manufacturing department," succeeded in removing Alfred as general manager, replacing him with Coleman's brother-in-law.

Coleman, in the meantime, was busy in New York City, the first Du Pont to appear there with business in mind. He built the McAlpin Hotel (now the Sheraton-Atlantic) in partnership with President Taft's brother, Charles P., and on the hostelry's twenty-first floor he established a New York rookery for himself, where he entertained a gay crowd, quite unlike Delaware. In 1913 he spent thirty million dollars in company with a syndicate to put up what was then the world's largest office structure, the Equitable Building.

Before it was finished Coleman went to the hospital for an intestinal operation, from which he made a slow recovery. He could not help to counter the sudden panic in the money market as the First World War began, nor could he be of any immediate help in the feud with Alfred. Alarmed, he wrote to Pierre and offered to sell his Du Pont holdings, as the largest stockholder.

There began a cat-and-mouse game among Coleman, Pierre, Alfred and William, who had also risen to prominence in the company. Coleman's offer was to be accepted, but there was a serious argument as to how much Du Pont stock was worth. For the first time Pierre demonstrated fully how practiced the conservative mind can become. He made a secret deal with Coleman, by which he and his associates bought out the senior Du Pont for fourteen million dollars, thus giving him working control of the company. Alfred and William learned of this transaction from the newspapers, along with some other Du Ponts who were equally ignorant of what Pierre had been up to.

Pierre then performed a feat of financial sleight of hand worthy of Coleman himself. In a few months he had reorganized the corporation into a new company with a capitalization of $240,000,000, so that in the exchange of stock he and his associates were able to quadruple their investment. By this time, too, he had succeeded in displacing Alfred both as a vice-president and as a member of the finance committee. Alfred was understandably bitter. Not that he was hurt financially—his income for the first half of 1916, reflecting heavy war orders, was nearly $4,000,000—but he resented deeply the conspiracy between Coleman and Pierre to oust him, the last and worst blow of the feud.

Alfred sought revenge, in the courts and out of them. With other family members, he brought suit against Pierre, charging breach of trust, but the case was lost in every court, and the Supreme Court refused to review it. Frustrated, Alfred turned the editorial guns of his newspaper, the Wilmington *Daily News,* which he had bought a few years earlier, against the triumphant figure of Coleman, who had recovered from illness and whose incessant ambition now urged him toward the White House.

For once Alfred was successful. The *News,* with the aid of a batch of smaller papers Alfred had formed into a chain, so discomfited Coleman that his political hopes were killed. Perhaps to his own surprise, Alfred found himself named to the seat at the Republican national convention which Coleman had sought.

Misfortune was still lying in wait for Alfred, however. His two children by Alicia had died in infancy, and the wife for whom he had fought so hard also died in 1920. He married again, a childhood sweetheart named Jessie Ball, of Ball's Neck, Virginia, a lady who established somewhat better relations with the family. But Alfred was sick of the battle. He moved to Florida to nurse his wounds but, being a Du Pont, he could not help making more money with new enterprises, so that when he died in 1935 his estate was estimated at nearly $33,000,000.

A substantial part of this fortune was profits from the First World War, when the company expanded its capacity from 8,000,000 to 500,000,000 pounds annually, making forty per cent of all explosives used by the Allies, and making for the stockholders a net profit during the war years of $237,-000,000, or four hundred and fifty-eight per cent dividends on the par value of Du Pont stock.

The war, indeed, produced so great a surplus in the corporation, something like $100,000,000, that a place had to be found to invest it, and John J. Raskob, now the company treasurer, found just the place. It was, of course, General Motors. Du Pont began to buy into the motor empire in 1915; by 1918, Raskob was chairman of G.M.'s financial committee, and two years later he succeeded in increasing the company's capitalization to 56,100,000 shares, with a ten-to-one split. Later, Pierre Du Pont served a term as G.M. president, utilizing his talents to tide it over the postwar depression, which he did with the help of J. P. Morgan & Co., who helped float a bond issue.

General Motors was the best investment the Du Pont Company ever made. In the first fifteen years it returned $250,000,-000 in dividends, and when Du Pont created a chemical empire, General Motors became its best customer. The company had begun experimenting with synthetic materials as early as 1906. By the end of World War I, it was in the burgeoning plastics business, and substantially in rayon manufacture as well. In 1924 the horizon was broadened to include cellophane, and soon after, G.M. formed the Ethyl Gasoline Corporation in company with Standard Oil of New Jersey, making a fuel for which the Du Ponts supplied tetraethyl lead.

Such giantism made an inviting target. When the unavoidable investigation of war profits occurred in 1935, the Du Ponts were once more accused of fattening themselves on blood, as they had been for a century and a half, although no one explained how the war could have been fought without explosives. The argument was that the Du Pont profits were excessive, which might have been debatable, but the "merchants of death" label which was fastened on the company by Senator Gerald P. Nye's investigating committee was as emotional as it was unrealistic. It was only a matter of six years before the government had to turn to the Du Ponts once again for the vital materials without which a war could not be fought.

Once more, inevitably, the profits were large, but the investment was larger. To supply government orders the company spent a billion dollars to build fifty-four plants, for which their net fee was only one-fifteenth of one per cent of the construction cost. Out of these plants came smokeless powder, at the rate of a ton a minute; parachute yarn, thirty-six million yards of it; and elements for the first atomic bomb.

By 1951, with the added industries resulting from wartime research and development, Du Pont could boast of a breathtaking operating investment of one and a half billion dollars. In these later years another generation of Du Ponts—the three brothers, Pierre, Irénée III and Lammot—ruled company and corporation affairs. It was not until 1940 that a non-Du Pont, Walter Carpenter, became president of the company. Crawford Greenewalt, who succeeded him in 1948, was a Du Pont by marriage, however, having entered the family by way of the last Irénée's daughter.

It is impossible to estimate the wealth of the Du Pont family today, simply because there are so many of them—at least sixteen hundred, and about a hundred more born every year. Seven generations of them have lived and inter-bred in feudal Delaware. Only a relative few are really rich, in present-day terms; many more are moderately well to do, and some have merely average incomes. The best guess of their aggregate wealth would be that it is no less than a billion dollars, and quite possibly twice as much.

The frustrated Alfred Irénée could not have been thinking of money, or of his family's superb talent for making it and conserving it, when he advised one of his cousins: "Never form a habit, good or bad. There is no such thing as a good habit. All habits impair will, initiative and free agency."

$ 10 $

Expansion in Chicago:
McCormicks and Fields

If there is an impression thus far in this chronicle that the accumulation of great wealth was a talent confined to the eastern United States, it can only be said that there is an inherent snobbery even in accumulating. No doubt about it, the great accumulators were Easterners, by the accidents of history and industrial geography. So provincial was their outlook that the inheritors of the wealth have been inclined to look upon Chicago money as somehow—well, *different,* and Chicago society as not quite.

Nothing in the history of accumulating supports this thesis. The Middle Western giants, most of whom were born in the East, came from poor families, like everyone else, and they were just as ruthless and relentless in the acquisition of money as their Eastern counterparts. Nor have their inheritors demonstrated, on the whole, any special abilities in handling the wealth entrusted to them. It would not be difficult to find spenders among them, but the Chicago mood is different. What may be spending in the East looks more like expansion in the Middle West, because the atmosphere is expansive. The getting and spending have been integral parts of a dynamism peculiar to Chicago.

Perhaps the best example of the Chicago syndrome is the McCormick family, that many-pronged and fascinating collection of human beings whose varying personalities have made an imprint on the nation as well as on their own city. The family's Scotch-Irish forebears migrated to America in 1735 in the persons of Thomas and Elizabeth McCormick, a young weaver and his wife, who settled on the frontier at Cumberland, Pennsylvania. The fifth son of this union, Robert, was the immediate progenitor of those McCormicks who have made so profound an impression on American life.

On a comparative basis, the family began to be rich with Robert, who always kept a weather eye toward improving his fortunes, and did so not only through the acquisition of property but by marrying well. His bride was Martha Sanderson, the daughter of a Scotch-Irish landowner who lived nearby. After the Revolution, in which Robert fought with distinction, these two moved to the Valley of Virginia, where they bought 450 acres and a log house. By 1800, Robert owned three slaves and eight horses, as well as a substantial amount of property, and was the second-ranking accumulator in the valley.

Robert's sixth child was a boy, who inherited his name and his acquisitive talents. In 1808 he married a girl named Mary Ann Hall, who brought a dowry of horses and cattle worth a thousand dollars, and infused the blood of still another Scotch-Irish clan into the deepening McCormick stream. This second Robert sired eight children, of whom two influenced family history. One of these, the first-born in 1809, was Cyrus Hall McCormick, who left an enduring monument to his name in the reaper he invented, accumulated an imposing fortune, and sired in turn a colorful branch of the line whose members Colonel Robert R. McCormick, late publisher of the Chicago *Tribune,* was said to call "the mad McCormicks." Robert's other son was William Sanderson McCormick, whose son Robert married into the Medill family and produced among his grandchildren the Colonel and Medill McCormick, a United States senator.

All these descendants were influenced by the dominating figure of Mary Ann, the second Robert's wife, who was called Polly. It was Polly who inspired her children to make a place for themselves in the world; it was she who set the standard of rich living which her grandchildren carried to the height of *fin de siècle* elegance in Chicago.

Polly was a proud woman, and her rich dowry soon made possible the kind of life she required. She liked to see the shimmer of the family silver and admire the peacocks as they strutted across the lawns of the country home which replaced the log house she had come to as a bride. In her handsome carriage she whipped her fine horses at a dashing speed along the rough country roads. She wore lovely dresses and ornamented herself in a way that inspired the gossip of poorer neighbors. Her ivy-covered home at Walnut Grove, overlooking the lush Virginia hills, was the scene of a good many gay parties.

Overshadowed by his wife, Robert McCormick was nevertheless an admired and respected man in his quiet way. He was honest and pious but, like so many good Calvinists, he did not let his religious tenets hamper his business. With one hand he took away his workers' liquor ration and with the other he sold homemade whiskey for twenty-five cents a gallon. Moreover, he had the business ability to double the size of his father's estate. The original McCormick estate flourished under his hand. He bought the 532-acre home farm from his aging father, who lived with him. By 1812 he owned four slaves and seven horses. He built the two-story red brick Walnut Grove house, sixty-five feet across and fifty feet deep, complete with a porch, a service wing and windows with white casements. Polly filled the eight rooms with splendid furniture, from the stores of Richmond and Lynchburg, designed to blend elegantly with the house's high wainscoting, carved wooden mantels and big fireplaces.

Robert was master of this house, and of workshops, barns, slave quarters and mills. His estate was self-sufficient. Its flax, hemp and sheep fed the busy spinning wheels and looms. Brine barrel and smokehouse were filled with meat from the farm's animals, and with such by-products as tallow for candles and oil for soap. Hides from slaughtered animals were tanned nearby and made into shoes and harness. The harvested grain was turned into flour at Robert's own gristmill, and into whiskey at his distillery. The fruit went into cider. He had a sawmill to cut up his own timber whenever he needed lumber. There was always more than enough stone for building and the limekiln. Robert turned out numerous inventions at the forge and anvil of his smithy, where Cyrus got his apprenticeship in invention. By 1830 the Walnut Grove estate contained about twelve hundred acres of land, nine slaves and eighteen horses.

If Cyrus McCormick had remained the quiet inventor he started out to be at Walnut Grove, he might never have precipitated the family into history, but money and fame made it possible for him to back up his political convictions. If he found himself in a fight, he quickly displayed the dominant McCormick family characteristic, an inability to admit that he might be wrong. When his Virginia conservatism came into conflict with expanding, radical Chicago the results were paradoxical; his political defeats were more than balanced by the mark he left upon the city's business and social life.

Cyrus was only fifteen when he invented a light cradle to help him compete with the grownups in the harvest fields of

Walnut Grove Farm. Seven years later he was demonstrating his first reaper at the famous public trial on a field near Steele's Tavern, Virginia.

In 1835 his father gave Cyrus a farm on South River, nine miles from Walnut Grove. In the following year the young man built an iron furnace in Augusta County and entered into a partnership with his father, meanwhile improving his reaper. Five years later he sold the furnace, as the result of losses in the panic of 1837. Both he and his father were heavily in debt. By that time, however, his reaper was beginning to sell, mostly because of Cyrus' own salesmanship and demonstrations.

The business began to expand in 1845. Cyrus had made connections with Backus Fitch & Co., of Brockport, New York, and with A. C. Brown, of Cincinnati, to sell reapers in upper New York State and Ohio. Within two more years he was able to enter into a partnership with C. M. Gray, of Chicago, for the sale of reapers, and established a factory on the north bank of the Chicago River, near its mouth. The plant was the marvel of its day, shown proudly to visitors by resident Chicagoans. Three stories high, the brick building was a hundred by thirty feet in ground area, and in it a steam engine operated saws, lathes, planing machines and grinding stones. Thirty-three men worked at these machines and the plant's six forges. In eight years the factory grew so rapidly that it had a daily capacity of forty machines; it built four thousand reapers in 1856.

Cyrus had pulled up his roots in 1847 and gone to Chicago to live. Two years later he sent for his brothers, William and Leander. While these men ran the plant and made the family a power in Chicago real estate, Cyrus himself was drawn into the political arena. As an old-school Presbyterian, he was against the Civil War. In his mind patriotism, party loyalty and his religion were inextricably entangled. He believed that the Union could not be preserved by force, and in January 1861 he predicted that failure to reach a compromise would mean "all the horrors of a civil war." Still, he shared Douglas' view that coercion was the next best thing if it was not possible to avoid the issue.

Denounced by the Chicago *Tribune,* which was a Republican organ and consequently favored war, Cyrus was defended by his brother William in a letter to a friend: "We have helped to build this city by hundreds of thousands & these Editors though strong politically are without body or soul substantially. . . . We are not secessionists by a good deal, but are for the South having her rights."

Cyrus fought his battle against war by buying the Chicago *Times,* transferring a Presbyterian monthly from St. Louis to Chicago, and endowing four professorships in the Presbyterian Theological Seminary of New Albany, Indiana, to guarantee its removal to Chicago, where he expected it to preach old-school anti-war doctrine. This removal led to a long fight within the church and the seminary. It came to a climax with the Chicago fire, which came at a moment when a fund-raising campaign to finance the institution was drawing to a successful close. Many of the pledges were, of course, instantly worthless. McCormick's unyielding character was never better demonstrated than in that moment. While his own factory burned he wrote out a check for forty-five thousand dollars. The fire reached the edge of the seminary grounds, but nearly all the buildings were saved. It brought victory to McCormick, because the seminary and church authorities realized there was only one man who could save them in their crisis.

Cyrus' views did not prevail ultimately either in the Presbyterian Church or in politics, but his powerful, willful personality nevertheless made him outstanding in a city full of strong men. His family created an era of elegance in Chicago society which has persisted into our own time, an era whose external evidences of wealth and privilege made a mockery of Cyrus' pronouncement: "I have throughout my life been opposed to all measures which tend to raise one class of American people upon the ruin of others." This was the man whose patriarchal home on the near North Side was surrounded by the stately Victorian dwellings of his family, so that the neighborhood around Rush and Erie streets came to be known as "McCormickville."

Cyrus' mansion, dominating McCormickville, was one of the great town houses of the Gilded Age. Remembering his comparatively humble Virginia birthplace, Cyrus determined that the home his wealth would build must be the equal of any built by Chicago tycoons of the seventies. The architects he engaged outdid themselves but, sadly, Cyrus lived to enjoy his hard-won splendor only five years.

The mistress of this house was Nancy ("Nettie") Fowler, of Jefferson County, New York, a sweet and gentle woman who sometimes bewildered her friends by her odd behavior, which appeared to be a characteristic of her son Harold. Nettie gave her husband seven children: Cyrus Hall, Jr., Mary Virginia, Robert Fowler, Anita, Alice, Harold Fowler, and Stanley. These were the inheritors of Cyrus' $200,000,000 fortune when he died in 1884, at seventy-five, still believing the Civil War could and should have been avoided, still the enemy of Presbyterian liberalism. At his death the family he had established was numbered among the first in Chicago and his business was one of the nation's leaders. These things may have compensated somewhat for the political failures of his life, and the stubborn resistance to change for which he paid so heavy a price.

On the whole, however, Cyrus was a successful man, who died admired and grieved by many people. In contrast, the life of his brother, William Sanderson McCormick, was a tragedy, a minute cameo of unhappiness in a setting of tremendous events. He would have liked to stay at Walnut Grove, which he inherited in 1847, and where he had settled down with the neighbor girl he married, Mary Ann Grigsby. But in 1848 Cyrus summoned both him and his brother Leander to Chicago.

The brothers discovered that Cyrus paid only modest salaries. Astutely, they invested what money they could in city houses and lots. At the plant, William soon took on numerous responsibilities, investing much of the company's money and acting in general as a buffer for Cyrus during the hectic war years. He was in general charge of the office, which had to handle a rapidly increasing flow of business. But he hated the confinement of an office. Constantly in his mind was the thought of the quiet and peace of his boyhood home.

Like Cyrus and many another McCormick before and after him, William could not relax. When he went hunting and fishing up in Wisconsin or Minnesota he took his business with him. After a long day at the office he went on working at home. Many times, after a sleepless night, he rose at dawn and hurried away without breakfast to test a mower while the dew still remained on the grass. He had helped materially to develop a good McCormick mower.

William and Mary Ann were soon accepted by the inner circle of Chicago society, as he quickly accumulated a small fortune, but this recognition brought him no pleasure. He was only Chicagoan enough to acquire the tremendous faith every citizen had in the city's future. Aside from that, he was an unhappy, transplanted Southern farmer who lived mostly for the time he could retire to Virginia again.

The pressures on William were many and severe. His political convictions—he shared Cyrus' feeling about the war—and his nostalgia for the Virginia valley oppressed his mind. His body suffered from too much desk work. An additional factor, and again a paradoxical one for him, was the heavy responsibility of investing the reaper factory's money. With Leander's help these investments made the family a power in Chicago real estate, but they only added to William's worries.

Cyrus was the conservative member of the family in these matters. As early as 1862, William wanted to invest $1,000,000 in real estate; his brother said no. By the end of the war, McCormick properties in Chicago were valued at nearly that figure and paid off about $100,000 a year annually in rents. The brothers owned at least two dozen stores. Chicago regarded the three men as the city's biggest landlords, and even their bitterest enemies, the Abolitionists, could not help respecting them for what they had done to push the city's expanding fortunes.

But it was all too much for William. His health began to fail as early as 1856, and by 1865 he was in the State Hospital for the Insane at Jacksonville, Illinois, where he died within a few weeks, of "dysentery of a typhoid nature," according to his doctor. As he lay dying, the mistakes of his life were more than ever in his mind. His brain cleared and he called upon his brothers to realize that money-making was folly. With almost the last breath he drew, on September 27, 1865, he urged Cyrus and Leander to "forbear one another in love."

William's death was a blow to Cyrus. They had been closer than any other members of the family. But neither Cyrus nor Leander paid much attention to their brother's admonition, and William's last earthly effort ended in futility. The two surviving brothers quarreled sharply over the administration of the estate.

Leander was unlike both Cyrus and William. Less interested in business, and presumably less talented in it, he preferred his art collection and his interest in science, which led him to donate an observatory to the University of Virginia. These interests he bequeathed to his sons, Leander Hamilton, who dropped his first name most of the time, and Robert Hall McCormick.

Hamilton was one of the most versatile of all McCormicks. Born in Chicago in 1859, he graduated from Amherst in 1881 and studied law at Columbia, after which he took up architecture. In his lifetime he dabbled in invention, sculpturing and art collecting. His hundred or so inventions included airplanes, an aerial torpedo, motorcycles and a watch that recorded time all over the world. His art collection contained fine examples of the early English and old Dutch schools.

He married Constance Plummer, of Canterbury, England, in 1887 and the $125,000 mansion he built for her became the center of Chicago society. Their dinners were famous events. Hamilton and his wife did not stay long in this luxury, however. They moved to England about 1900 and did not come back until shortly after the outbreak of the First World War. While they were abroad, living in London for the most part, the two collected pictures, bronzes, enamels, statuary, armor and old furniture, most of which they brought back to Chicago and installed in their residence.

Hamilton's brother, Robert Hall, was also much more interested in collecting art than in adding to the family fortune. He lived in still another famed McCormick mansion, at the northwest corner of Rush and Erie streets. It did not have an impressive exterior, like Hamilton's mansion, but inside there was not only the customary luxury but one of the country's largest and most expensive private collections of art, mostly of the English school and including Constable, Van Dyck,

Gainsborough, Herring, Hogarth, Holbein, Jannsen, Raeburn, Romney and Watts.

Four years after the Great Fire, Robert moved into his three-and-a-half-story residence, where he lived for forty-two years until he died in 1917 at the age of seventy. The mistress of the place was Sarah Lord Day McCormick, daughter of a noted New York attorney. Like her sister-in-law, Sarah was an outstanding hostess who entertained an imposing list of great names from Chicago and the nation.

The unlucky William, who had died yearning for Virginia and disdaining money, left a son who surpassed Leander's sons in distinction. Robert Sanderson McCormick married Katharine Medill, daughter of the Chicago *Tribune's* editor, Joseph Medill, who had attacked his father and the whole McCormick clan so violently. Robert was one of the few McCormicks not interested in Chicago. He became the first American Ambassador to Austria-Hungary, and later Ambassador to Russia, during the Russo-Japanese War.

Of the three brothers, however, it was Cyrus who had the most interesting inheritors. They ranged from Cyrus, Jr., to Harold Fowler, and a wider range would be difficult to find. Cyrus, Jr., was a man who took the business his father had founded with the utmost seriousness. Reserved and a hard worker, he was president of the company by the time he was twenty-five; it was then the largest of its kind in the world. It was Cyrus, Jr., who persuaded J. P. Morgan to underwrite the formation of the International Harvester Company in 1902, of which he became president. Thus Cyrus both expanded and conserved his father's great fortune, preserving it against the assaults of other members of the family. He first married the daughter of a Massachusetts sea captain, was married a second time, to his secretary, and died in 1936.

The contrast between him and his brother, Harold Fowler,

was marked. Harold is described in the official records as a manufacturer and capitalist, but he devoted considerable time to lighter occupations. Harold had no more than graduated from Princeton in 1896 when he married in November the amazing Edith Rockefeller, daughter of the financier. Edith had been educated by private tutors, had lived abroad and was interested in just about everything. The marriage was unostentatious. It took place in a New York hotel and was followed by a wedding trip to Europe.

Harold and Edith did not come to Chicago until several years after they married, and when they did they settled in a magnificent home at 1000 Lake Shore Drive. It was rumored persistently that the bride's father had bought the place and given it to the couple as a wedding present, but Edith denied it.

She ascended, nearly at once, to the tottering throne which was slipping away from Mrs. Potter Palmer, long acknowledged as the queen of Chicago society, but now frequently absent from the city. The new queen reigned until her death in 1932.

Her incredible castle on the Drive had turrets, an arched entrance and wide stone steps; it was protected by a highly ornamental grillwork iron gate. In the years before the First World War, Edith held court there and raised her three children, Muriel, Mathilde and Fowler. She also installed the objects of art which placed her among the world's foremost collectors. In the huge reception hall, called the Empire Room, she entertained such royal personages as Queen Marie of Rumania in 1926, and Prince William of Sweden in the following year. Royalty walked in this room on the Emperor's carpet, a rug which cost $125,000, had been made in Persia six hundred years before and had once been the property of Peter the Great.

There were art treasures everywhere in the house: gilded chairs given by Napoleon to the Princess Pauline Borghese, a rug internationally known for its beauty, a private library of first editions and other literary rarities, a collection of old lace surpassed only by the Vatican's, and priceless jewels.

Edith had a nervous breakdown in 1913. The illness stimulated an already extraordinary interest in herself, and she went to Switzerland to study psychology under Jung for eight years. When she came back to Chicago a young Swiss architect named Edwin Krenn accompanied her, and shortly afterward, in 1921, she divorced Harold, charging desertion.

When Edith died at the age of fifty-nine, they opened the gray stone house on the Drive and placed her body in state in the Empire Room. The coffin was surrounded by Claude Pernet roses, her favorite flowers.

She left more than a financial legacy. Edith, for all her eccentricities, had used some of her money for worthy purposes. With her husband she was a founder of the John Mc-Cormick Institution for Infectious Diseases, established in memory of their first son, John, who died in infancy of scarlet fever. Antitoxin to treat the disease was developed in this institution. In addition Edith was an original promoter of civic opera in Chicago, a founder of the Chicago Zoological Gardens, and a patroness of opera in English.

When the experts got around to cataloguing her possessions at 1000 Lake Shore Drive, they were amazed by the endless quantity of antiques and rare porcelains, silver and first editions crammed into every corner of the mansion. But the place was, they agreed, overdone. The dining room was paneled in dark wood and filled with ornately carved furniture. With appalling lack of taste, the owner had priceless Chinese vases made into lamps, surmounted by fringed shades. Edith was not of McCormick blood, but she had one dominant

McCormick family characteristic: she loved to collect things.

Meanwhile, Harold pursued his eccentric way. He married Ganna Walska, the Polish opera star, a year after his divorce. To achieve this union, so the story goes, he resorted to the then popular Steinach operation, a gland rejuvenation process alleged to restore sexual vigor to aging men. But there appeared to be little mutual rejuvenation in the marriage. Madame Walska never achieved her desire to sing opera in Chicago. She retired to Europe and lived there most of the time until 1931, when Harold divorced her on a charge of desertion. He had one more try at matrimony. In 1938, in his sixty-sixth year, he married Adah Wilson, his nurse and former attendant.

Harold's business career was full of titles: executive posts in the International Harvester Company, director of the First National Bank, trustee of the University of Chicago, the McCormick Theological Seminary (which Cyrus had founded) and the Chicago Orchestral Association, and director of the Chicago Civic Opera Company. He belonged to ten of the right clubs. Harold died in 1941 in Beverly Hills, California, of a cerebral hemorrhage, aged sixty-nine. *The New York Times* obituary noted solemnly that he was "a talented amateur" musician who often entertained his friends by whistling difficult classical pieces. What was left of his $7,500,000 estate (a comparatively small McCormick fortune), after half of it had been taken by taxes, went to Adah and the three children.

His brothers and sisters were not nearly so well known, and one is scarcely spoken of at all. Robert and Alice died in infancy. Mary Virginia, who was said to be a woman of rather strange behavior, died in the early forties, leaving an estate estimated at $13,000,000. Anita, who became Mrs. Emmons Blaine, also had numerous eccentricities of dress and behavior, but she was an extremely generous inheritor, who was devoted to charity and employed three secretaries to give away her money to worthy causes. She was so selfless in this endeavor that she neglected her own appearance and never dressed in accordance with her wealth and position.

The greatest expander of all the McCormicks, however, was Robert Rutherford, son of Robert Sanderson and Katharine Medill, who became publisher of the Chicago *Tribune*. Until his death in 1955 he was the voice of Middle West isolationism, a man who was not interested in the McCormick fortune or in wealth itself, but one who was profoundly in love with his own opinions, one of the great egotists of his generation. The newspaper he built, for all its McCormick-like eccentricities, political malpractice and sheer fatuity, was nevertheless a journalistic model in other respects, sheltering at various times a long and distinguished list of Chicago newspapermen and women. Along with Hearst, McCormick was the only publisher of any consequence who practiced nineteenth-century personal journalism in this century.

There is no reason to rehearse the rights and wrongs of his controversial life in these pages, but it should be noted that his ability as a businessman, which was generally overlooked in the uproar over his politics, resulted in a formidable expansion of the McCormick fortune. For the Colonel had a talent for accumulating that would undoubtedly have made him a fortune in any other business, but with wealth already behind him and one of the most prosperous newspaper properties in the nation handed to him on a platter, it was inevitable that he should materially increase his assets.

How much they increased is difficult to determine, because the Tribune Company has always been extremely reticent about disclosing the details of its corporate structure or its ledger books. But the company itself, when all its assets are added up—the *Tribune;* the New York *Daily News,* founded by McCormick's cousin, Joseph Patterson; radio and television in Chicago; paper mills; steamships to carry the paper; and various other properties—must be worth, at a rough estimate, well over $100,000,000, possibly twice that amount. The original capital of the Tribune Company was $200,000. In seventy-three years it appreciated more than $38,400,000—an eloquent argument for single-family control.

No one knows how much money Colonel McCormick made from the company, although it is certain that, under its rules, his stock in it could not be inherited but had to be returned after his death. It is equally certain that there were no divorcing children to fragment the fortune and spend it extravagantly. He was married twice, both times to women who divorced their husbands for him, but he had no children by either one. Thus, except for what his widow inherited, and what went to various institutions in his beloved Chicago— the new McCormick Plaza, a vast exhibition center on the lake front, is a memorial to him—it must be assumed that the remainder, in Tribune Company stock, reverted to that many-tentacled octopus and is currently enriching the heirs of Captain Joseph Patterson and his sister Eleanor, late publisher of the late Washington *Times-Herald*, who were the other principal stockholders.

By an odd circumstance, the only major challenge McCormick faced in his publishing career came from the grandson and great-grandson of another noted Chicago accumulator, who also started out in a completely different line. This was, of course, Marshall Field I, who founded the famous department store bearing his name and accumulated the fortune that the Marshall Fields III and IV used to confront the *Tribune* successfully.

The first Marshall Field has been dismissed by some liberals as a hardheaded titan of the old school whose economic misdeeds were later undone. This estimate is based on the fact that the man who made the fortune allied himself in name, if not always in deed, with those ruthless defenders of wealth who symbolize the tyranny against which the labor heroes of the late 1800's struggled on the bloody battlegrounds of the Midwest. In reality, Field I was important and necessary to his times; his social actions, however wrong some of them may have been, were understandably motivated, and the estate he created was, on the whole, an honorable one.

He followed a traditional path, beginning as a farm boy in Conway, Massachusetts, and started his career clerking in a general store, whose proprietor made one of the most profound mistakes in judging another human being ever recorded when he told young Field's father, "John, your boy Marsh is a well-meaning boy, but he'll never learn to keep store in a thousand years. You'd better put him back on the farm."

Instead, he served a five-year apprenticeship at a dry-goods store in Pittsfield, where he began to demonstrate that encyclopedic knowledge of stock and special way with customers which were to guarantee him success. He was diffident and shy, with a normal youthful bashfulness so exaggerated that few people were attracted to him. Yet he was painstaking, courteous, considerate and eager, and these qualities endeared him to the customers. With his associates in and out of the store he was reticent. That was the mold in which he remained for the rest of his life. Those who worked closely at his side for years in the great institution he built respected and admired him, but they could not give him love and affection. As the father's religion had been hard work, the son's was success.

On a late fall afternoon in 1856 the proprietor of the Pittsfield store did him what he plainly considered the unprecedented honor of proposing to take him in as a partner, but that was the moment young Marshall, only twenty-two, chose to break the news that he intended to go west and make his own fortune. Like a Horatio Alger hero, he walked the plank sidewalks of booming Chicago until he went to work for Cooley, Wadsworth and Co., wondering if he hadn't made a mistake by not trying to work for the rival firm of Potter Palmer.

His salary for the first year was four hundred dollars, but he saved half of it by sleeping in the store and buying no new clothes except some overalls. He worked eighteen hours a day, and as he had done in Pittsfield, he acquired almost at once a thorough knowledge of the merchandise, and made friends with the out-of-town buyers. By 1860 he was able to buy a junior partnership and to move from the store into the Metropolitan Hotel, at the corner of Randolph and Wells streets.

Soon after, he married Nannie Douglas Scott, the twenty-three-year-old daughter of an Ironton, Ohio, ironmaster. Nannie was pretty and delicate, a well-turned product of Miss Willard's School for Young Ladies, in Troy, New York. Field's courtship of her was the single impulsive act of his life. He lived in happy anticipation until a fashionable wedding bound Nannie to him and he had set her up in a house at 306 Michigan Avenue, whereupon he immediately plunged again into his business career. No record exists of what happened to Nannie after this event, except the formal record of a woman moving in society, but it is possible to deduce that she found being married to a man like Field something less than what the romantic circumstances of her betrothal had led her to expect.

But the bridegroom resumed his career with a new zest, and was soon buried in it to the exclusion of everything human in his life. By the time he was thirty-nine he was already worth about thirty thousand dollars, an embryo fortune he had acquired in just seven years. All the classic virtues were present in this hard-working, modest young man. He neither drank nor smoked; he did not associate with the young rake-hells who constituted Chicago's younger set; and he shunned the gambling element. Yet he was not above dropping into a saloon when he could meet buyers by doing so.

Two courses were open to him. He could get a job with Potter Palmer, whose store he so much admired, or he could establish one of his own. Looking about for capital, he approached Cyrus McCormick with an offer to enter into partnership. William urged his brother to forsake the "grain gamblers" and join the "quiet, gentlemanly capitalists" of the dry-goods business, to the extent of a $200,000 investment, but Cyrus, who regarded William as a dreamer, refused to have anything to do with such an arrangement.

Field was disappointed, but early in 1865 he learned that Palmer had decided to retire from active work in the store, and went to him with a proposition to buy a part interest. Palmer sold him one and at the same time took in Levi Leiter of the Cooley store to form the new firm of Field, Palmer and Leiter, with a capitalization of $600,000. Field could afford it, because the Civil War boom had doubled his personal fortune. In eight years he had risen from a clerk's job at four hundred a year to become the head of a successful business, in which his interest was $260,000. He was thirty years old, and his career had only begun.

By 1867, Field was ready for two more significant steps. Palmer, turning his attention to real estate, sold his share in the store to Field and Leiter, who now owned about two thirds of the entire capital stock. Fashioning the new firm of Field, Leiter and Co., Field took into the business his two brothers, Joseph and Henry. The articles of copartnership,

dated January 1, 1867, were written in longhand. Of a $1,200,-
000 capitalization, Marshall and Levi Leiter were to furnish
$400,000 each, and the other four partners $100,000 each.
Something of the return these lesser partners got on their
money can be determined from the case of Henry Field, who
died twenty-three years later and left an estate of $2,000,000.
Joseph Field remained in the firm until his death in 1914.

The second step Field took in 1867 was to back George
Pullman in the formation of the Pullman Palace Car Co. It
was his first excursion into the business world beyond the
bounds of merchandising, and it could hardly have been a
more profitable one.

Field had been in the new store only two years before he
took the final step in the creation of his empire. He foresaw
uninterrupted years of growing prosperity if he could have
unimpeded control of the business. The only obstacle was
Levi Leiter. From long association, Field knew that the most
effective way of dealing with Levi was to confront him suddenly, and so he remarked abruptly one day: "Levi, I've concluded that it's time we part."

Leiter was startled and would have made some reply, but
his partner went on smoothly, in his calm, dry voice:

"Here's my proposition. I'll name a figure that will cover a
half interest here, and at which either of us may buy or sell
the business. I'll give you first choice—buy or sell."

The idea seemed so obviously fair that Levi agreed at once.
Field named the figure. It was so low that Leiter decided immediately to buy, but he cannily asked for time to consider,
as his partner knew he would, and Field gave him twenty-
four hours. In that period Levi discovered something that
Field had foreseen: none of the key men in the organization
wanted to stay in the company if Field were going to leave it.
Field had made the price low purposely and now he held Levi

to their bargain. If Leiter would not buy at the agreed figure, Field would—and he did. By this piece of Yankee horse trading, Field got rid of his partner at a handsome profit.

Field felt well satisfied with himself as he signed the papers dissolving the partnership. Now it would be Marshall Field and Company, and he experienced a sense of completion as he realized that at forty-seven he was one of the richest men in America, director of one of the nation's leading business houses—in brief, a success.

The store that Field built, like the builder himself, reached its full blooming in the nineties. More than three thousand employees swarmed over the thirteen acres of floor space in the wholesale store by 1893, and the retail store now covered all but one small corner of the State Street block. Besides the goods he bought from the usual sources, supplies came from factories scattered everywhere in the country, all bought or built by Field; still other plants were under contract to sell him everything they produced. The store had offices in Paris and in other strategic European capitals.

The flow of money in expanding Chicago was making it increasingly a luxury market. Its newly rich men began collecting things, indiscriminately for the most part, but a few with excellent taste. Their wives, many of them accustomed to shopping in London and Paris, Vienna and Rome, knew what to buy when they were at home in Chicago, and Marshall Field knew what to sell them. The business was never in debt, as most other stores were at one time or another, because of Field's devotion to the debt-free dollar.

Field moved his employees about like checkers on a board, without the least regard for them as human beings, but he could not believe that this was wrong because he conceived of it as his right as an employer. According to his own lights, he treated his employees well—and he did, indeed, by the standards of that day—but he also believed that the men and women employed by him and his fellows were treated as well as they deserved, and if they objected, they were always free to work elsewhere. Consequently the whole concept of trade unionism was deeply offensive to him. "The customer is always right," the slogan Field made famous, was suspended if someone prominent in the labor movement entered the store, even if he came only to make a purchase. Before he could state his errand, he was ushered firmly from the premises.

It was the founding of the University of Chicago that brought Field out of the shell of self-sufficiency and began to make of him a man who could understand the importance and satisfaction of translating wealth into enduring public service institutions. Eventually, after considerable prodding, he gave twenty-five acres of land on which to build the university, and that gift was the decisive factor in securing the remaining funds needed. A donation from a man like Field was enough to start a wave of support.

Once he grasped the concept of philanthropic giving, Field began to be more accessible. He gave another $100,000 to the university in 1892. In the following year he was approached to help found a natural history museum, using the collections at the Columbian Exposition as a nucleus. He gave a million dollars and his name to the now famous Field Museum. His will bequeathed it $8,000,000 more, added to a total of $2,000,000 given in his lifetime.

After that it came easy. In 1898 he contributed $136,000 to a joint gift with Rockefeller of a site for an athletic field at the university, making his total gifts to the institution a sum of $361,000, thus placing him among the twelve largest benefactors.

In 1899, having fitted out Chicago with a university, a museum and no one knew how many other minor appurtenances, Field decided that he should do something for his home town. He suggested to the startled village officials of Conway that he give them a free library, a proposition almost overwhelming to a community that had been trying to support a makeshift kind of library for nearly eighty years. Field visited Conway and took a landscape architect with him, chose the site, hired a leading firm of architects to design the building, and the cornerstone was laid on the Fourth of July, 1900. At the dedication ceremony, July 13, 1901, Field appeared with his two sisters and several friends, and made a brief presentation speech. It was, he said, the first public address he had ever given. The gift had been made in memory of his father and mother, and it had cost him $200,000. As he meditated upon the classic Greek design of Field Memorial Library on its dedication day, there is little doubt that the aging merchant felt his money had never been better spent.

Looking back over his first decade of giving, from 1890 to nearly 1901, Field estimated that he had contributed about $2,500,000 to various causes. The transformation in that side of his character had resulted in great service to his community; it is equally certain that it had drawn Field out of himself and made him, to some extent, a human part of the world he lived in. Of course he did not become less remote and dignified, to any appreciable degree, nor did he alter his business code an iota, but at least he was aware that there were other uses for money than the simple accumulation of it. After years of taking, he knew at last the joy of giving.

He called in his nephew Stanley in 1905 and declared he was making a will different in several important particulars from the one he had made the year before. The first will had named only four charitable and public service institutions in Chicago as recipients of bequests; now he made out a much longer list, and the amounts were not miserly. As for the

museum, even the eight million dollars he had previously decided to bequeath it would not be enough, he declared, and
so he had determined to double the bequest, the second half
of it to be used for maintenance.

These were not belated gestures made in the imminence of
death, although Field's time on earth had only a few more
days to run. At this late hour he had simply come to realize
fully what money could do in the world besides buying position and privilege. It was the final irony of his life that death
cut short his beneficent intentions before they could be carried out.

Field had given nearly all his time and energy to the creation of his empire. He had little left for a life of his own. The
logical result was an emptiness that engulfed him in the last
decade of his life, when there were no more worlds to conquer
and all that remained was to safeguard the money he had
made. A close acquaintance, describing those ten years, called
them "the epitome of loneliness." Almost desperately he
grasped for the love and affection that the pursuit of money
had always denied him.

Nannie had been lost in that pursuit. She had become little
more than a social fixture in his home and the dutiful mother
of his children. After the Fire, she had gone to Europe, osten-
sibly for her health, and gradually spent more and more of
her time abroad, until she died in Nice, in 1896.

Now Field was completely alone in his great mansion on
Prairie Avenue. Ethel, his daughter, had married Arthur
Magie Tree and gone to live in England. Later they were divorced and she married a dashing British Navy officer, Captain (later Admiral) David Beatty.

Field's other offspring, Marshall Field II, was a figure as
pathetic as his mother. Any young man growing up in the
shadow of such a father would have had to be an exception-

A gay quartet of Vanderbilts watches the start of the America's Cup races from the New York Yacht Club landing in Newport. Mrs. Cornelius Vanderbilt III (second from right) is flanked by her son, Cornelius, Jr. (IV), and her daughter, Mrs. Henry G. Davis, 3rd. Cornelius's wife is at left.

Mr. and Mrs. George Gould being rowed out to their yacht by crewmen of Mr. Gould's private navy.

TOP: *The epitome of inheritors' boredom: Mr. and Mrs. William K. Vanderbilt, recently arrived in Miami on their yacht* Ara, *watch the races at Hialeah.*

BOTTOM: *Scarlett O'Hara fails to move John Jacob Astor VI at the premiere of* Gone With The Wind. *With him was his first wife (one of five—or six), the former Ellen "Tuckie" French.*

TOP: *The fabled Chicago residence of Potter Palmer, pioneer Chicago merchant. In this medieval splendor, his wife reigned as queen of Chicago society for decades.*

BOTTOM: *Marble House, summer cottage of Mrs. Oliver Hazard Perry Belmont, at Newport. She had acquired it as Alva Vanderbilt, William K.'s wife.*

Underwood and Underwood

A trio of Belmonts at the opening of the racing season in Belmont Park. From left to right: Mrs. Perry Belmont, Perry Belmont and August Belmont.

The estate of Henry Morrison Flagler, built with Rockefeller and Florida real estate money, in Palm Beach.

Brown Broth

A flight of Goulds embarking for Europe. From left to right: Kingdon Gould, Edith Gould, Mrs. George Jay Gould, Gloria Gould, George Jay Gould, Jr., George Jay Gould and Jay Gould, Jr.

Father and son, John D. Rockefeller, Senior and Junior, not long before the founder's death.

At the time Congress dared to investigate him in 1912, J. P. Morgan, Sr. (center) arrives with his son, J. P. Morgan, Jr., and his daughter, Mrs. Satterlee, at the hearing in Washington.

At the Yale-Harvard races in New London, Conn., a gay couple from 871 Fifth Avenue, Mr. and Mrs. Cornelius Vanderbilt Whitney.

Marshall Field III and his third wife, Ruth Pruyn Phipps, at the races at Jamaica, where his Tintagel nosed out Seabiscuit in the third race.

This is Mrs. George Gould.

The Fragonard Room in Henry Clay Frick's mansion on Fifth Avenue, now a museum. The room was considered a triumph of the uninhibited decorator's art.

Biltmore, the estate of George W. Vanderbilt, near Asheville, North Carolina, regarded at the time it was built as the finest country home in America.

ally strong personality to emerge as an individual. Young Field never had a chance. His father had made what seemed like all the money in the world; he was already a legendary figure. His son had nothing to look forward to but a life of complete subservience and service to a business he had had no part in creating. It is understandable that Field II grew to have a profound loathing for any kind of business. From a study of the available evidence, it appears certain that he suffered from a neurosis. In those days he was simply put down as a queer one who had failed to take advantage of his opportunities, and his father quite naturally had little sympathy or patience with a boy who showed no interest whatever in business.

The young man drifted off to Harvard in 1889, not because he wanted an education but because there seemed nothing else to do. Not long after, he met and married Albertine Huck, daughter of a Chicago brewer. He took his dark and lovely bride to England, thinking perhaps to escape the stultifying atmosphere of Prairie Avenue. They leased an estate near Ethel's, in Leamington, Warwickshire, and lived there most of the year, spending only a few months in Chicago. Albertine bore him four children: Marshall, who died in infancy; Marshall III, Henry and Gwendolin.

Field the founder enjoyed playing with his grandchildren whenever he visited them, but he was enjoying a new interest in Chicago, an entirely platonic affair with the beautiful wife of his neighbor, Arthur J. Caton. He had known her for thirty years, but their friendship had blossomed anew in these later, more relaxed years. Then abruptly their relationship changed in November 1904, when Arthur Caton died suddenly in the Waldorf-Astoria, and Delia Caton became a widow at fifty. In the summer of 1905 he proposed, and the wedding was set for September 5, eighteen days after his seventy-first birthday.

They were married in Westminster Abbey on a gray morning, before a distinguished group of witnesses, including Ambassador Whitelaw Reid and Ethel Field, who cried at the end of the ceremony. Returning to Chicago, the Fields made their only public appearance in that city, at the annual horse show, before a series of disasters struck the man who seemed rejuvenated and reclaimed.

The first tragedy was the suicide of Marshall II, which became a major scandal because the family tried to pass it off as an accidental shooting, thus giving the gossipers and Field's enemies an opportunity to circulate rumors so thoroughly that some of them are sworn to as truth until the present day, although there is incontrovertible proof that young Field did indeed end his life. It was a terrible blow to his father, who really loved the boy, although it was not in his nature to show it or to comprehend how his position and personality had shadowed his son's life.

When Field II's widow recovered somewhat from her grief, she made a statement which indicated that she well understood the tragedy of her husband's life. "American wealth is too often a curse," she said. "I want it to be the means of the greatest blessing to my sons, the means of fulfillment of the highest patriotic ambitions. I should like to see them grow up into politicians, for then they would, it seems to me, employ their wealth to the greatest good for their countrymen."

Mrs. Field undertook to fulfill this ideal in a rather peculiar way. Soon after the funeral she removed her offspring to England, where she bought a fine London house at 2 Carleton Terrace and entered the three children in English schools.

Back in Chicago, Field could not seem to recover from the shock of his son's death, or from the bitter fight with photographers and reporters which had gone on for three days before young Field died of his self-inflicted wound, an invasion of his privacy the elder Field could not understand, and which drove him to impotent rage. His health began to slip and shortly after New Year's Day, 1906, he came down with a bad cold. On January 17 he died of pneumonia. When reporters begged his wife, widowed again so soon, for Field's last words, she kept the old man's faith to the end. "Mr. Field's last words were for me and not for the world," she said.

When Field's will was filed, it proved to be approximately 22,000 words long, the most comprehensive such document the court had ever recorded. It was the handiwork of William Beale, a corporation lawyer whose specialty was drawing up for rich clients wills which could be guaranteed to withstand the efforts of disappointed relatives to break them. In Field's case, instructed to draw up an airtight will, he overdid it. A tide of public feeling welled up against its terms, and the resulting pressure forced changes in the state and federal inheritance tax laws. At that, the will showed that Field had not taken the time to make changes after his son's death.

There were several attempts to break it. When Henry Field, Marshall III's brother, died in 1917, there was some dispute about who should inherit what part of his $40,000,000 share of the Field Trust. The will had to be construed and the court ruled that Marshall III was entitled to the income from this share, as well as that from his own $60,000,000 portion. To the nine law firms representing the five parties involved, fees amounting to $960,000 were allowed by the Circuit Court.

The meat of the will was in the directions for the residuary trust. Summarizing these unusual provisions, a writer for *World's Work* noted in a March 1906 article that the bulk of the estate was left to the two grandsons, who would not come into personal possession of it until they were fifty, and "by that time they will have had such experience as men of fortune as to be unlikely to dissipate the vast wealth they will then become possessed of. If the estate is conservatively managed in the meantime, it will then be among the largest private fortunes in the world; and its owners will be men of fixed habits and of large experience." The article went on to speculate as to whether people a century later would consider Field's plan wise. According to the old theory, said the writer, great fortunes did not remain in the family for more than two generations, but in the new dispensation, more and more families might have "the rare quality of conserving great wealth."

Time did not deal kindly with Field I's plan that his grandsons, at fifty, would carry on the conservative management of the estate in the manner prescribed by the economic rituals of his day. Henry did not live long enough to become a major inheritor, and Field III, by the time he was fifty, had ideas about how to spend a fortune that would certainly have shocked his grandfather. In a little less than four decades the concept of the use of wealth had changed in a way that would probably have seemed incomprehensible to the accumulator of the Field fortune.

In spite of the great care with which it was drawn, Field's will was eventually flouted in more ways than one by the individuality of the inheritors. The merchant left his Prairie Avenue mansion to Marshall II, but Delia acquired it by the default of young Field's death. She lived there for a few years with her niece. In the early 1900's, however, she left the house in charge of a caretaker and housekeeper and moved permanently to Washington. The fine old mansion forthwith lapsed into a state of melancholy decay, in which condition it passed to Marshall III when Mrs. Field died in 1937. By that time it had ceased to have anything more than historical interest, and Field deeded it to the Association of Arts and Industries, with the understanding that it be used as an industrial school.

Before that occurred, however, the house had a moment of remembered glory in May 1936, when a covey of young Chicago socialites borrowed it for an 1885 ball. For one night the place glittered with the grandeur it had once known, as the guests, dressed in period costumes, paraded up and down the splendid circular staircase and danced beneath the magnificent chandeliers. Then the splendor vanished forever, and with that night passed the last visible remembrance of the life Marshall Field had created from the mud and struggle of early Chicago.

Marshall Field III, the chief inheritor of the Field fortune, was aptly summarized by *The New Yorker* magazine in 1943 as "a socially conscious man who is lousy with dough and is trying to make the best of it in a changing world." As an open combatant on the field of ideas, Field had to endure a kind of treatment spared his fellow millionaires, who fought for *their* ideas behind a screen of lobbies, associations and public relations counseling. Field also suffered the peculiar kind of public contempt reserved for idealists, a contempt enhanced by the fact that he had the money to do something about his convictions.

At the beginning, however, he had to do something about himself. For Marshall III grew up with severe psychic handicaps. There was, first, the suicide of his father; he was old enough at the time to understand what had happened, and had heard the fatal shot as he played downstairs. Even before that, his doting grandfather and possessive mother had taken the place of his melancholy and ailing father. To have a beloved grandfather and a father die within two months would have been enough in themselves to wreck another man's psychic life, and it did not leave Field unmarked. Then too, at twelve he was the richest boy in the United States, with a three-fifths interest in his grandfather's estate, then in the neighborhood of $130,000,000. Youngsters with far less money had translated their prospective inheritances into worthless, empty lives.

Field later believed that what saved him was his mother's removal to England, and his education there. He got his more liberal ideas, he said, from a most unlikely place—Eton. By the time he was called upon to take over the trusteeship of the Field estate in 1914, he was prepared for it, and he had some idea of how to spend the money. He met a pleasant New York girl, Evelyn Marshall, on the way over from England on the *Lusitania,* and they were married a year later. Field was now a handsome, athletic man, a thorough gentleman—no longer the shy, ill, buffeted youngster he had been when he left America twelve years before.

For a time he interested himself in investment banking, after the First World War, but in the twenties he succumbed to the glittering life of the rich. He had a Long Island country place, Caumsett, a 1750-acre estate much like those he had seen in England. He had a racing stable, went pheasant hunting, and played hard at a half dozen other sports. His wife, meanwhile, presented him with three children, Marshall Field IV, Barbara and Bettine. Then, in 1930, there was the inevitable divorce, with a settlement likely to give a lawyer indigestion. Evelyn got a $3,000,000 town house and approximately $1,000,000 a year. Undaunted, Field married again in the same month he got the divorce, this time Audrey James Coats, a goddaughter of Edward VII and widow of Captain Dudley Coats. They were married in London and honeymooned on an African safari.

Audrey was a restless girl. The Fields went hunting in England and yachting on the Mediterranean with the international set; they rehabilitated an ancient Virginia plantation to its ante-bellum splendor, and once they even leased a ranch in Wyoming for a single house party. These preoccupations went on in the slowly darkening world of the thirties, while Field grew more and more uncomfortable and discontented with his life. It surprised no one, including Field, when Audrey went to Reno in 1934 and lived in the same villa that Evelyn had inhabited while she waited for her divorce.

A year after his second divorce Field turned to psychoanalysis as a sensible means of straightening out his life. There was a good deal of nonsense circulated about this event by his enemies. The truth was that Field undertook psychoanalysis because he felt, and accurately, that there must be something wrong with him if he could not make either of his marriages stick. This was a tribute to Field's intelligence, because on all sides of him he saw the men and women of his social class making and breaking marriages casually. If their extroverted minds were troubled by this lack of emotional stability, they showed few signs of it. To Field, however, his unsuccessful marriages were the major portion of an increasingly doubtful picture of himself that his naturally introspective nature was showing him.

After analysis by the late Dr. Gregory Zilboorg, Field was a new man who could utter a truism like, "Mere possession of wealth is not in itself creative," and understand its implications. He was beginning to realize how creative wealth could be; his life was beginning to take on form and purpose. Moreover, Zilboorg had helped him clear away a quantity of emotional deadwood in his life. He was no longer puzzled and disturbed by the failure of his marriages, and he had learned to accept the psychic conditions imposed upon him by his childhood.

His first step was to get out of the investment banking business, which he had entered more out of a sense of duty than because he enjoyed it. Next he married Ruth Pruyn Phipps,

Ogden Phipps's ex-wife, in 1936, a marriage which proved to be singularly happy. For the first time in his existence, Field had a happy domestic life and he turned to other matters with a clear mind.

The first matter he turned to was the establishment of the experimental newspaper *PM*, in which Field got into the newspaper business with both feet, although he modestly refrained from playing the role of publisher. He became, indeed, perhaps the only publisher in this country ever to take responsibility for a paper over which he deliberately exercised no control. That paradoxical state of affairs occurred because of Field's notion that he could learn to swim without getting his feet wet. Readily confessing his ignorance of the newspaper business, he proposed to let others do the work while he studied the results. It was enough for the moment, in his estimation, that he should make a New York liberal newspaper possible, without entering the battle personally.

The result of his rigidly observed non-interference policy was very nearly disastrous to him. He took a large share of the blame for all the sins, real and imaginary, of the paper he had thought would be a daring success, and after he became sole owner he saw the newspaper *PM* become the journalistic whipping boy of the forties.

It sometimes startled Field to observe the profoundly irritating effect his first journalistic child had on so many different kinds of people. *PM* was all things to its enemies. To the professional anti-Stalinists it was a classic example of the Communist wrecking crew's work. To conservative businessmen it was proof of what happened when a wealthy man deserted his class. To all orthodox practitioners of the profession it was a shocking example of lamentable unorthodoxy. To other publishers it became in time a comforting reassurance that adless newspapers do not succeed. In brief, *PM* annoyed more people than had any other newspaper since the days of James Gordon Bennett's *Herald*.

PM eventually took advertising, but nothing could save it from the general indifference of the audience to which it was addressed. It is the sad history of all liberal publications that in terms of circulation they are betrayed by the very people who are called upon to support them.

Soon after he started *PM* in 1940, Field turned to orthodox journalism in Chicago with the publication of the Chicago *Sun*. Where he had made the mistake with *PM* of entrusting all the responsibility to one man, Ralph Ingersoll, whose brain child *PM* had been, he entrusted the *Sun* to several men, extremely able newspapermen who still could not come up with the circulation formula needed to compete with such solidly entrenched opposition as the *Tribune*. Drastic measures were taken eventually. The *Sun* went tabloid and bought the Chicago *Times* in 1947, making it an around-the-clock publication. In 1959 the *Sun-Times* bought the Chicago *Daily News* from John S. Knight, and the *Tribune* countered by purchasing the *Herald-American* from Hearst, giving it the unlikely new name of *Chicago's American*, and reducing Chicago to a two-publisher city.

There were two major results of Marshall Field III's excursion into journalism. One was the reduction of the family fortune by at least five million dollars; no one knows exactly how much was actually invested in the two papers before *PM* ceased publication and the *Sun-Times* began to make money. The other was the providing of a career for Marshall Field IV, who prefers to be called Marshall Field, Jr.

When Field III died in 1956, his son was already virtually in full control of the Field properties. Field, Jr., a man remarkably like his great-grandfather in many respects, proved to have the first Field's cold, steady judgment, an ability to assess other people accurately, and an essentially conservative temper which found him disagreeing publicly with his father in the columns of the *Sun-Times* over the presidential candidates of 1952.

Combating difficulties of every variety and seriousness, Field, Jr., has turned out in the end to be the kind of man needed by the estate's interests. Coming into a position of tremendous responsibility before he was forty, he has survived a sea of troubles and emerged as the first member of the family since Field I to qualify as an accumulator. Thus the Fields have come full cycle.

There has been some trimming of the Field interests, but they still include the estate itself, with its real estate and stock-and-bond activities; Field Enterprises, including the World Book Encyclopedia and four radio stations, as well as the newspapers; and the Field Foundation, which Field III set up in 1940 as a directive agency for Field philanthropies.

Field the founder left to his inheritors an inheritance of about $125,000,000, after taxes. In approximate figures, $50,-000,000 has gone into stocks and bonds and real estate; another $50,000,000 is in various philanthropies, trust funds for Field III's five children and Field, Jr.'s five, and the Field Foundation; and about $25,000,000 in the communications properties. A formidable array of lawyers and other experts help to administer this estate.

The figures can be only approximate because of the constantly shifting value of properties, and the trimming and paring which takes place from time to time. Comparatively little of the estate is in fluid capital; it is symptomatic of the times that Field, Jr., could not today afford to write checks for large sums to aid causes, good or bad, as his father and great-grandfather could. Nevertheless, while Marshall Field I's fortune has not been expanded in a financial sense, the money has been used in an expansive way, and the estate the founder handed down has remained relatively intact and held within the family, unlike so many others.

The man who made the fortune lived honorably according to his lights, but he lived by the ideals of a predominantly acquisitive society. The man entrusted with spending the fortune proved himself to be one of the few inheritors who was conscious that the old order had changed, and who attempted to insure the democracy of the new one. His son, it appears, has successfully constructed a bridge between both worlds.

11

Conservation in Philadelphia and Pittsburgh:
Drexels, Mellons, Phippses, Fricks

The word "conservation" pairs naturally with the place names "Philadelphia" and "Pittsburgh." There is nothing of New York glitter or Chicago dynamism about these two old Pennsylvania cities, which are more often the subject of bad jokes than synonyms for inherited wealth.

To anyone who comes within proximity of society in either city, however, it is apparent that their wealth is like a feudal system, closely held within a few families and socially impregnable. In this respect Philadelphia is much like Boston, with which it is often compared, and its old families have conserved their wealth in the same way.

Of all the Philadelphia families, it is the Drexels who have come to represent the city in the public consciousness, although some might argue for the Biddles. Both families have a tradition of public service which has made them well known, but the Drexels, probably through their family connections with the Morgans, have been better known.

The family's founder was Francis Martin Drexel, who migrated to Philadelphia from the Austrian Tyrol and set himself up as an artist, painting portraits of city notables and giving lessons in art. It was as difficult for artists to earn a living in the early nineteenth century as at any other moment in history, and Francis, casting an eye about a city celebrated in its day for the close attention of its citizens to money-making, concluded that he would be far better off as a stockbroker. He began modestly in Louisville, Kentucky, in 1837, but moved the following year to Philadelphia, where he opened the firm which became noted all over the world as Drexel and Company. When the gold rush occurred, he added to his fortune through the operation of banks in the West. No doubt he would have gone on making money to an even more advanced age, but a railroad train struck and killed him when he was seventy-two. He left two sons to finish the accumulating.

One of the sons was Joseph William Drexel, who gave his portion of the inherited estate the kind of conservation that only a man capable of inviting J. P. Morgan to join him in business could give it. He married into another old Philadelphia family when he took Lucy Wharton as his bride, and thereafter divided his time between his Philadelphia and New York interests, but especially New York. Besides directing the powerful firm of Drexel, Morgan & Co., he was also a director of eleven banks and acted as a kind of liaison between the financiers of Philadelphia and New York, and between the financial institutions of these strongholds and their counterparts in Europe.

But Joseph had inherited more from his father than financial ability. From his boyhood he shared Francis' interest in languages, art and music, and he had constructive ideas about the uses of money. Much in the manner of Andrew Carnegie, he withdrew entirely from business in 1876 so that he could devote himself to philanthropy, and to various public and artistic activities. The result was a series of superb collections. One was a music library. Another consisted of important manuscripts and autographs. Etchings constituted still another. All of these were bequeathed to the Lenox Library and the Metropolitan Museum, of which he was a director. He was also president of the Philharmonic Society.

Joseph was equipped with a healthy social conscience. It disturbed him to see wealth in the midst of poverty, although it was a common American paradox of the century, and he conducted investigations of public health conditions, of the unemployed, and of poor people generally, particularly families of men in prison. A good part of his money was spent for the relief of these people.

The hope he saw for them was one so many other reformers have shared. If the poor could only be removed from city slums and transported back to the land, he thought, they would be far better off. Apparently it did not occur to him to do something about the conditions which had produced the slums. Instead, he fostered a movement to buy substantial pieces of acreage—what would now be called a subdivision— and to set up on them five-room houses, which would be sold at cost on easy terms to the deserving poor. Nothing much came of the idea before Joseph died at fifty-five, leaving a substantial fortune to his inheritors, who had other ideas of how to use it.

His brother Anthony was far more interested in business, and began working in his father's office when he was only thirteen. What education he had was obtained there and at home, but he learned enough to become a member of the firm at twenty-one, and to take over as chief developer of its interests after his father died. The subsequent early death of Joseph gave him full control of the company, which he exercised not only in the firm's banking activities but also in Philadelphia real estate, where his dealings added materially to the Drexel wealth.

Taking up where his father had stopped on the housing problem, he proceeded along more conventional lines and with much more success in providing better living conditions for Philadelphia workers. More adventurous than the other Drexels, he branched out into fields far from banking and became owner of the Philadelphia *Public Ledger,* a publication which was to take a substantial slice out of Cyrus H. K. Curtis' wealth. This venture led to his aid in founding the Home for Aged Printers at Colorado Springs. His special philanthropy, however, when the hospitals, churches and other institutions were cared for, was industrial education. Drexel Institute, in Philadelphia, stands as a monument to this interest. Anthony gave more than three million dollars to found and sustain it.

Some indication of the kind of man Anthony Drexel was can be seen in the fact that he was a member in good standing of the Union League, even influential in its affairs, yet the Institute he founded was declared open to people of any religion, sex, race or social class. That was the way he wanted it, conservative Republican businessman though he was.

The Drexel inheritors in this century took their accumulation of nearly $100,000,000 and conserved it with care, undoubtedly expanding it as well, but what it may be today is not known, so carefully has the money been handled. These inheritors are the kind who do not get into the newspapers, are not involved in extravagances and manipulations which are likely to get them into trouble, have a low divorce rate and are practically never touched by scandal.

The only other Philadelphia fortune to compare with Drexel money is the one accumulated by Cyrus H. K. Curtis, which was augmented through the marriage of his daughter to Edward Bok, the noted editor of the *Ladies' Home Journal.* The Curtis Publishing Company, which then included the *Saturday Evening Post, Ladies' Home Journal* and the *Country*

Gentleman, returned to its owner during his lifetime an estimated $174,000,000, and presumably went on swelling the fortunes of Cyrus' inheritors after his death in 1933. Like the Drexels' fortune, it has been carefully conserved.

Much the same situation has prevailed in Pittsburgh. The chief inheritor of Andrew Mellon's millions, his son Paul (Ailsa, his sister, had become Mrs. David Bruce), did not pretend to the financial genius his father possessed. He was, he said, more like his Irish mother, Nora McMullen, although he had none of the bitterness toward making money that made poor Nora exclaim in her divorce statement: ". . . Always new plans, bigger plans for more dollars, bigger dollars, dollars that robbed him and his family of the time he could have devoted far more profitably to a mere, 'Thank God, we are living.'"

Paul enjoyed his inheritance, especially the part of it that went into his Rockaby Stables, to which he devoted much of his time after Choate and Yale; and there were abortive attempts in other directions. He was content to entrust the management of the fortune to his cousin, Richard King Mellon, the son of his father's brother Richard, who had been carefully trained for the job.

After going to school at Culver Military Academy and Princeton, Richard K. started in traditional fashion, regardless of the fact that times had changed since his father's day, as a messenger boy in the Mellon National Bank. Carefully following the pattern, he rose to the management of the Mellon interests that his father and uncle had intended for him from the beginning. He even married a banker's daughter in 1936, the widowed Constance Prosser, whose father was Seward Prosser, at that time board chairman of the Bankers Trust Company.

As a Mellon, Richard K. displayed none of the family's well-known shyness about publicity, but fortunately most of it had to do with his efforts to rescue Pittsburgh from smog and urban decay, a civic enterprise in which he was one of the prime movers. A hard worker, he proved to be exactly the kind of Mellon needed to conserve the immense Mellon fortune.

In Pittsburgh, the Phippses have always ranked next to the Mellons, not only socially but in the size of their fortune, which is not as monumental but has been estimated at more than a half billion, certainly one of the largest in the country.

Henry Phipps followed the Philadelphia-Pittsburgh pattern of cautious conservatism, probably the natural result of having been born in one city and making his money in the other. One supposes that Henry would have been a very rich man in any case, but at the same time it is fascinating to speculate what his life would have been like if his neighbors in Allegheny City, Pennsylvania, to which his family moved from Philadelphia, had been other than the Carnegie family. Both families were poor at the time. Henry's father, a master shoemaker (as Carnegie's grandfather had been), helped his neighbors by giving Andrew's mother four dollars a week to bind shoes for him. Ties were close between the families, but it was some time before the two sons came together. While young Carnegie was learning the telegraph business, Henry Phipps was equally remote from steel in the jewelry store where he began work at thirteen, and then as clerk for a merchandise dealer.

Once he got into business at seventeen, as office boy for Dilworth & Bidwell, who were Pittsburgh agents for the Du Ponts and sold iron and spikes on the side, his way upward held true to course, in the manner of other accumulators. First clerk, then bookkeeper, next a silent partner in another firm, manufacturing scales, into which he bought with a one-sixth interest, costing him a borrowed eight hundred dollars. This was the company that joined Carnegie after the Civil War in the formation of the Union Iron Mills. Thus the paths of the two neighbor boys came together, not to separate again until both retired in 1901.

Phipps has been described as crafty, cautious and close-mouthed. In that he was an ideal Carnegie partner, because the steel business demanded those qualities. But he was also highly resistant to change, and in that he was not like Carnegie at all. This quality and his extreme caution prevented him from being anything but a money man. He wanted nothing except his income from the iron industry, and he contributed nothing to that industry except sound financial management. To the business of making steel he made what appears to be an entirely characteristic contribution, the discovery of how to use a waste product, scale.

It is hardly surprising that Phipps made more money than Carnegie himself, but if his philanthropies were not in the grand manner of his partner, they at least were directed toward the same humanitarian ends. A lover of parks, he decorated those in Allegheny and Pittsburgh with playgrounds, conservatories, reading rooms and public baths. These were his first gifts. What he really wanted to do with his money was to give it to help combat tuberculosis and mental illness, but it was typical of his nature that he would not do so until he had studied for some time what was being done in these fields, and at first he did no more than to make certain anonymous contributions. He even made an investigative trip to Europe before he would commit himself to any large-scale philanthropy.

When he did, however, he was generous. In 1903 he established in Philadelphia the Henry Phipps Institute for the

Study, Treatment and Prevention of Tuberculosis, later a part of the University of Pennsylvania, and two years later he founded in Baltimore the Phipps Tuberculosis Dispensary, at the Johns Hopkins. At this hospital he met Dr. William H. Welch, a distinguished figure in the study of mental disease, and after much consultation with him, he founded at the hospital the Henry Phipps Psychiatric Clinic, which was opened in 1913. Emulating the Drexels, Phipps also investigated housing, especially in New York City, where he gave a million dollars to put up new tenement houses.

His marriage to Anne Childs Shaffer, daughter of a Pittsburgh manufacturer, gave him five inheritors, three sons and two daughters. The third generation of Phippses demonstrated the usual watering-down process—not of wealth, because it was so large as to be nearly unassailable, like Mellon's, but of business ability. Henry's grandsons were twice as well known as he, although not for making money. Hubert and Michael Phipps and Raymond and Winston Guest were among the best polo players in the country. The Phipps family members and their associates who continued in business made substantial gains in the family fortune by far-reaching real estate operations through a Phipps-owned corporation, Bessemer Industries, which contrived to gobble up valuable properties from Long Island to Florida.

One family member, Lawrence C. Phipps, retired when he was thirty-nine from the money-making of Pittsburgh and fled to Colorado, where he became the nation's richest senator. Cleveland Amory describes his son, Lawrence C. Phipps, Jr., as "Master of Foxhounds of one of the most unusual hunts in the world—the Arapahoe. Meeting at Highland Ranch, on the Phipps estate, the Phipps hounds hunt, not fox, but coyote."

Old Henry lived to see some of these wild departures from

conservative Pittsburgh accumulation. An extremely well-preserved man, perhaps the result of his lifelong caution, he lived to be nearly ninety-one before he died in 1930 at his home, Bonnie Blink, in Great Neck, Long Island. What he thought of his grandsons and the general disposition of the Phipps fortune is, unfortunately, not recorded. Comparing his own with other dynasties, however, he had little to worry about. Henry had conserved too well.

As a final example of Pittsburgh conservation, the Frick family will do as well as any to demonstrate how strongly the pattern has persisted. Henry Clay Frick's fortune did not compare with that of Phipps or Carnegie, his partners in the Carnegie Steel Company, but in some ways he was the strongest of the three, an accumulator as hard as the product, although he was a slight man who had indigestion and rheumatism all his life. He was a born conservationist, with a considerable talent for it.

Frick was a farm boy from Westmoreland County, Pennsylvania, who was doing chores on his father's farm when he was only eight. His schooling was limited to thirty months snatched during the winter when there was no work on the farm. For a while he worked in his uncle's store, for which the pay was his board and the opportunity to sleep on the counter.

But Henry Clay Frick had a good deal of the determination which had been a characteristic of the Whig Party leader for whom he had been named. He got a job with his grandfather, at a thousand dollars a year, in the distillery the old man owned, known down to the present generation for the splendid product it produced, Old Overholt. While he made liquor, Henry looked about the countryside for opportunities and found one in the new business of making coke. With a few associates, he began at twenty-one to build and operate coke ovens in the nearby Connellsville coke region.

Seeking to buy coal land, he went to another hard man, Judge Thomas Mellon, of Pittsburgh, and got an initial loan of ten thousand dollars, then still more from the canny judge, and with a final lift from his family, he was able to buy, as the result of the panic of 1873, most of the coal land and coke ovens that could profitably be operated. He had to keep them going through three depression years, but he went on increasing his holdings until the Pittsburgh steel men learned that Connellsville coke was the best they could get to make steel, and that four fifths of the available output was under the control of Henry C. Frick, a young man who was president of H. C. Frick & Co. Meanwhile the price of coke had risen from less than a dollar to five dollars a ton. No wonder Henry Frick was able to realize a boyhood ambition—to be a millionaire by the time he was thirty.

In getting the loans from Judge Mellon to buy coke ovens and coal land, Frick had come to know the judge's son, Andrew, and through him that other Andrew, Carnegie. When he married Adelaide Howard Childs, Frick took his bride to New York on the honeymoon and they had a friendly dinner with Carnegie and his mother. Naturally the men talked business over the brandy and cigars. Carnegie was interested in the other man's work, and as a result of their meeting he acquired a modest amount of Frick stock.

The two men were far apart in their personalities. Frick was a man who intended to stand no nonsense from labor; Carnegie was conciliatory and essentially humanitarian. Frick wanted to increase the capitalization of his company by a million dollars, but Carnegie could not approve of his method and told him so in a letter. "I do not like the tone of your letter," Frick answered, and went ahead.

Carnegie was astute enough to see, however, that a man like this could be valuable to his organization, and offered to make him general manager of all his properties, as well as a stockholder in the company. Frick accepted without visible enthusiasm, but he did his job well. It was Frick who organized the Carnegie Company from a number of diverse parts into a smoothly functioning whole.

The difference between the men was never better illustrated than in the celebrated Homestead labor battle and its aftermath. The Homestead Works were the nerve center of the Carnegie Company, and in 1892 were the target of a union organizing drive by the Amalgamated Association of Iron and Steel Workers. Carnegie would doubtless have pursued a course of conciliation; Frick meant to wipe out the union.

A cut in wages, ordered by Carnegie, precipitated the battle. Carnegie had given the order and then sailed away to Scotland on vacation, leaving Frick to execute it. When the union rejected the wage cut, Frick simply closed the plant and hired three hundred Pinkerton men to defend it. The Pinkertons arrived on two armored scows, found the union men waiting for them, and for the next six days there was mob rule in Homestead. A violent battle raged on the first day between the unionists and the embattled Pinkertons, who stayed on their scows and fired back, while the enraged steel men bombarded them with dynamite and an old Civil War cannon. When the Pinkertons surrendered and asked for safe conduct, they considered themselves saved from certain death, but still the mob dragged them from their line of march to beat them savagely. Before state troops took over five days later, fourteen men had been killed and one hundred and sixty-three others seriously wounded.

At first Frick was damned by press and public alike, as a conscienceless enemy of the workingman. Then, abruptly, in the most dramatic incident of Henry's otherwise unmarred life, he won an equal amount of public praise by a display of raw courage. Little more than a week after the Homestead battle, a Polish-Russian immigrant whose untutored sympathies had been aroused by the incident crept into Frick's office in downtown Pittsburgh and fired twice at him, clipping off part of an ear and lodging another bullet in Frick's neck.

As Henry tried to grapple with the assassin he saw a knife flash in the other's hand and felt himself stabbed repeatedly. Still he refused to fall, as office workers poured in and grabbed the man, but pointed at his assailant's mouth and gasped hoarsely, "What is he chewing?" It proved to be a capsule containing enough fulminate of mercury to blow up the office.

From the union standpoint, it was an unfortunate episode. It turned public opinion in favor of Frick and the other steel masters, and against unionism in general. Who could help but admire a man like Frick, who stayed in the office until his day's work was done, bound up with bloody bandages, and even refused to let the doctors give him an anesthetic when they removed the bullet from his neck? He followed that up with a statement from his home: "I do not think I shall die, but whether I do or not, the Carnegie Company will pursue the same policy and it will win." A liberal paper like the New York *World* could only say admiringly, "Those who hate him most admire the nerve and stamina of this man of steel whom nothing seems to be able to move."

The incident set back the union movement in the steel mills a good forty-five years, and gave the Pinkerton men a bad name from which it took them nearly as long to recover. Even Carnegie had to endure a brief period of unpopularity, when it was charged that he had stayed in Scotland and let Frick take the blame for the Homestead battle. Although both men knew this was not the case, still it did not improve the always delicate state of affairs between them. Their differences increased until at last Frick resigned as chairman, after which he was one of those most instrumental in forming the United States Steel Corporation; in addition, he acted as an intermediary between Morgan and Rockefeller.

Pittsburgh had a 150-acre park to remember him by, which cost Frick two million dollars of his fortune, and Princeton had much to thank him for, but it was the people of New York who became his ultimate chief inheritors. Following Carnegie's example—not by design, one may assume—he moved to New York and built a mansion for himself at Fifth Avenue and Seventieth Street, a safe twenty blocks from the partner to whom he no longer spoke.

Frick began to fill this Greek temple with an outstanding collection of art. With dealers more than eager to advise him, it was easy for him to buy Turners, Van Dycks, Rembrandts, Fragonards and Bouchers. A better index to his taste, however, lies in what is known of the amusements he chose for himself. Seated alone in the great mansion, among one of the best private art collections in the world, he could be found, as one of his biographers reported, "seated on a Renaissance throne under a baldachino, holding in his little hand a copy of the *Saturday Evening Post.*" The mansion possessed a splendid organ, on which Frick loved to hear his favorites, "Silver Threads among the Gold" and "The Rosary," played by an organist hired to come and perform on Saturday afternoons.

Nevertheless, Frick was proud of his home and determined to give it to the public when he died. The gift was the most generous act of his life, since a $15,000,000 endowment went with it, a substantial part of his estate. But his death, in 1919, did not open the way immediately to the public's enjoyment of his treasures. The money was left to a corporation known as the Frick Collection, with the stipulation that the house could not be opened to the public until the death of his widow, who died in 1931. It was 1935 before the place was opened at last, but it has since been attended by many thousands of people who come to see the art and to hear the Sunday afternoon recitals by eminent musicians, who have replaced "Silver Threads" with Bach and Beethoven.

A curious provision of the will was overlooked until 1945, when a controversy arose which put the Frick inheritors into the headlines, although in a comparatively dignified way. Until that time they had been obscure. In that year an anonymous inquiry came to the Board of Trustees of the collection, inquiring whether it would receive gifts. Frick's daughter Helen, who was serving on the board with two other family members, her brother Childs and her nephew Dr. Henry Clay Frick, declared that no gifts could be accepted because her father had forbidden it in his will. She had the question tested in the courts, since the other trustees were not in agreement, but the New York Supreme Court held that the collection had a right to accept any gifts it chose. Unconvinced, Miss Frick took the case to the Court of Appeals, which upheld the Supreme Court.

Nothing more was heard of the controversy until a morning early in 1961 when Miss Frick resigned from the Board of Trustees in the most public way, by means of a letter sent to the New York *Herald Tribune*. The immediate cause was the acceptance by the board of art objects left to the collection in the will of John D. Rockefeller, Jr. It was said the vote of the board had been five to three, with the Frick heirs presumably on the losing side. Rockefeller had been a member of the board for more than twenty-five years.

One paragraph in Miss Frick's letter (she was seventy at the time) stood out. "It was never Mr. Frick's plan," she wrote, "to have other persons give or bequeath their works of art to his Collection, which he had formed with love and understanding throughout a long period of years."

That expressed Frick's personality perfectly, and guaranteed the line had not yet died out. Miss Frick's father would have been proud of her statement.

12

Conservation in New York:
Guggenheims and Morgans

Scholars who benefit from the Guggenheim Foundation's bounty today owe their good fortune to one of the most singular accumulators in the history of American wealth, whose money was conserved by an equally extraordinary family which underwent a more profound transformation, perhaps, than any of the other inheritors. The Vanderbilts and the Astors may be far better known, but nothing matches the Guggenheim story for sheer variety.

At the center of the stage stands that small wisp of a man, Meyer Guggenheim, reticent, suspicious, alone, his life wholly dedicated to making money. Meyer did not play the game for the game's sake, as did so many other nineteenth-century barons. His love of money bordered on the pathological, and his career in acquiring it is a case history in what a man can and will do to make himself rich and, having done so, to conserve and shape his fortune for the benefit of his family.

A Swiss-born Jew from the ghetto of Langnau, Meyer came to America in 1847 with no more than the clothes on his back, friendless, nearly penniless. No man could have started on his way to a great fortune with less than Meyer Guggenheim. At twenty he was little more than a beggar, peddling shoestrings, laces, ribbons and other notions as he walked through the drab towns of the anthracite region in Pennsylvania. He had only two people to care for in the world. One was his old father, Simon, who had come with him to America; the other was a young girl named Barbara Myers, his stepsister, with whom he had fallen in love on the boat.

Meyer demonstrated one of his best talents at the beginning. He knew how to sell. This man who trusted almost no one and believed only in getting ahead at whatever cost possessed a cheerful, friendly manner when he approached customers. They looked upon the bearded young chap in his foreign clothes as an earnest, good-natured fellow making a hard way in the world as he slogged along through the mountain towns, and the women especially became sympathetic buyers.

Behind the smile and the beard, Meyer was assessing the products he sold with a mind that worked like a calculating machine. The product to which he devoted special attention was stove polish, which he sold for a dime, with a penny profit. To his horror, he discovered that the man who made it took a profit of seven cents. Now he demonstrated the second of his admirable talents. Meyer carried a sample of the polish to a chemist in Bethlehem and asked him to analyze it. With the formula in his pocket he went home to Philadelphia and set up a factory at home in which father, stepmother and stepsisters were busy turning out stove polish. Having married his stepsister Barbara by this time, he had a truly ingrown organization working for him. But the formula had been established: to make a product or create a service and let other people carry it out for him. It was a logical step to other products—spices, a coffee essence, a household lye.

Meyer saw the same possibilities in lye that he had seen in stove polish and was soon manufacturing it himself, successfully, until he was sued for patent infringement by the Pennsylvania Salt Company, its original maker. Meyer not only won the suit, but the larger company paid him $150,000 to get out of the business.

If he was rich in money-making talents, Meyer Guggenheim was even richer in inheritors. Of the eight sons and three daughters Barbara gave him, seven sons grew up to be his faithful disciples, and he trained each one to serve him, deploying them with the skill of a general over the terrain of acquisition. These sons were Isaac, Daniel, Murry, Solomon, Benjamin, Simon and William. The girls were Jeanette, Rose and Cora.

From the beginning the sons were directed in the way Meyer ordained. He had decided that the four oldest should go into the lace embroidery business, an occupation he knew from his Old World experience was always, or nearly always, profitable. The sons did so well with it that by 1881 they were able to form M. Guggenheim's Sons. The four were equal partners, with their father excluded, but he held himself ready to act as financial counselor and ever present aid in time of need, at five per cent.

The sons hardly needed their father's financial generosity. They became adept at underselling their competitors, sometimes by as much as twenty per cent, and the Guggenheim fortune began to grow apace. It had grown so much by 1888 that the whole family left Philadelphia to its own resources and moved to New York. They were now ready to turn their talents in another direction.

Meyer had something to contribute to whatever new venture might be decided upon. While the boys were making money in lace, he gave them a virtuoso exhibition of how to accumulate, one that must have impressed them. He invested $84,000 in two thousand shares of a decrepit Missouri railroad, the Hannibal & St. Joseph, which looked like the worst of investments, having passed dividends and appearing to be on the point of bankruptcy. Meyer must have heard that Jay Gould was casting avaricious eyes at it, because he had no sooner bought the stock at $42 a share than Gould began an attempt to get control of the line, so that he could use it as a connecting link between his Wabash and the Union Pacific. The stock soared to more than $200 a share, and Meyer sold for $400,000. "You see, boys?" the father might have said. "In lace, where could you get profits like this?"

Where, indeed? But Meyer was not content with this simple exercise. He saw even larger profits in other sagging, apparently worthless properties. When a man who had been involved with him in the lace business told him about how much money there was to be made in Western mining, Meyer went out to see for himself, presenting a somewhat ludicrous picture in rough and tough Leadville, where his parted rabbinical whiskers, long coat and flapping hat made him look like a character in some stereotyped drama. Meyer had no better view of booming Leadville. "What a place!" he complained to the man who had brought him there.

Typically, the properties Meyer owned in the rich boomtown were two flooded mines, the A.Y. and the Minnie, which had cost him $5000 for a half interest. Even Meyer was aghast when he stood on the scene and saw the dismal aspect of the shafts, in which only a few men were working. He refused to go below ground and look for evidences of treasure. "I know there is a mine here; more I cannot know," he said. They had to be "unwatered," as he phrased it.

Unwatering proved to be a costly, uncertain process. Meyer

had to part with $25,000 immediately, which caused him some anguish, and then there was a further delay caused by a miners' strike. While the miners were out, the water crept back in again and that cost Meyer $50,000 more.

Then, within a year, the mines began to produce. In another five years they had disgorged more than 9,000,000 ounces of silver and another 86,000 tons of lead. Meyer took a net profit of $1,383,000. For a total investment which could not have exceeded $100,000, he soon had valuable mining properties worth about $15,000,000.

But Meyer had not forgotten the basic lesson of the stove polish. He saw that the people who were making the real money in mining were those who owned the smelters, the middlemen, since they made a profit both from the smelting and from selling the refined ore. Obviously a man should have a smelter if he wanted to stay in business. Meyer could have bought several smelters out of hand, but it was typical of him that he made careful preparation by deploying a son in the new direction his accumulating was to take. He sent Benjamin to the School of Mines at Columbia, and William to the University of Pennsylvania, where he majored in metallurgy, while Daniel was brought back from the lace business in Europe to be on the spot in Colorado. Murry soon joined him at Pueblo, where Meyer meant to build his smelter. The sons were to construct the smelter as a company, which Meyer would finance with Guggenheim money, lent at the usual five per cent interest. All his sons were to participate in this new enterprise, he decreed, because that was where the money was. In the new Philadelphia Smelting & Refining Company, capitalized at $1,500,000, all of it family money, Isaac was to be treasurer, Benjamin general manager, Simon the buyer of ore, William Simon's assistant, Solomon and Daniel general production men, and Murry president.

When Congress embargoed Mexican silver in 1890 the Guggenheims simply sent Daniel and Murry to organize the Great National Mexican Smelter Company, and after that was accomplished Sol and Will went down to run it. By this time the Philadelphia operation in Colorado was earning $50,000 a month. After the Mexican smelter opened in 1892 it cleared $60,000 the first month, and within a year had earned back its investment.

It appeared, sometimes, that the Guggenheim boys were everywhere, behind every industrial bush. While he was in Mexico, Daniel had bought a copper mine and set Solomon and William to building a smelter that would take both copper and lead. Meanwhile, Benjamin had returned East, to New Jersey, where he supervised the building of a refinery at Perth Amboy. The eight flying Guggenheims were now masters of an empire dealing in silver, copper and lead from mine to refined metal, from which they were taking more than a million dollars a year.

To their rivals, it was an empire which could be fought only by consolidation, and the opportunity came when Henry H. Rogers, who had already created a highly successful copper trust, proposed to organize all the principal American smelting companies into the American Smelting & Refining Co. Into this new Rogers trust came all the major companies— except the Guggenheim interests. It was against Meyer's deepest convictions to permit his company to get out of the family; he flatly refused to sell. But now the family was on the defensive, for the first time, or so it seemed until Daniel Guggenheim, at forty-three the family head in place of his aging father, began to carry out his plans to fight back. The result was a battle of giants which utterly absorbed the financial world while it lasted.

Daniel's first gambit was bold but logical. He planned to

organize the Guggenheim Exploration Company, which would, in effect, corner the best mines in North America, beginning with Mexico and moving on to the United States, Alaska and Canada. To finance the imaginative gamble, Daniel intended to risk no more of the family's money than he could help. He looked about for a willing speculator who could afford to toy with a million dollars, and his eye fell upon William C. Whitney, who had risen from a Massachusetts small town into realms of glory, first by marrying the sister of one of Standard Oil's most substantial stockholders, Oliver H. Payne. Later he had been Secretary of the Navy in Cleveland's first administration. There was a less distinguished aspect to his career. With Ryan and Widener he had been involved in the risky, odorous but highly profitable business of the New York street railway franchises. A man who could indulge in this kind of speculation was the kind of man Daniel Guggenheim was looking for. He soon had Whitney and his speculative million.

Meanwhile, as the Exploration Company began to buy up properties, its task was made easier by a crippling strike in the trust's properties. This development also made American Smelting temporarily vulnerable, and the Guggenheims took advantage of it by unloading great quantities of lead on the market, compelling the trust to sell below cost.

It was a no-quarter battle in which the shrewd, savage strokes of Daniel Guggenheim were decisive. The trust gave up in December 1900 and tried to buy him out. But now that he had his enemies where he wanted them, Daniel turned the final screw. He and his brothers would sell, but they insisted on control. The trust had no real choice and accepted a hard bargain, by which, for $45,200,000, it got all the Guggenheim properties except the best ones—the Colorado and Mexican mines, and the Exploration Company. With the properties came the Guggenheims, who were now the trust.

The whole affair had been a smooth, swift operation. When Henry Rogers, creator of the trust, understood what had been done to him, he was understandably agitated, and vengeful as well. He turned to David Lamar, one of the several speculators who have been given the title "Wolf of Wall Street," and instructed him to drive American's stock down until it went through the floor and ruined the company. It was the kind of assignment Lamar enjoyed, but Daniel had a speculator of much the same stripe on his side in Whitney. By the time the two wolves had fought each other to a standstill, American stock had dropped no more than seven points and the bears were in full retreat.

Rogers was a resourceful battler. He appealed to the courts and got an injunction temporarily blocking the Guggenheims' merger with the trust, pending a decision as to its legality. Rogers had the law on his side, at least in some respects, but the Guggenheim lawyers behaved as though the law had been invented for their benefit, and it was obvious after a time that a compromise would have to be arranged if any of the litigants were to live long enough to survive the suit. As usual, the compromise came out in favor of the Guggenheims. They made some unimportant concessions, but they were still in control of American when the smoke cleared. No better evidence of their grip could have been produced than the composition of the trust's new board of directors. There were five Guggenheim brothers on it; Daniel was chairman, and Simon was treasurer.

This was the high point of the Guggenheim family's activities. In a sense, there were no more worlds to conquer and so perhaps it was inevitable that family solidarity, hitherto an impregnable front, should begin to crack. When it began to dissolve, however, the dissolution took unpredictable directions and Guggenheims were observed in situations where no one would ever have expected to find them. True, there was nothing especially remarkable about Benjamin's decision to go into the mine machinery business for himself; it had, after all, been one of his interests for years, and it was closely allied to the family business. But what sense could be made of William's decision to marry a gentile?

None at all, the brothers decided, and they took drastic measures. William was virtually exiled to Europe, while the brothers arranged a divorce for him in the Illinois courts. He could not, or would not, fight against the heavy weight of family tyranny but his bride would not be cast aside so easily. She displayed a disposition to fight back, which the brothers termed blackmail, but it appeared that she was on far more substantial ground. The divorce itself was of questionable legality, and with this as basis, William's ex-wife kept the Guggenheims in court intermittently until 1914. It was the first divorce in the family, and the only one in the second generation. William never forgave the interference with his life. He refused to go back into business with his brothers.

Not long after this scandal the incredible occurred and old Meyer found himself in court, on the uncomfortable end of a breach-of-promise suit filed by a lady named Hanna Mc-Namara, who claimed what she termed a "constant intimate association" with the smelter king for the past quarter century. Those who knew of Meyer's devotion to business could scarcely believe that he had ever been devoted to anything or anyone else. Nearly inarticulate with indignant rage, he offered $10,000 reward to anyone who had ever seen him with the plaintiff, and this action in itself was considered convincing proof of Meyer's innocence. The court did not believe Hanna's story either.

Meyer subsequently had to undergo an operation, tossing off one of his much-quoted aphorisms in the process: "You can't sell a Jew anesthetics or life insurance." He had neither, but survived the operation, only to die a little later in March 1905, at seventy-eight, the first of the family to go. It is difficult to say how much Meyer passed on to his inheritors, because the family's business affairs were so closely guarded, but certainly the estimate of $2,250,000 was a serious understatement of his true wealth.

His sons were already multimillionaires, and the customary decay had begun to set in. The fortune had been accumulated; it was large and growing steadily of its own momentum. The patriarch was dead. He had held the family together by virtue of his Old World insistence on his position and, beyond that, his commanding, unyielding personality. With that influence removed, the sons began to live like other rich men's sons. Benjamin's case was not untypical. His mistresses were well known, and when he went down on the *Titanic* his companion who survived was a young blond singer, registered as his wife.

Barbara, one of the three daughters who survived Benjamin, was deeply affected not only by his tragic death but by the hardly concealed facts of his private life. She was married while still in college, went to England with her author husband to live, returned to New York after he asked for a divorce, and took her two sons to the apartment of a relative, from which the children fell sixteen stories to their deaths, which were officially ruled as accidental, after two investigations. Barbara was later married twice more.

Her sister Peggy has become an international celebrity because of her salon on the Grand Canal in Venice, which *avant garde* artists from all over the world have made a gathering place.

Meanwhile, however, the second generation of Guggenheims had not yet played itself out. After Meyer's death Daniel began to push the activities of the Exploration Company, along with the celebrated mining engineer, John Hays Hammond. The result was a steady flow of money-making additions to the Guggenheim empire—property in Mexico, Idaho and Washington; smelters, mines and refineries in San Francisco, Illinois, Baltimore and Utah, as well as ventures into the Yukon and Africa. It was entirely typical of family luck that the African expedition, intended to develop rubber properties, found little of this commodity but a great deal of gold and diamonds. Thomas Fortune Ryan was associated with the Guggenheims in the diamond operation, and the resulting loot from the Congo was a substantial part of the inheritance Ryan left behind him.

Of all the brothers' fortunes, however, Simon's was the largest, perhaps as high as fifty million dollars. When he went to the United States Senate from Colorado in 1907, joining a corrupt but affluent body which then numbered eighteen multimillionaires, Simon's wealth exceeded all the others, a fact duly noted by that part of the press which had begun to feel that the Guggenheims had overdone accumulation.

There seemed no end to the golden touch. Exploring the Wrangel Mountains in 1916, Daniel's men came upon one of the largest copper deposits in North America, which ultimately became the Kennecott Copper Mines. The discovery touched off a spectacular scramble to control these riches, but Daniel, with the help of J. P. Morgan & Co. and a $20,000,-000 investment, was first to complete in 1911 a rail line, the Copper River Railroad, which could haul the ore two hundred miles from mine to sea, where it had to be transported by water another twenty-five hundred miles to Puget Sound and a Guggenheim smelter. The first cargo netted $500,000.

The Alaska Syndicate, which brought all this to pass notwithstanding a homicidal warfare with rivals and a monopoly vs. conservation struggle which involved the United States government, also quietly acquired in the process Alaskan steamship companies, salmon canneries and coal fields which materially added to Guggenheim (and Morgan) wealth. Dividends from the Kennecott mine alone were $3,000,000 in the first year.

Still the money rolled in. In 1910 their Utah Copper Company earned $5,401,000, with dividends of $4,648,000. Their Chile Exploration Company opened a new copper source just before the First World War broke out, adding to the mines in Alaska, Idaho, Nevada, Utah, Arizona, New Mexico and Colorado, not to mention the Mexican properties and numerous smelters and refineries.

The Alaskan venture with the Morgan partners had been so successful that in 1916 the brothers decided on something old Meyer would never have approved—joining forces with an organization outside the family. Meyer would, however, have approved the result in this case, the creation of the Kennecott Copper Corporation. This company's shares removed from Morgans and Guggenheims part of the staggering cost of the Copper River Railroad by letting the public help pay for it. Guggenheim Exploration and its mines also went into the new corporation, although American Smelting was excluded. Three million shares of no par value were issued; they rose at once to fifty dollars per share, and the corporation's market value was estimated at nearly $200,000,000. At the end of the First World War it had paid out more than this sum in dividends.

Kennecott represented the peak of the accumulating. As the nation entered upon a new era after the war, the second generation of Guggenheims began to disappear. Isaac died in 1922, leaving a net estate of $10,000,000. Then Daniel went in 1930, and although the value of his estate was not recorded, something of its size could be guessed from the fact that each of his three children got $2,000,000. Murry, who died in 1939, paid gift taxes of $3,449,000, the largest ever assessed from an individual up to that time. William and Simon died in the same year, 1941. Long separated from the family, William presumably did not leave an estate to compare with those of his brothers.

Simon and Solomon were the last to go. Before he died Simon decided to perpetuate the family name through the John Simon Guggenheim Foundation, the best known of the several foundations established by the brothers. These included the Daniel Guggenheim Fund for the Promotion of Aeronautics, which spent its entire endowment of $2,500,000 in the fight for air power, both civil and military; and the Daniel and Florence Guggenheim Foundation, totaling $4,000,000, which has provided summer after summer of music for New York's city-bound dwellers who hear it at the Guggenheim Shell in Central Park, as well as money for heart research and space flight. But it was the bequest of Simon and his wife, in 1925, in memory of a son, which has made the family name well known to many who might otherwise not have heard it. This is, of course, the Foundation which provides annual fellowships "to assist research and artistic creation." Hundreds of the nation's foremost writers, artists, musicians and scholars have benefited from the fellowships.

Besides these endowments, Murry and his wife founded the Murry and Leonie Guggenheim Dental Clinic in New York with a $1,000,000 building and a $2,000,000 endowment. The clinic gives free dental care to thousands of school children every year.

Solomon, the last of the brothers to die, epitomized the rise of the Guggenheims from Meyer's penniless beginnings to a peak in accumulating. Remembering the bearded and somewhat ragged founder, peddling his stove polish, it was wonderful to behold Solomon in all his glory—a man who shot quail in Scotland, sent his daughters to good English schools, lived to see one of them marry into the nobility, and perhaps most miraculous of all, became himself one of the best-known patrons of non-objective art. His Foundation's Guggenheim Museum on upper Fifth Avenue, where this controversial art is on display in a Frank Lloyd Wright building which has probably created more uproar than any other public structure in the city, is a fitting monument to the last of the founding line.

After Solomon's death in 1949, at eighty-eight, the second generation was done. It was an extraordinary generation by any measurement, not to be equaled by any other American family. In the third generation, only two of the grandsons have demonstrated the family's superior talents for business or shown any special concern for carrying on its interests. Edmond, Murry's son, appeared content to concern himself with Kennecott Copper and the Guggenheim Nitrate Corporation. But Harry, Daniel's son, has had a distinguished and useful career as Ambassador to Cuba, under President Hoover, as one of those who has done much to promote aviation, and as an author and publisher. He is married to Alicia Patterson, the daughter of Captain Joseph Patterson, Colonel Robert R. McCormick's cousin, and with her is publisher of *Newsday*, most successful of the Long Island dailies.

It was Harry and Edmond who announced in 1951 that they had formed a new Guggenheim partnership to carry on

along traditional Guggenheim lines the mining and metal-
lurgical enterprises which had created so much wealth.

As for the other Guggenheim heirs, in the third and fourth
generations, it was a sad story of multiple divorces—in such
numbers that some historians believe they have set a record
for rich American families. Meyer and his sons would also
have been horrified by the unusual number of marriages with
gentiles.

It is significant, too, that the once plentiful supply of sons
has begun to run out. Isaac, Benjamin and Solomon had
none, one of William's two died, both of Simon's died before they could marry, and Murry's only son married twice
but could produce only a daughter. There were just three
sons in the fourth generation, and one of these died too
young to marry. As Amory puts it, most limbs of the family
tree have "dried up and died with the sap drained off by
too much money. . . ."

An exception has been Harry, as noted, and his sister
Gladys, who married the late Roger W. Straus, once president of American Smelting and active in education. Their
son, Roger, Jr., is founder and president of a respected Manhattan publishing house, Farrar, Straus and Cudahy, while
his brother Oscar, having served for a time as vice-president
of American Smelting, has carried on the family mining exploration interests. One of Harry's daughters, Joan, is married
to a member of Guggenheim Brothers, present name of the
family firm. Thus sons-in-law step in where an absence of
sons precludes more Guggenheims.

Harry once wrote to his daughter Nancy, "I believe there
is a responsibility to use inherited wealth for the progress of
man and not for mere self-gratification, which I am sure does
not lead to a happy life. . . ." Certainly the various Guggenheim foundations have exemplified that ideal, perhaps more

so than the inherited wealth of any other family. The Guggenheim accumulation, which approached a collective $200,-000,000, has been distributed through its foundations to art, music, aviation, medicine, scholarship, education, and in each case it has been done in imaginative ways. Whatever sins there may have been in accumulating the Guggenheim fortune, and these were no worse than the others of the century, they have been atoned for by the immense good which the money, conserved so well through the foundations, has done for so many Americans.

In contrast to the Guggenheims, the Morgan family has traced a relatively simple pattern of accumulation and conservation, but by one of those ironic accidents of American public life, it is the Morgans and not their contemporaries who have taken much of the blame for the excesses of the robber baron era. Somehow the Morgan name has become associated in the American mind with the far worse evils of acquisition practiced by Ryan, Hill, Jay Gould and some others. Similarly, the Morgan name is associated with great wealth, but the $68,000,000 John Pierpont left when he died in 1913 was far surpassed by the Guggenheim, Frick, Harriman, Mellon, Ryan and Whitney fortunes, and was not even in the same company with the Du Pont, Rockefeller or Ford accumulations.

There are other confusions about the Morgan family. To many Americans, J. P. Morgan is one man; they would be unable to distinguish father from son or grandson. Indeed, so symbolic has the name Morgan become that few people recall any fragment of family history. No specific scandal is associated with the family but, illogically, the collective scandals of a whole era are attached to it in the public consciousness.

In reality, the Morgans, father and son, were essentially middlemen, financiers of other people's ventures, whose profits they shared. The fortune did not begin with these activities, however. It was the work initially of Joseph Morgan, a Hartford entrepreneur of the late eighteenth century who employed the nineteenth-century method of pyramiding —stagecoaches, hotels and fire insurance companies—to pass on a substantial inheritance to his son, Junius Spencer Morgan, born in 1813.

Junius grew up in Hartford and always retained a sentimental fondness for the place, although he lived half his life abroad, where he had become a financial middleman between Great Britain and the United States by mid-nineteenth century. It was Junius who founded the great banking house which bore his son's name.

Although the fortune was not large at this point, Junius was relatively generous with it. He gave a free library to Hartford which cost him $100,000, and in memory of his mother he gave a further gift to the Hartford Orphan Asylum. His other benefactions were well distributed: a Reynolds to the Metropolitan, money to Guy's Hospital and the National Nurses' Pension Fund in England, a law professorship at Yale, and similar gifts. The bulk of the estate went to his surviving three daughters and one of two sons who lived, John Pierpont Morgan. (Junius, it may be added, died in a way that was incongruous for an international banker of such formidable dignity. Driving in his carriage along the Riviera, in Monte Carlo, he jumped out when the horses threatened to run away and was killed.)

John Pierpont, born in Hartford, went to an excellent Boston school, English High; a Swiss school; and the University of Göttingen. After this superior preparation he began his career in the usual way by starting at the bottom in his father's firm, to learn the business. In the course of several partnerships, with the Drexels and others, he came inevitably to that day in 1895 when, with several associates, he organized, on the solid foundation his father had laid, the powerful banking house of J. P. Morgan & Co. That was J. Pierpont's outstanding talent—organization. He was not an expander, a speculator, a buccaneer, like so many of the men around him, but a powerful force for integration and stabilization in an essentially unstable financial world.

He learned early what it meant to be unpopular. When President Cleveland had to appeal for help from the international bankers in 1895 to prevent the further outflow of gold, Morgan and August Belmont accommodated him, as noted earlier, but at their own terms in supplying the government with $65,000,000 in gold. In payment, they took bonds at 104½ and sold them at 112¼, after which Morgan bluntly refused to disclose his profits to an inquiring congressional committee. It was difficult to tell, at this juncture, whether Cleveland or Morgan was running the country, as far as the average citizen was concerned.

Morgan had a hand in the organization of United States Steel, the International Harvester Company, and the International Mercantile Marine, the latter one of the few projects in which he had a part that failed. No one could doubt his formidable power. At seventy-one, it was his influence alone, in the opinion of competent observers, which halted the panic of 1907 at a critical point. Only Harriman rivaled Morgan in eminence, and after the railroad empire builder died in 1909, Morgan stood alone.

Inevitably he became an object of congressional investigation, with the famous Pujo Committee of the House setting the stage for the final drama of his life in 1912. Much has been written about that conflict between the power of government and the power of money, but in retrospect the primary fact that emerges is the absolute belief of the accumulators in their accumulating. Morgan was not only incapable of "admitting" anything at all, but equally unable to believe that anything he had done was wrong.

The congressmen said he was in control of a "money trust," meaning that he had, in a sense, cornered the money market. Morgan denied the very existence of such a thing. The committee characterized him as a man of enormous financial power; Morgan asserted he did not even desire such power, let alone possess it. The congressmen cited the tight centralization of control his financial interests represented; Morgan described it as a reservoir of strength to provide adequate banking facilities. Did he favor even more concentration? Morgan could see nothing wrong with it. Did he not think this was dangerous? Power was dangerous only in the hands of evil men, Morgan said, and he stood firmly upon his own wisdom and character.

So it went in the duel between the committee's counsel, Samuel Untermeyer, and the men who were the epitome of financial power in America. In the end Morgan prevailed, largely because he was simply too formidable to attack. He was formidable physically, too, a man of rugged physique, with a craggy face, penetrating eyes and an aura of sheer indomitable energy. There was ice inside him and a mind closed to everything except what he himself believed, but it was also a mind of extraordinary brilliance in its sheer power to grasp, to organize, to command. Morgan was an aloof and lonely man, like most of the others whose only interest was money. If he made mistakes, they were rare and not of great moment. Those who struggle with the New Haven and Hartford Railroad today may take some consolation from the fact that not even a man of Morgan's exceptional talents could deal with it successfully, as its banker and a director of the line.

Morgan was a total defender of the status quo. He abhorred the idea of social reform, although convulsive changes were taking place everywhere about him in society. His taste, manners and outlook were those of an aristocrat; he had only contempt for the public, its opinions, or its needs, and he hated publicity with the same passion Marshall Field I displayed.

As did other rich men, Morgan collected art. In doing so he displayed a side of his nature that no one was permitted to see—a deep, sensuous appreciation of the rare and beautiful. A substantial part of his fortune went to gratify this appetite, and another part of it went to buy literary treasures. When he died in 1913—some said because of his profound shock at being subjected to the Pujo Committee—his son, J.P., Jr., inherited most of the collections. Junior authorized the famous loan exhibition of 1914–16, the first great art show of the century, after which most of the Morgan pictures and other art objects went to the Metropolitan Museum.

As for the 25,000 rare books and manuscripts, housed in a chaste white library next to his residence, the junior Morgan conveyed these to six trustees, who were to administer the collection as a public reference library.

The art collections and the library were valued at about $50,000,000, besides the $68,000,000-net estate, yet most people were astonished at the small size of the fortune, so accustomed were they to the image of Morgan as a man of incredible wealth. It surprised others to discover in his estate a good many worthless securities, representing misplaced friendships. This from the man who had said he would never lend money to a man he couldn't trust in spite "of all the bonds in Christendom."

Morgan's philanthropies were as highly individual as his personality. The churches, museums, cathedrals and hospitals which received gifts during his lifetime knew that these were the result of Morgan's methodical study of where such philanthropies should go. Other benefactions after his death reflected associations during his lifetime, and some were purely whims.

Like his father, he died abroad, in Rome, a prince of the realm to the last. He so overshadowed his family that the inheritors who remained—his second wife, his three daughters and his son—were little more than names to the public. J.P., Jr., as stiff and remote as his father but without the other Morgan's conspicuous abilities, spent some of his money on the largest private yacht afloat, a mansion larger than any his father owned, and luxuries for which the second Morgan had no time or inclination. When he died in 1943 he was still in the shadow of his father, as he had been all his life, although he was a worthy man in his own right.

The only visible evidence of the magnificent Morgan today is the marble mausoleum on East Thirty-sixth Street which houses the priceless collection of books and manuscripts known as the Morgan Library. All the Morgans, who insisted that time stand still when they were alive, are now the victims of it. They were the ultimate in conservation, of ingrown wealth which denies its creative use except for primarily selfish purposes.

Four

LORDS AND LADIES

BOUNTIFUL

$ 13 $

The Care and Feeding of Foundations

By far the largest part of the wealth accumulated in the nineteenth century has filtered down into foundations set up by individual inheritors, sometimes but not always with the aid and assistance of their families. More than eleven billion dollars has been handed down in this way, and in the past few years the annual grants from the 5202 foundations which control the money have exceeded a half billion dollars.

Clearly this transference of wealth is of far more social importance than the dispositions of the fortunes we have discussed in these pages until now, which were dissipated or conserved and expanded according to the highly individual temperaments of the men and women who inherited the money. Foundation money is directed entirely toward social purposes, by impersonal boards which may or may not have the guiding influence of an individual inheritor from the founding family.

The excellent definition of a foundation proposed by F. Emerson Andrews, director of the Russell Sage Foundation, is a lucid expression of this idea: "A foundation may be defined as a nongovernmental, nonprofit organization having a principal fund of its own, managed by its own trustees or directors, and established to maintain or aid social, educational, charitable, religious, or other activities serving the common welfare."

In brief, as Mr. Andrews has pointed out, a foundation in its broadest sense is a means by which private wealth is contributed to public purposes. This concept has found its fullest expression in our own century. In the era of accumulation, or until 1910, there was little public use of private wealth except through individual philanthropies. Before 1901 there were only eleven foundations in America with assets of $1,000,000 or more, and their combined assets were less than $200,000,000. By the end of 1910 the number had shrunk to eight. Then, in the next five years, both the Rockefeller Foundation and the Carnegie Corporation were established and the era of the modern foundation began.

The range of these modern devices for dispensing wealth is astonishing. In the records of the Foundation Library Center in New York about twelve thousand of them are listed, ranging from one which lists its total assets as twenty-six cents, up to the Ford Foundation, much the largest with its awesome stockpile of more than three billion dollars. Many of the foundations are too small to be included in the comprehensive list of 5202 included in the Center's Directory, published by, quite naturally, a foundation—Russell Sage. The Directory also excludes from its listings so-called foundations which make general public appeals for funds, and such other categories as those "which act as trade associations for industrial or other special groups; which are restricted by charter solely to aiding one or several named institutions; or which function as endowments set up for special purposes within colleges, churches, or other organizations and governed by the trustees of the parent institution."

What remain are the foundations which control nearly all the wealth in this country which has escaped the hands of individual inheritors. The names of the most important are familiar to everyone: Ford, far in the lead, as noted; Rockefeller second, with $648,000,000 in assets; and following, in order, the Duke Endowment, $414,000,000; the Hartford (John A.) Foundation, with a similar figure; the Carnegie Corporation of New York, $261,000,000; the Kellogg (W.K.) Foundation, $215,000,000; the Sloan (Alfred P.) Foundation, $176,000,000; the Lilly Endowment, $157,000,000; the Commonwealth Fund, $119,000,000; and the Danforth Foundation, $110,000,000.

Of these top ten foundations, only four were listed in a tabulation compiled in 1937, and only two of these could boast assets of more than $100,000,000 at that time, thus dispelling the common idea that great foundations could not arise in the economic climate of the forties and fifties, an idea as erroneous as the notion that taxes preclude the acquisition of large fortunes in our day.

Where does this staggering inheritance go—this nearly six billion dollars controlled by the ten largest, and the nearly equivalent figure in the hands of the other 5192 foundations listed in the Directory? Certainly not always in directions which would be approved by the accumulators, who were essentially anti-social in their attitudes and profoundly disinterested in most "activities concerning the common welfare."

It has often been remarked, for example, that Henry Ford would have been shocked to the marrow by the liberal activities of the Fund for the Republic (now the Center for the Study of Democratic Institutions), before the Fund was turned loose to die by its embarrassed parent, the Ford Foundation, and thenceforth became, as the phrase went, "a wholly disowned subsidiary." But it is less often noted that the first Henry would also view with horror many of the present activities of the foundation which bears his name— activities which are not now considered radical except by the radical right.

Most of the large foundations, like those in the top ten, function as general research organizations, and their grants are directed toward research in education, health and welfare, of a kind familiar to everyone because of the generous publicity which accompanies them. They are staffed by experts drawn from a good many fields, who seek out and evaluate projects which are then weighed and approved, or declined, by a board of trustees likely to be made up of transplanted university administrators and professors, with a sprinkling of upper-echelon corporation personnel. The Foundation Directory records that 178 foundations are in this category, controlling sixty-six per cent of the assets of all foundations, and therefore to be considered as "leaders and standard-setters."

Other foundations are set up for special purposes, usually through wills or trusts. The special purpose may be extremely broad, as in those designed only to aid education, or as specialized (the Directory records) as the Dr. Coles Trust Fund for Ice Cream for the Pupils of Scotch Plains and Fanwood. The 584 foundations in this category control approximately thirteen per cent of total foundation endowments.

Still another kind of foundation is the community foundation, most often a trust controlled by a community, its resources drawn from numerous individuals and distributed through municipal committees or local banks and trust companies. There are already 101 foundations of this kind, whose active capital totals $340,000,000, and whose assets appear to be increasing steadily.

A fourth type is the company-sponsored foundation, designed for corporate giving and customarily administered by a corporation's own officers. These foundations are phenomena of the past fifteen years, although they existed before that time. They are largely the outcome of increased federal taxes on corporate income after the Second World War, but they also offer an additional channel for individual accumulators in family corporations. Some of them are large and beginning to be well known—the Ford Motor Company Fund, General Electric Foundation, Standard Oil Foundation and United States Steel Foundation are examples—and their assets total more than $700,000,000.

Finally, there are family foundations, which seemingly do not properly belong within the scope of this book because they are set up by the living rather than the dead. But they are the modern expression of personal philanthropy—unincorporated giving. It may be noted that these foundations, like the company-sponsored type, have also primarily resulted from high taxes.

The tremendous outpouring of wealth from all these foundations flows into a variety of fields, of which education is clearly the leader, followed by health, social welfare and scientific research. The lower categories are revealing in their descent through the humanities to government, international affairs and religion, which has always been the recipient of less foundation money than any other kind of activity, leading perhaps to the conclusion that the entrepreneurs of philanthropy do not believe that money will save souls.

More specifically, the wealth of the accumulators is being directed, through the inheritor foundations, principally into improving man's education and health, with somewhat less attention paid to his way of living and his capacity to find out new things about the physical world he lives in.

In education, the money goes for higher education and aid to teachers, for buildings and equipment, adult education, the dissemination of knowledge, educational research, fellowships, libraries, museums, scholarships, elementary and secondary schools, and even into endowments, although this kind of giving is not characteristic of large foundations.

Foundation money for health is concentrated primarily in health services and hospitals, with such categories as mental health and public health far in the rear. Social welfare grants are concentrated in youth agencies, community funds and child welfare, with a comparative disinterest in the aged, delinquency and crime, and family service; housing rests in the lowest place of all. Scientific research grants go to the life sciences, physical sciences and social sciences in that order, with medicine, physics and economics leading the respective fields.

When the uses of foundation wealth are summarized, according to F. Emerson Andrews' introduction to the Foundation Directory, it is apparent that education is the favorite philanthropy of the inheritors, most of whom are college graduates, but this was also true of the accumulators, few of whom went to college at all. Of total foundation grants, about forty-one per cent go to education, compared with sixteen per cent for health, fifteen per cent for social welfare, eleven per cent for scientific research, five per cent for humanities, slightly more than five per cent for international relations, somewhat less than that figure for religion, and only two per cent for government.

As Mr. Andrews points out, these totals are not impressive "against the background of our economy; foundations are able to spend for all purposes only about 8 cents of the annual dollar of private philanthropy." But, he continues, "because they have had long experience in giving and most of them disburse their funds with care, they have built an enviable record of accomplishment from relatively meager resources."

That is the best answer, perhaps, to the charge from some quarters that foundations are mere tax devices which enable the rich to cheat the government out of its due. While no one doubts that tax evasion is involved in their creation, it can hardly be argued that the use of wealth through foundation giving is not infinitely more constructive than the haphazard philanthropic patterns of the earlier accumulators, and far better in a social sense than its use by the waster inheritors, or by those who used their money simply to make more money.

Foundations are certainly not without fault, and may be criticized legitimately on several counts which do not concern us here, but an excellent measure of the beneficent use of their inherited wealth may be the kind of criticism directed at them. It is, in more cases than not, the kind which deplores use of money for any educational or humanitarian purpose. Consider, for example, the stated intent of the Ford Foundation, which is to "advance human welfare by trying to identify problems of importance to the nation and the world and by supplying funds on a limited scale for efforts directed at their solution." This is more than enough to cause a rise in the hackles of the radical right, if they had not already been raised by the declaration in the Rockefeller Foundation's charter that it is interested in promoting "the well-being of mankind throughout the world."

The concept of foundation giving has changed, and is changing, the use of inherited wealth in America. Tax structures today preclude the general practice of the nineteenth-century accumulators of handing down immense fortunes within the family, at least in the manner in which it was once accomplished. The day of reigning families like the Astors and Vanderbilts is vanishing, if it is not already gone. Inheritors now get comfortable fortunes after the inheritance taxes are paid, but the bulk of personal fortunes tends to go into a family foundation.

Besides the compelling motive of tax avoidance, there are unquestionably human factors at work here. A foundation perpetuates a family name and does it honor in a way nothing else could do. The name of John D. Rockefeller, once a swear word among intellectuals and a synonym for the sins of the rich, is now well respected because of the uses of his money by the foundation which bears his name, as well as because of the exemplary lives of his inheritors. Henry Ford's provincialism, eccentricities and ingrown hostility to the advancement of human welfare are far overshadowed by the work of the Ford Foundation.

The growth of large foundations from small ones illustrates the modern use of wealth by inheritors. A family establishes a small foundation to place its personal charities on a more organized basis than the old-fashioned haphazard giving, and to centralize its philanthropy in an agency under family control yet operating on its own responsibility.

While the family members live, they may make further annual additions to the foundation principal; interest and income from investment also add to it. As the members die, still further additions are made through bequests and the fund grows. In some cases the assets become substantial and the initial limited program undergoes a gradual expansion; the number of trustees may increase to include people from other fields than the original; and soon the foundation begins to take on nationally important projects.

Thus a large general research foundation is created out of a small family philanthropic program.

$ 14 $

Philosophies of Giving:
Carnegie, Rockefellers, Harknesses,
Rosenwald and Fords

Emerson may well have been commenting on a society already devoted to the material (besides composing a splendid nineteenth-century homily) when he wrote, "The only gift is a portion of thyself." There was little in nineteenth-century life, here or abroad, to encourage this humanitarian notion, which has for centuries been a keystone in the philosophies of selflessness. The giving of wealth by those who had it was extremely limited, in comparison with the philanthropy of today, and the giving itself was motivated almost entirely by the personal whims of those rich men who cared to consider it at all.

It was a contemporary of Emerson's, Andrew Carnegie, who introduced to his fellow accumulators the proposition that it was an obligation of the rich to share their wealth with the less fortunate. While there were almost none then (and only a few now) who shared his views on the same lofty level, Carnegie was a disturber of consciences and led the way to the first flush of real philanthropy, which occurred toward the end of the century.

"Philanthropy" was a word Carnegie disliked. There was a

condescension in it that alienated this good man, who preferred to think of himself as a distributor of wealth "for the improvement of mankind." Students of environmental influences find in Andrew Carnegie one of those baffling instances in which a man is subjected to the same kind of early life as a whole category of human beings, yet turns out to be fundamentally different in his reaction to it, and in his later conduct.

Carnegie was born to poverty, like most of the other accumulators, but where the reaction of the others was to devote their lives toward a single-minded effort to make money, the young Scotsman desired wealth so that he might fight privilege and its consequent evils. It is difficult, of course, in the context of our society to believe in such idealism, and some historians have attempted to ascribe less noble motives to Carnegie's altruism. Yet it is as difficult to denigrate Carnegie's words as it would be to minimize his actions, which are so well known.

Hear him in 1868, long before he had even begun to make his great fortune in steel. "Thirty-three, and an income of $50,000 per annum!" he exclaimed, in a memo to himself. Then he went on to instruct himself as to his future course: "Beyond this never earn—make no effort to increase fortune, but spend the surplus each year for benevolent purposes. Cast aside business for ever, except for others. Settle in Oxford and get a thorough education, making the acquaintance of literary men—this will take three years' active work—pay especial attention to speaking in public. Settle then in London and purchase a controlling interest in some newspaper or live review and give the general management of it attention, taking a part in public matters, especially those connected with education and improvement of the poorer classes. Man must have an idol—the amassing of wealth is one of the worst species of idolatry—no idol more debasing than the worship of money.

Whatever I engage in I must push inordinately; therefore should I be careful to choose that life which will be the most elevating in character. To continue much longer overwhelmed by business cares and with most of my thoughts wholly upon the way to make more money in the shortest time, must degrade me beyond hope of permanent recovery. I will resign business at thirty-five, but during the ensuing two years I wish to spend the afternoons in receiving instruction and reading systematically."

Those who sneer at Carnegie's idealism note with satisfaction that he went on making money for more than thirty years after he wrote these words. A psychoanalyst would find the motivation for it in Carnegie's childhood. A literate, sensitive child, strongly attached to his mother, perhaps abnormally so, he hated the makers of power and longed for their strength to correct the wrongs they had created, and even more he yearned to be rich enough to provide his mother with fine clothes and carriages. This childish adoration and devotion persisted into middle life; he did not marry until his mother died.

Carnegie was unlike other accumulators in his passionate attachment to his fellow humans and his acute understanding of them. It was this, as much as sheer business ability, which enabled him to build the Carnegie Steel Corporation and sell it at an enormous profit in 1901, getting $250,000,000 in five-per-cent fifty-year gold bonds for his share. At this juncture Carnegie could have anticipated Mellon, Rockefeller and Ford and become the nation's first billionaire. Instead, he chose to be the first great philanthropist, much as he scorned the word.

What he intended had been foreshadowed in June 1899, when his article, titled "Wealth," appeared in the pages of that distinguishd magazine, the *North American Review*. It caused a sensation, both here and in England, where it appeared in the *Pall Mall Gazette* under a different title, "The Gospel of Wealth." The gospel, according to Carnegie, was that a rich man should divide his life into two parts, getting his wealth in the first period and distributing it in the second, after he had provided properly for his family.

Carnegie's distribution was on a magnificent scale, his benefactions amounting to $350,000,000 in all. Into them went his annual income of more than $12,500,000, and such substantial portions of the principal as well that when he died in 1919 his estate was extremely modest, considering that he had been one of the nation's richest men.

Who were Carnegie's inheritors in the twentieth century? Not his wife and daughter, who were left enough to live on comfortably after the amiable Scot had been laid to rest in Sleepy Hollow, on the Hudson River. The real inheritors were the American people, to whom he entrusted his wealth in a variety of ways. These heirs are most familiar with the libraries which bear his name, and which have meant so much to generations of children and book-starved inhabitants of small towns. Yet the $60,000,000 that went into creating libraries was only a small part of the $228,000,000 which passed into American hands, $62,000,000 having gone to the British Empire. The largest single portion of the fortune, $125,000,000, went to the Carnegie Corporation, the foundation which has carried on the ideals of its donor perhaps more successfully than any other.

The Corporation's purpose is simply stated: "The advancement and diffusion of knowledge and understanding among the people of the United States and of the British Dominions and Colonies." That was the high purpose Andrew Carnegie always intended for his money. Today it is carried out in supporting training and research programs in higher education and international affairs in colleges and universities. In 1959 such support totaled nearly eight million dollars.

Operating separately, and carrying out another aspect of the founder's idealism, is the Carnegie Endowment for International Peace, whose purpose is "to promote international peace and understanding through research, publications, educational activities, and cooperation with organizations having a similar objective." Currently its emphasis is on international organization, with a natural empathy for the United Nations. Its International Center Building is a familiar part of the UN complex in New York City, while its European work is administered through the European Centre in Geneva.

Still another phase of Andrew Carnegie's legacy to the people is the Carnegie Foundation for the Advancement of Teaching. Its purpose is "to provide retiring allowances for teachers of universities, colleges, and technical schools in the United States and Canada; and in general, to do and perform all things necessary to encourage, uphold, and dignify the profession of teaching and the cause of higher education within the United States and Canada." So much needed was this foundation that its list of those eligible to receive pensions closed in 1928, and nearly all of the income from its twenty million dollars in assets today goes into the pension program. Expenditures from capital are not permitted.

Thus millions of Americans have become the inheritors of Andrew Carnegie's wealth, from the three foundations, the libraries and such relatively small benefactions as six million dollars given for church and cultural institutions like Carnegie Hall.

In the philanthropic uses of wealth, Carnegie showed the way to others, but he was surpassed in our time by the master inheritor of them all, John D. Rockefeller, Jr., who gave away $450,901,000 between 1917 and 1958, in a career devoted almost entirely to philanthropy. In doing so, he and his sons made the name of Rockefeller honored where it had once been despised.

No one was more conscious of this transformation than John D., Jr., whose inspiration was his father's methods of accumulating, which had made the founder of the Standard Oil fortune one of the most hated men of his time. After the oil empire was dissolved by Supreme Court decree in 1910, following the pitiless exposure of its practices by Ida Tarbell and other early-century muckrakers, John D., Jr., withdrew from the family business, placed himself at the head of the Rockefeller Foundation which his father had created, and began a spectacular career in philanthropy that did not end until he died in 1960 at the age of eighty-six.

"What concerned him was the hard, practical problem of how to dispose of his wealth in ways that would advance the public good," says his biographer, Raymond B. Fosdick. How much else there was of a deep guilt sense in his motivations no one knows, but perhaps it is implied in his later pronouncement: "My father created an organization for the making of wealth. I regard it as my responsibility to see that the vast amount of money he accumulated is used for the good of humanity." He expressed this idea often, in other ways, as convinced as Carnegie had been that money had potentials for both good and evil. "Wealth, when unwisely used," he noted, "is likely to be a stone around a man's neck, a power for destruction." And again, "Money itself is lifeless, impotent, sterile . . . but man with his brain, brawn and imagination, using money as servant, may feed the hungry, cure the diseased, make the desert places bloom, and bring beauty into life."

That was exactly what Rockefeller money did for its inheritors, the American people. The largest portion, $81,708,000, went to feed the intellectually hungry, in gifts to education. Brown, John D., Jr.'s alma mater, got $8,679,000, while $5,-000,000 went to the Harvard School of Business Administration. With $21,062,000, the International Education Board was created, to support educational institutions abroad, from the American School of Classical Studies, in Athens, to the Imperial University of Tokyo.

But Rockefeller was as aware as Carnegie that man did not live by intellectual bread alone, and nearly as large a sum, $80,617,000, went to charities of various kinds, to alleviate want and suffering. A comparable amount, $79,832,000, was devoted to religion, in which Rockefeller backed up his belief in church unity with $1,525,000 to the Interchurch World Movement of North America, and $23,231,000 to the inter-denominational Riverside Church and its predecessors on Fifth and Park Avenues. Combining religion and learning in one splendid gift, he created a fund that gave $22,164,000 to institutions of theological education.

Historic structures were the fourth major category of Rocke-feller benefactions, reflecting his belief in preserving beauty, whether it was natural or man-made. The best known of his preservations in the man-made category was also his favorite project, the restoration of colonial Williamsburg, at a cost of $52,599,000. Abroad, he gave $3,080,000 for the care of Versailles Palace, Rheims Cathedral and other French monuments. At home, he was as solicitous on behalf of America's natural beauty, financing a campaign to save the California redwoods ($2,027,000), and helping create the nature preserve in Jackson Hole, Wyoming, at a cost of $17,497,000, as well as Acadia National Park, in Maine, for $3,568,000. Allied with these ventures, and ranking fifth in the hierarchy of giving, was the $42,480,000 he gave for public parks, roads and similar items.

Museums and libraries, more conventional types of philanthropy, ranked sixth, with $34,721,000, while hospitals and
health organizations came next with $20,765,000, including
support for medical research through the Rockefeller Institute and the Memorial Center for Cancer and Allied Diseases.

His religious interests were reflected again in the eighth
largest category, $14,616,000 to the YMCA and the YWCA.
He believed in international organizations, and gave $11,493,-
000 to them, with an additional gift of $8,515,000 worth of
Manhattan real estate on which to build the United Nations.

After these came the arts. Here the people of New York
benefited from the beauty of the Cloisters Museum, costing
$15,741,000, and its surrounding acreage of Fort Tryon Park,
worth $5,930,000. Rockefeller did not care much for contem-
porary art, yet he gave $5,353,000 to the Museum of Modern
Art in New York. A final sum of $3,820,000 went to various
zoological and horticultural interests, and there still remained
the substantial fortune of $8,428,000 to be given to miscella-
neous causes.

The guiding philosophy behind this massive giving was expressed by Rockefeller in this way: "Our endeavor has been
not so much to relieve poverty but to prevent poverty through
making it possible for the largest possible number of people to
live in healthful surroundings and to obtain educational opportunities fitting them to earn their own livelihood."

He approached giving in what he conceived as a business-
like way: "I have been brought up to believe, and the conviction only grows upon me, that giving ought to be entered
into in just the same careful way as investing—that giving is
investing, and that it should be tested by the same intelligent
standards." But the basic concept was humanitarian: "The
health and well-being of the human race is rapidly becoming

the common problem of all nations. Whether we choose to be or not, we are our brother's keeper."

Rockefeller was always conscious of his role of inheritor. "I was born into it," he once said of his overpowering inheritance. "There was nothing I could do about it. It was there, like air or food or any other element. The only question with wealth is what you do with it. It can be used for evil purposes or it can be an instrumentality for constructive social living."

At first, however, young Rockefeller intended to do nothing more with his immense wealth than hang onto it. As Cleveland Amory points out, he was initially an introverted boy dominated by his mother, then a tight-fisted young man under the influence of his father, and it was only after he met and married Abby Aldrich, a young woman of extraordinary generosity, that he learned to give and fully developed the philosophy of giving described previously. It was Abby who taught him *how* to give and, by further teaching and her own example, guided him until she died in April 1948, at the age of seventy-four.

Her five sons—John, Nelson, Laurance, Winthrop and David—have, with the possible exception of Winthrop, often described as the "maverick" of the family, carried on the family image created by their mother and father, which has now largely replaced the nineteenth-century bugaboo useful for so long in frightening recalcitrant proletarian children. Only in the Soviet mind, which still clings to nineteenth-century American images, is the word "Rockefeller" synonymous with sinister capitalist machinations and hidden power. When Nikita Khrushchev in 1961 solemnly declared that the Rockefellers controlled America, it produced only exasperated smiles in a country where Governor Nelson Rockefeller, of New York, is a symbol of liberal Republicanism but nevertheless failed to win a presidential nomination, and where David represents the most enlightened variety of capitalism, which opposes the kind of sinister power the Soviet leader had in mind. But if the Russian charge had been made sixty years ago, a great many Americans would have believed it, and there would have been, moreover, an element of truth in it.

As William Manchester observes in his book, *A Rockefeller Family Portrait,* history has been confounded by the Rockefellers. He writes: "It [history] first watched the amassing of the world's mightiest fortune and the concentration of its enormous power in one family of strong men. It has since seen their benefactions grow until one of them has been entrusted by the public with the only power in America greater than wealth, and it has seen this happen in an eventful century.

"Society needed someone who could manage money, and nobody managed it better than John D. He invested it so cannily that the billion which has passed into public hands has grown today to be two-and-a-half billions. Society required something else. It wanted of the Rockefellers a social wisdom that John D., with his benevolent despotism, could not provide. It found its own way of getting that, through Junior and his sons, and today the true Rockefeller heir is the public. It earned what it has, for it made demands Junior could not deny. Yet even here some credit must be given to John D. He did not make Junior a social creature, but he made him a good man and therefore susceptible to social pressure. In his son the old titan ended his life well, which, as Solon told Croesus, is the best way to be blessed. In his grandsons his blessings, like his riches, go right on multiplying."

The Rockefeller family, indeed, multiplied its influence many times over in its effect on other families which became part of the vast Standard Oil empire created by John D., Sr. The most important of these families was that of Stephen Harkness (like Carnegie, a Scot, though not native-born), who in 1866, as the owner of a prosperous distillery in Republic, Ohio, lent $70,000 to John D., thereby creating generation after generation of rich Harknesses.

One of the richest, and certainly the most important, of these inheritors was the late Edward Stephen Harkness, Stephen's son, who is credited with observing, "A dollar misspent is a dollar lost, and we must not forget that some man's work made the dollar." The man who uttered that aphorism, the apotheosis of conservatism, gave away more than $100,-000,000 in his own name.

While the Rockefellers became what has been called "institutional philanthropists," Harkness preferred more personal giving, although he did not slight the Rockefeller variety. Married to a banker's daughter by whom he had no children, he emulated John D., Jr., in devoting his life to philanthropy, shyly and modestly, which was the Harkness manner, distributing his wealth where he hoped it would do the most good. The Commonwealth Fund, providing money for child health and guidance on an international basis, was one of his inspirations. A more visible monument was the gray city on the Hudson known as the Columbia-Presbyterian Medical Center, among the best of its kind in the world. In education, he made the Harvard and Yale "House" Plans possible.

The idea of using inherited wealth for the well-being of mankind, exemplified by the Rockefellers and the Harknesses, was also the motivating force in the life of Julius Rosenwald, whose birthplace in Springfield, Illinois, was across the street from the Lincoln house, a fact which profoundly influenced the growing boy who ultimately became president of Sears, Roebuck.

It is a measure of Rosenwald's success as a humanitarian that he is better remembered for his use of money than for the business genius which enabled him to establish a great mail-order business. To both endeavors he brought a certain humility, along with a social vision and a profound understanding of people.

As a Jew, he did much for his faith but he was not a Zionist nor was he sympathetic with Jewish nationalism of any variety. Jews, he said, were a people, not a nation. In any case, his philosophy of giving included all races, creeds, countries and nationalities, the money pouring out of the Julius Rosenwald Fund he created in 1917 for "the well-being of mankind."

Rosenwald had positive ideas above giving. He did not, for example, believe in endowments, and he tried to persuade other foundation givers not to perpetuate huge principals as static wealth. "I believe that large gifts should not be restricted to narrowly specified objects," he said, "and that under no circumstances should funds be held in perpetuity. . . . I have confidence in future generations and in their ability to meet their own needs wisely and generously." To make certain this would happen with his own fortune, he provided in his will that both principal and interest must be spent within a quarter century after his death.

There were other aspects of Rosenwald's giving that set him apart from most of his fellow philanthropists. In his philosophy, it was fundamentally wrong for a rich man to give simply for the sake of giving. The gift should impel others to give and, more specifically, he insisted that the recipient do something to help himself.

Because his contributions to Negroes were so outstanding, the extraordinary range of Rosenwald's other philanthropies is often overlooked. They were international in scope. Hebrew Union College, in Cincinnati, and Jewish Theological Seminary of America, in New York, owe their initial financial health to this man who did not endow. Hebrew University of Jerusalem and various cultural agencies in Palestine benefited from his attention. Colleges in Assyria and Constantinople might never have been created without his aid. The hungry children of Berlin knew his generosity after the First World War, and adult Berliners went to the dental clinic he established.

At home, in his own Chicago, he founded the Municipal Voters' League and fought the graft and corruption which have moved so many other civic-minded citizens to earnest if unprofitable battle against sin along the lower shores of Lake Michigan. Rosenwald was ardently against prostitution and equally as ardent on behalf of the Chicago Planning Commission. He strove to bring reason into the intermittent conflicts between white and Negro in Chicago. The city received from him a splendid Museum of Science and Industry, and the University of Chicago, where he was trustee for two decades, was five million dollars richer as the result of his various benefactions. What remained of his wealth, after the many distributions of it, went to his second wife (he married his oldest son's mother-in-law after his first wife's death) and his five children. There was enough to go around. Julius Rosenwald was a wise man as well as a generous one. In many ways he was like Carnegie, an accumulator who made the American people his inheritors and became in himself a kind of inheritor, taking the social responsibility for his wealth as John D., Jr., had done.

The antithesis of his kind of personal philanthropy may be observed in the giving of Henry Ford's sons. To the public, at least, the Ford Foundation is a large, impersonal organization which seems remote from the personalities of the Ford inheritors, although not as remote as it is from the accumulator himself, who made it all possible.

When the first Henry Ford died, he was so firmly established as a folk legend in America that many people were not aware of his descendants, except for the unfortunate Edsel, who had been popularly thought of as the weak son of a strong father, although in fact he was a hard-working, able and conscientious man whose conflict with the old eccentric may well have contributed to his untimely death. The two grandsons, Henry Ford II and Benson, were too young to have made any impression on the public mind, and it was widely supposed that the enormous Ford fortune would be handled by some kind of regency, acting on behalf of the two scions, who could certainly not be counted upon to control and direct the Ford empire.

There was, indeed, no lack of advisers to help the two young men who thus came to power, but in the end they demonstrated that they were quite capable of gathering up the reins themselves, particularly Henry II, who became president and later board chairman of the company. He and his brother had been well schooled in the uses of wealth. With the help of a small army of advisers, they presented to the public not only the bright face of the Ford Foundation, but an entirely new impression of the Ford Motor Company itself, which was transformed from a kind of industrial concentration camp to a place as inhabitable for workers as an automotive plant can be, considering its built-in limitations.

Henry II showed himself to be a most conscientious inheritor. With the Foundation operating virtually autonomously, and the company itself at last in the hands of men who spent more time making automobiles than indulging in company politics, he worked actively in the United States delegation to the United Nations and allied himself with other worthy causes, meanwhile speaking his mind occasionally, with sharpness and clarity, on the shortcomings of his fellow capitalists. Benson, less in the public eye, meanwhile became a hard-working company executive who appeared to be as progressive as his brother.

These attributes and activities overshadow the displays of wealth, reminiscent of another day, which have attended the debuts of Henry II's two daughters. Charlotte, the eldest, made her debut on December 21, 1959, at an eighteenth-century French ball, the lavish decorations for which were done by Jacques Frank, of Paris, where Charlotte went to study at the Sorbonne immediately after her introduction to society.

In June 1961, Monsieur Frank performed a reprise for Charlotte's sister Anne, and outdid himself. A dance pavilion and two summerhouses were built into the magnificent Georgian mansion of the Fords, resplendent with fifty thousand red and white roses and decorated further with a splendid collection of Du Ponts, Firestones, British royalty and movie stars. The eighteen-year-old debutante, inspiration of this splendor, had dined earlier with two hundred guests and later danced with them, tripping lightly in slippers imported from Rome. Perhaps indicating a latter-day trend among the rich, Anne had designed the white silk organza gown she wore. But the old trends were apparent, too, in her hairdo, created by an artiste brought directly from New York, and in the cost of the affair, $250,000, which had been the estimated expense of Charlotte's debut. A half million dollars to launch a brace of daughters was a phenomenon not seen since the far more opulent days of the Vanderbilts and Astors. Inheritor spending, in the old sense, was not entirely dead, it appeared.

Some Meditations on the State of Wealth
in America Today

The rich man's house on the hill, lonely and proud, overlooking the town and the factory which produced his wealth, was a nineteenth-century symbol of American life, heavy with meaning for novelists and poets as well as reformers. The gulf between people like the Vanderbilts and Astors and everyone else was such an omnipresent fact of life that it interpenetrated American humor, folklore, satire, politics, fiction, theater, poetry, and of course the entire range of sociological writing, as well as the American language itself. "Astorbilt," "swell" (used as a noun), "Mrs. Gotrocks," "Astor's pet horse" (sometimes "Mrs. Astor's pet horse," a delicate distinction), "plushy"—these were only a few of the enrichments produced by the dichotomy between haves and have-nots.

It was an essentially feudal concept, however, and contrary to the American spirit, which is undoubtedly why Americans had to treat it with scorn and heavy-handed satire. There were many who feared the rich and what they could do, and some who hated them, but to most citizens the rich man on the hill was simply too remote from their own lives for comprehension, unless they were living in a company town, where cause and effect were directly observable every day.

Today it is a common observation that the gap has narrowed. True, there are still men of great wealth in this country, and there are huddled masses in the slums of every city, as well as thousands who live substandard lives in rural areas. But the rise of the middle class, one of the significant social phenomena of this century, has made the extremes less obvious. Pleasures and luxuries which were once the exclusive property of the rich are now enjoyed by increasing numbers of people, while some of the comforts of the old middle class have filtered down to the poor. In spite of taxes, there are more millionaires in America today than there were at the turn of the century, but there are also many more people who have what used to be described as "a comfortable income."

Among the numerous changes in attitude which this altered situation has produced is a difference in the outlook, and even the way of life, of the inheritors—that is, the inheritors of the old fortunes, not those who in the future will inherit the fortunes being accumulated today.

As we have seen in the case of the Fords, the "old" present-day inheritors are a different breed from those who came into wealth during the early years of the century. Their responsibilities are not the same, since the institutionalizing of wealth has tended to place inheritances more and more in the hands of banks, of law firms, of foundation trustees and boards. There is no need today for an inheritor to get down to the office every morning and be the responsible manager of an enormous estate, but there are numerous inheritors who *do* go down to Wall Street or a factory office and deal in business simply because they like it. The day of the polo-playing, free-spending, luxury-loving, indolent rich man appears to be ending, if it has not already gone. Society itself has changed, as Cleveland Amory, its indefatigable chronicler, has pointed out, primarily because of the distribution of money. Taxes do

not preclude young men from becoming millionaires, but they
do deprive the rich of the kind of spending money that enabled Edward T. Stotesbury to build his 145-room, 14-eleva-
tor palace in Philadelphia, and Mrs. George Westinghouse to
fold hundred-dollar bills within the napkins of each of her
hundred guests at a Washington dinner party. This kind of
ostentation has disappeared with the personal fortunes that
made it possible, but the resulting redistribution of wealth
has, as Amory remarks, given money to too many people and
thus collapsed the world of the old guard.

It is, one must say, a good thing. That world is amusing to
look back upon today, and the era in which it existed is a
fascinating part of our history in retrospect, yet it must be
remembered that it was a world and an era whose values were
wrong in the context of a democratic society.

Inheritors look upon money in a different and healthier
sense today. This viewpoint has never been better expressed
than in the words of Louis Lorillard, great-great-grandson of
Pierre, first man to be called a millionaire when he died in
1843. Amory quotes Louis in *Who Killed Society?* as follows:
"In the old days, they passed money from generation to generation like a good after-dinner liqueur. Now it's more like a
hot potato. A lot of people have it, sure, in oil and in stocks,
and in tankers and Black Angus and even in expense accounts.
But it's not the uncommon denominator it once was. People
just don't look up to it the way they used to. Even with the
people who may have more than anybody had in the good
old days it means a good deal less—and not only to other
people but to them too."

Thus the cycle has come around. The nineteenth-century
accumulators and the first generation of their inheritors created a gaudy era of personal spending and personal philanthropy, but then, as wars, depression and taxation changed

the fabric of American life, the second and third generations of inheritors found themselves the possessors of wealth that had been largely institutionalized, much of it fragmented by divorce and taxes, more of it diverted to foundations, and comparatively little remaining to spend. The inheritor of today lives well but not magnificently, except in a few instances, and he is forever conscious that his material assets are more in the nature of future tax exemptions, destined for museums, trust funds or the institutional philanthropy of foundations. Celebrity has replaced money as the criterion in America, and while this may be exchanging one false value for another, the new outlook toward inherited wealth is salutary, as far as the common good is concerned.

But a new cycle, with unpredictable consequences, is beginning. Today there is a whole new generation of accumulators, and some of them have amassed money to equal the robber barons themselves. A few of them appear in the public view—a new billionaire, like Paul Getty; or a man making a million dollars a day, like the Texas oil Croesus, Roy Cullen. Other Texas oil barons emerge above the surface from time to time, usually by reason of their support of right-wing causes and ideas, in their unremitting effort to return to the nineteenth century, where things were much better arranged for rich men. The money of these men has kept hard-core conservatism alive in America, along with the contributions of old-line corporations.

There are other accumulators the public seldom hears about. The stock market produces new millionaires with an ease unheard of in former days. International trade has created substantial fortunes (incredible ones, in a few cases) during the past twenty-five years. There is a class of bold business entrepreneurs who manipulate corporations on a scale Thomas Fortune Ryan would have admired, and perhaps envied, resulting in fortunes whose ramifications only a battery of lawyers would be able to unravel. The communications industry, particularly television and motion pictures, has produced its quota of new accumulators.

Most of the men who made this money are middle-aged. Soon there will be new generations of inheritors and another cycle of getting and spending will be in full bloom. Have the tax laws effectively ended old-style inheriting forever? Do the new rich automatically think in terms of tax exemption rather than of handing down to their children as much as legal ingenuity can devise? No one really knows. Perhaps the real question is whether the tax experts of the new rich can outguess the tax experts of the federal government. The future of wealth in America has so many dark imponderables that it would be idle to speculate.

One thing is certain, however. Another era of accumulating and inheriting has begun. People are creating new personal accumulations of wealth, and something will become of the money. Fifty years from now the author of another book about inheritors may be able to tell us where it has gone.

Index